THE HUNTING GROUNDS OF THE OLD WORLD

THE HUNTING GROUNDS OF THE OLD WORLD.

HENERY ASTBURY LEVESON

"THE OLD SHEKARRY,"

NEW EDITION

WITH ILLUSTRATIONS BY E. LAW.

GYAN

Published by

Gyan Publishing House
5, Ansari Road
Daryaganj, New Delhi-110002
Phone: 011-47034999, 9811692060
E-mail: books@gyanbooks.com

Distribution Network
gyanbooks.com
India, USA, Canada, UK, Australia, France

ISBN : 978-81-212-9644-1(PB)
First Published, 1860

2nd Impression 2023

Printed at: Gyan Press, Delhi.

THE HUNTING GROUNDS OF THE OLD WORLD
Author: HENRY ASTBURY LEVESON

TIGER HEAD.

THE HUNTING GROUNDS OF THE OLD WORLD.

BY

"THE OLD SHEKARRY,"

AUTHOR OF

"THE FOREST AND THE FIELD," "THE CAMP FIRE," "WRINKLES," ETC.

New Edition.

WITH ILLUSTRATIONS BY E. LAW.

1871.

PREFACE.

THE following pages, descriptive of different incidents in a Hunter's life, are selections from the journal of a wanderer over many lands, which, having excited a certain degree of interest amongst a class who have themselves participated in similar scenes, the Author has laid before the Public; in the hope that some of his comrades, many of whom are "mighty hunters," and abler with the pen than himself, will follow his example, and disseminate the knowledge they have acquired by experience during their sojourn in "the pathless woods," as their accounts cannot fail to be of intense interest to their brother sportsmen, and a great assistance to the uninitiated who may wish to follow in their footsteps.

LIST OF ILLUSTRATIONS.

CONTENTS.

PART I.—INDIA.

SECTION I.—THE DECCAN.

CHAPTER I.

HYDRABAD.—MY FIRST DAY'S DEER-STALKING.

CHAPTER II.

HOG-HUNTING IN THE DECCAN.

CHAPTER X.

THE SHEVEROYS.

CHAPTER XI.

BEAR-HUNTING.

CHAPTER XII.

BOWANI.

CHAPTER XIII.

THE COMBEI JUNGLE.

SECTION III.—THE MOUNTAIN RANGES.

CHAPTER XIV.

THE NEILGHERRIES.

CHAPTER XV.

THE NEILGHERRIES, *continued.*—A NIGHT AFFAIR.

CHAPTER XVI.

ELEPHANT-HUNTING IN THE FOREST AROUND THE BASE OF THE NEILGHERRIES.

CHAPTER XVII.

ELEPHANT-HUNTING IN THE ANNAMULLAY FOREST.

CHAPTER XVIII

THE GREAT ANNAMULLAY FOREST.—TIGER-HUNTING.

CHAPTER XIX.

THE GREAT ANNAMULLAY FOREST, *continued.*—BISON-HUNTING.

CHAPTER XX.

THE GREAT ANNAMULLAY FOREST, *continued.*—A ROGUE ELEPHANT.

PART II.—CIRCASSIA.

CHAPTER XXI.

CHAPTER XXII.

CIRCASSIA—*continued.*

CHAPTER XXIII.

CIRCASSIA—*continued.*

PART IV.

PRACTICAL HINTS ON FIREARMS AND THEIR USE.

CHAPTER XXVI.

THE HUNTING GROUNDS

OF

THE OLD WORLD.

PART I.—INDIA.

Section 1.—*The Deccan.*

CHAPTER I.

HYDRABAD.—MY FIRST DAY'S DEER-STALKING.

Leave of absence obtained.—My Mentor.—Departure.—Abdulla-ben-Ali, the Killadar.—A Banian.—The hill-fort of Bhoonghir.—Old cannon.—Native hospitality.—Visions of deer.—The start.—Plenty of "slots" but no deer.—The Sambur described.—His habits.—A deer-stalker's qualifications.—Hints.—The trail.—Walter's companion.—Tracking.—The sambur's instinct.—The bark of a buck elk.—The game in view.—An anxious moment.—My first stag.—Two harts die, a third hard hit.—The chase.—Ponto brings him to bay.—A good shot.—Return to camp.

In the year 184— I was a jolly sub. in the old —th Regiment, then forming part of the Hydrabad subsidiary force, and having got over the early troubles of my griffinage (*i.e.*, the goose step, adjutant's drill, &c.) in a weak moment after dinner I obtained three days' division leave from my colonel (a regular Tartar) who during the temporary absence of General A——n, was in command of the garrison, in order to accompany my great chum, Walter M., in a sporting expedition to the Jaghir of the Killadar* of the hill-fort of Bhoonghir, which was about twenty miles from our cantonments.

Walter, who commanded the company to which I was attached, had been my Mentor in all duty matters from the day I first joined the regiment, and he now undertook to initiate me in the mysteries of "Shekar," in all its branches, a task which he of all others was well qualified to perform, being well known as the most fearless hunter and unerring shot in a country pre-eminent for the excellence of its sportsmen.

Years have rolled since poor Walter went to "that bourne from whence no traveller returns;" and the kindest heart that ever warmed human bosom has ceased to beat, for my friend sleeps his last under the shade of a giant forest tree, and his name is seldom called to mind, save when, at the close of day, his old comrades assemble round the social board and speak of "moving incidents by flood and field;" of hair-breadth "'scapes," of mighty feats and daring deeds, and an old hand pointing to

* Killadar, the governor of a fort.

some grim trophy of the chase hanging in the mess-room, will tell how the daring spirit that is gone plunged in some angry torrent, "and did buffet it with lusty sinews" after his quarry, bearded the tiger in his lair, and slew him single-handed, or saved a comrade from inevitable death by the fatal accuracy of his deadly aim.

Mais revenons à nos moutons. We left cantonment at the first indication of dawn, and accompanied by all our people and baggage, which was furthermore escorted by a corporal and three sepoys, as the country was hardly deemed safe, on account of predatory bands of Rohillas and Puthans, we proceeded along the bank or embankment of the Hussain Sauger Tallow, an artificial lake which was upwards of thirty miles in circumference in the rainy season, and passing by the princely palace of the Resident of Hydrabad, we arrived at the bungalow of Captain M——, the Assistant Resident, with whom we breakfasted; and having rested a few hours, until the heat of the day was past, we again set out, leaving the city of Hydrabad behind, crossing the Moosa river by a ford, and after a ride of three hours arrived at Shajehanpoor, where we remained for the night, and from which place the lofty hill-fort of Bhoonghir was pointed out to us, looming high above the surrounding hills.

At daybreak the next morning we were again in the saddle, and after a pleasant ride through low jungle arrived at an immense banian tree, where we found Abdulla-ben-Ali, the Killadar, and his son, waiting for us with "Saindee" (the sap of the date palm, which, when fresh, is a delightful beverage) and trays of fruits and sweetmeats of different kinds.

He offered us accommodation, for ourselves and followers, in the fort, but we preferred encamping under this magnificent banian tree, which in itself was quite a grove, being of amazing size. Contrary to most other vegetable productions, this tree seems to be exempted from decay; for every branch from the main body throws out its own roots, at first in small tender fibres several yards from the ground, which continually grow thicker, until by a gradual descent they reach its surface, where striking in they take root, and receiving nourishment from the earth, increase to large trunks, which themselves become parent trees, shooting forth other branches; thus continuing in a state of progression, independent of the first parent of them all. A banian tree, with its many trunks, forms the most beautiful walks, vistas, and cool recesses that can be imagined, for the leaves are large, soft, and of a lively green, and the grateful shade it affords is infinitely preferable to that of any building. The fruit is a small fig, which is of a bright scarlet colour when ripe, affording sustenance to monkeys and birds of various kinds, which dwell among the branches. We killed several dozen green pigeons, besides others of different kinds, the morning of our arrival, but the next day they came just as numerous as ever.

Having seen that our tents were properly pitched and our horses firmly picketed, we accompanied the Killadar to his quarters in the fort, the ascent of which is very steep, and almost impracticable for horses, and he took us round the fortifications, which were tolerably strong for a native fort, consisting, as usual, of a loop-holed wall, with square bastions of masonry, and a kind of *fausse* brae, with a line of interior defences, which form the citadel. He appeared to think the place impregnable, and neither Walter nor myself cared to undeceive him, although we both made up our minds that it would take our troops something less than an hour to get into it.

He showed us some curious old native guns, one of which was of very large calibre, being formed of bars of iron welded together and fastened with large iron hoops, and the shot, which were of stone, we found to be rather heavier than we could lift.

After our inspection we adjourned to the Killadar's house, which appeared to have been formerly the gateway of an old Hindoo temple, but all the images had been destroyed and replaced by stone slabs bearing Persian inscriptions. We were shown into the "dewan-khana," or guest-room, where a very nice dinner, in the native style, was served, and our host conversed with us whilst we partook of his hospitality, and appeared much amused at my awkward attempts to convey the food to my mouth with my fingers, a feat which I was not then accustomed to perform, although it is the ordinary mode of eating among all classes and castes in India. I had my turn when he came to visit us afterwards, and attempted to eat with a knife and fork for the first time.

After we had dined, sherbet and sweetmeats were handed round, with hubble-bubbles and hookahs (water-pipes,) and the Killadar informed us that his shekarries * had not returned from the jungles, whither he had sent them to try and find out the whereabouts of a large tiger, who had been committing a good deal of depredation among the herds in the low country; but that if we would like a day's sambur † shooting, he would accompany us on the morrow, and show us a place where we should be nearly certain to find.

Of course we were agreeable, and after expending a good deal of breath in interchanging compliments, &c., we took our leave and returned to our tents, the Killadar having promised to be with us before daybreak with masaltjies or torch-bearers, as it was some short distance to the jungle where we were to hunt, and early dawn was the best time to catch the deer feeding.

I had never killed a deer, or, indeed, any other large game (except a hyena, that ventured into my compound, or garden, one night, after my dogs, and

* Shekarries, hunters. † Sambur, elk (*Rusa Aristoteles.*)

which I managed to knock over with a charge of buck-shot,) and consequently I was in too excited a state to rest much during the night, for visions of deer came and vanished amidst broken slumbers, and I awoke dreaming that, after a long and weary chase over mountains and across ravines, I came upon a monstrous stag, put up my rifle and pulled, but all in vain—it would not go off.

I had only just dropped into a refreshing sleep, when I was awakened by Walter beating the "British Grenadiers" with his hair-brush on a huge brass basin, which was formed out of one of the gongs taken from the Pagoda at Rangoon. I sprung from my bed as if the deer were already before me, and donning my toggery, which was of moleskin of most approved colour and cut, buckled on my spurs and examined my rifles, whilst my servant poured out some hot coffee, flavoured with but just a "threatening of cognac," and in a few minutes we were joined by the Killadar, his son, and three or four "juwans," (young men in attendance,) and, mounting our horses, we wound round the scarped side of the hill-fort, and entered a long narrow defile between two hills, by a narrow path running along the banks of a mountain stream then nearly dry.

After a tedious ride of about two hours' duration, by torchlight, the gray dawn broke over the mount-tain tops, and a gentle breeze arose, just moving with its refreshing breath the leaves of the loftier trees; now and then a hare or a covey of partridges sprang up on either side, and vanished amid the gloom of the surrounding thickets, alarmed at the noise made by the feet of our horses over the rocky path.

At last the ravine opened into a beautiful glen, in which there were small patches of cultivation, and here the Killadar begged us to dismount and keep quiet, as the dun tenants of the waste were in the habit of quitting the dense jungle during the night, and browsing upon the young cholum (Indian corn) in the early morning.

He sent two of his people that knew the ground to reconnoitre, who, after a few minutes, came back with the information that they had seen a sounder of hog, but that there were no sambur on the ground, although there were several places covered over with fresh slots (the marks of a deer's tread,) showing that they had been there during the night.

The Killadar gave vent to his disappointment by a volley of strange oaths, and was for returning home, but Walter begged him to remain and enjoy a quiet smoke under the shade of a tree, whilst we followed up tracks and attempted to stalk them. This he was delighted to do, as he did not like the thoughts of following up the game through the thick jungle, being a stout, thick-set, phlegmatic individual, hardly fit for such work.

Walter divested himself of his extraneous clothing, substituting a pair of thin elk-skin shoes for his ordinary riding-boots, and I followed his example;

then unloosening the girths of our saddles, we gave strict injunctions to our people to remain quiet, and sallied into the glen, accompanied by one of the men who had seen the fresh slots.

I was so impatient to get on the trail, and plunge at once, as it were, *in medias res*, that I have omitted to describe the sambur, and also to point out the properties requisite for a deer-stalker. This species of deer, which is to be met with in almost all the large jungles throughout India, is considerably larger than the Scotch red deer, and cannot be mistaken for the same species. The horns are rather upright, having two short brow antlers *only*, and at three years old two points at the extremities of each beam; the eyes are large and very prominent; the ears rounded; the tail longer, and the arm more muscular than our red stags. The hair immediately next to the jaw is longer than any other part of the neck, and when he is alarmed or excited it stands on end, and forms a kind of ruff, sometimes called the mane. The colour varies slightly, but is usually of very dark slate, mingled with gray, nearly black about the face and points, and a light buff between the haunches and underneath. The female is much smaller than the male, and is of a lighter colour.

The horns vary in size, according to the age of the animal, and are cast annually, not, however, always at the same time, for one generally drops a day or two after the other. The new horns attain their full growth in about three months, appearing about a week after the old ones are shed, and are covered with a thick, leaden-coloured skin, called the velvet, which, after a time, begins to fall off. At this period the horns are very sensitive, and the stags avoid bringing them into collision with any substance.

The period of gestation in the hinds is eight months. She drops the fawn in some secluded and shady spot, making it lay down by pressing her nose and forehead against it, after which it will never stir until she comes again, for she leaves it until the close of day, remaining a short distance to windward, so as to be at hand in case it should be found out by foxes or jackals.

The natives say, and I believe with some truth, that if you find a young fawn that has never followed its dam, take it up and breath in its nostrils, allowing it to suck your fingers for a few moments, that it will follow you for miles, becoming instantly tame; but if it has once followed its dam, for ever so small a time before you found it, it will never follow a human being.

The female does not cohabit with the male until three years old, and never has more than one fawn at a time. During the rutting season, which period lasts about a week, the harts are extremely vicious, and may be heard roaring all over the forests, calling and answering each other. When they meet they engage in savage conflicts, rearing themselves on their hind legs, sparring with their fore-feet, and butting each other with their antlers, until one feels himself worsted, and leaves the herd; the hinds, who generally watch the engagement with the utmost nonchalance, bestowing their favours on the conqueror.

There is no animal more shy or solitary by nature than the sambur. He takes alarm from every living thing in the forest; the slightest sound, be it only the fall of a leaf or the scratching of a jungle fowl, will scare and set him off in a moment. Except in certain embarrassed situations, *they always run up wind*, their great security lying in their extreme keenness of scent, for they can smell a taint in the air at an almost incredible distance.

When a hart is disabled or run down by dogs, and he feels that he cannot escape by speed, he will choose the best position he can, and defend himself to the last extremity with his antlers. Powerful dogs may pull down a full-grown stag when running and breathless, but not a *cold hart* (one that has not been wounded) when he stands at bay, for he takes such a sweep with his antlers that he could exterminate a whole pack, should they attack in front only.

The sambur, like many other animals, seems to foresee every change of weather, for they leave the hills and descend into the plains whenever any rough weather is about to take place.

The deer-stalker should not only be able to run like an antelope, but he should possess the bottom of an Arab horse, to enable him to keep the game in view; he should be able to creep like a leopard, and to run with his back bent almost double, and at a pinch to wriggle himself along the ground, *ventre à terre*, like an eel. He should be able to wade or swim torrents, to keep his footing on slippery water-worn stones, remembering, if he does fall, to keep his rifle dry, whatever becomes of his wretched carcass. He should never go *rashly* to work, keeping always *cool*, *wary*, and *steady*, never allowing any untoward circumstances to interfere with his equanimity and self-possession.

Before commencing operations, he should carefully survey his line of route, marking any cover that inequalities in the ground, or bushes, rocks, &c., might give. I need not add, that temperance and moderation go a long way to keep *the hand in* and the nerves steady. When I first began deer-stalking, my Mentor endeavoured to instil the following general rules in my mind, and several years subsequent experience has proved to me that his theory is correct. *Be on your ground betimes in the morning; consult the clouds, and keep well to the leeward, even if you have to make a circuit of miles; be silent as the grave; when you step on stones or dry leaves, &c., tread as lightly as a ghost; keep under cover; exercise extreme judgment in approaching your game, which is a happy mixture of wary caution combined with prompt decision and boldness of execution. Memo. All this is useless, if you do not use straight powder.*

When we arrived at the cultivated ground in the bed of the glen, we found marks showing that a large herd of sambur had been very lately feeding on the young shoots of the Indian corn, for the slots were quite fresh, and Walter pointed me out the difference between the tread of the harts to that of the hinds, the former being much larger and broad, and round at the point, whereas the latter is long and narrow.

One impression, which was very deeply indented in the ground, measured three inches and a half at the heel, and the hind feet appeared to have been brought up to the same mark as that made by the fore, on which account Walter concluded the slot to belong to a heavy hart, who was most likely the leader of the herd; so we agreed to follow it up.

We were accompanied by a curious nondescript kind of dog, a cross between an English foxhound and a Bringarry greyhound, which had its ears and tail cropped close to the roots, to enable it to get through the jungle. He was Walter's inseparable companion, and the most highly educated dog I ever saw; like his master, being perfectly *au fait* at every kind of sport. In the jungle he never left his master's heel except when set by him on the trail. On scent, no jungle, however thick, or rocks, however steep, could check his course; no stream, however rapid, would discourage him; he would enter without splashing, cross and double about until he recovered the scent and came up with his quarry, which he would keep at bay until his master came. He was also first-rate after small game as a retriever, and was very successful in putting up florakin, (or the lesser bustard), which bird generally makes a practice of running when disturbed.

Walter was an adept at tracking, and under his guidance we had no difficulty in following up the trail, the slots not being more than an hour old. I remember being much struck with the extraordinary facility he had in discerning the trail over the most difficult ground; the slightest mark, an upturned stone, a bruised leaf, or a bent twig, being sufficient to indicate the route pursued by the game with the greatest certainty.

The gift of *tracking* or *following up spoor*, appears to be innate, or a kind of instinct, in the red men of the "Far West," and to certain jungle tribes of Hindostan; but it takes careful study, great observation, and long experience, before "dwellers of cities" are able to mark and understand *forest signs* with any certainty.

We found the elk had left the cholum fields and made for a steep ravine, at the bottom of which wound a mountain torrent, sometimes creeping silently among mossy stones, and at others dashing down over huge boulders of greenish granite, with a roar like distant thunder.

"The deer evidently know this ground well, Hal," exclaimed Walter, breaking silence after an hour's heavy pull up and down hill, "for see, they have gone up stream to find a more convenient ford, as the current here is so strong that the fawns, not, being able to keep their legs, would have been swept away in crossing, so if you are not out of breath, we will after them at once, as the quicker we get over the ground the less will we have to cover, provided we go about it quietly and cautiously."

On we went, sometimes on our hands and knees, creeping through dense underwood, and at others climbing rocks or wading watercourses, until we came to place where the stream was a shallow, and here it was evident that the deer had crossed very lately, as water was still flowing into the deep imprints made by their feet in the soft sands near the banks.

"Take care not to make any splash as you go over, and tread carefully, Hal," whispered Walter; "the trail is warm, and the herd cannot be far off, for the slots indicate they have been going slowly, browsing as they went, so they cannot have taken alarm." "Go ahead," I replied, feeling, I must own, rather nervous and excited, as who would not be, when after his first stag; and on we went, creeping along with the utmost caution for a quarter of an hour, when suddenly we heard a sharp noise, like the barking of a dog, which seemed to come from a dense thicket some short distance in our front.

Walter pulled up at once, and I noticed Ponto, his canine friend, had also caught up the sound, for he had his head knowingly cocked on one side, as if he was listening carefully, and his nose elevated, as if he was trying to sniff the air, whilst a small stump—an apology for a tail—made sundry eccentric movements, indicating that something was in the wind.

After a moment's pause, Walter touched my shoulder, and whispered below his breath, "That was the bark of a buck elk, so cock your rifle and step in front, as I want you to kill him; he cannot be far off, therefore keep a bright look-out, and be very careful not to make the slightest noise."

I stole noiselessly along the run, following the slots, which were distinctly visible, until I came to a more open spot, where the jungle had been burnt the preceding year, and, crouching behind a thick bush, I had the extreme satisfaction of seeing the herd, consisting of three harts and fourteen or fifteen hinds, some of which had fawns at heel, quietly cropping the herbage about two hundred yards distant.

It was a glorious sight, and I felt my heart thump against my ribs as I gazed for some seconds, too full of admiration to think of firing, when Walter, touching my shoulder, whispered, "They are too far off to make certain, so try and crawl under cover of the bushes to that thick clump, and you will get an easy shot. If you go carefully you will not be discovered, as the wind blows strong from them to us, and I will follow when I see you safely posted."

I did as he desired, and we were now about a hundred and twenty yards distant from the herd, which, still unaware of our presence, continued browsing on the young wood and tender shoots.

This was the anxious moment — everything hitherto had succeeded; much time had been spent in tracking; the game was before us; and all now depended on a steady hand. "Take the nearest, Hal," whispered Walter, "and leave the further one to me—fire when I whistle. Are you ready?"

I had covered the shoulder of a stately stag, with towering antlers and a large black ruff round his neck, and on the signal being given, let drive. He made a bound, staggered, then fell forward, and was instantly dead.

Walter, who had a very much longer shot, brought another fine hart to the ground, hitting him through the hind quarters, and paralysing them, and as the herd rushed by, wounded another as it sprang from an adjoining thicket, where it must have been lying down unobserved. I heard the "thud" as the ball struck against his dun side, and, jumping on a rock close by, let fly with my second barrel, but the shot was too high, it only cracked against his horns and stunned him for a moment, for he soon recovered and went off with the rest, seemingly as well as ever. "A splendid shot, by Jupiter!" exclaimed Walter, "for he was a good three hundred yards when you fired, but you were not quick enough, and as it has failed to stop him, we will first 'pay the last offices to the fallen,' and then send Ponto on his track, for I feel sure he is hard hit, and if we do not urge him whilst the wound is fresh, but give it time to stiffen, he will be obliged to slacken his pace and fall out from the rest of the herd."

Walter had shot his stag through the small of the back, and although completely disabled, so as not to be able to drag itself along, it was not dead, and it was with some difficulty that he managed, with Ponto's assistance, to plunge his long knife in his chest and finish him. After we had bled, opened, and "gralloched" both, we covered the carcasses over with thorny bushes and stones, to preserve them from the vultures, without which precaution we should only have found the bones when we returned with the coolies to carry away the game; and having refreshed the inner man with a nip of "brandy panee," we reloaded our rifles and tracked up the hart Walter had wounded, which, from the size of the slots, appeared to be larger than either of those we had killed.

Here and there we found the ground dyed with drops of blood, and where he rolled over when my bullet struck his horn there was a bright crimson pool, which showed that he was hard hit. "He cannot travel far, Hal, in that state," said Walter, "so we will set the dog after him, and I do not doubt but that he will soon bring him to bay. Hey, Ponto! fetch him, boy." The intelligent animal looked up in his master's face, as if he could there read what was required of him, then made a cast with his nose along the ground, until he got scent of the wounded deer, when off he set at speed.

We followed at our best pace, and after a sharp run, had the gratification of hearing Ponto's deep tongue echoing among the rocks. "Bravo, my dog!" cried Walter; "keep up, Hal, for five minutes longer, for by that cry I know the stag is at bay." We tore down the slope of the hill leading to the river, and there he was, standing in the torrent, every now and then menacing Ponto with his antlers, who was swimming in the stream, and had enough to do to evade his frantic rushes.

I was quite out of breath and powerless with the run, but Walter, standing up, at once firm and collected, took a deliberate aim with his unerring rifle; an echo was heard rumbling among the rocks, and the stag, taking a mighty spring, plunged into the stream, shot through the brain, and rose a lifeless thing.

The current, which was extremely rapid, bore the carcass down for some distance, dashing it amongst the rocks and whirling it in the eddies, and we had considerable difficulty in getting down to drag it out, as the ravine was very steep and full of precipices and huge rocks. At last we managed to haul him high and dry on the bank, and having gralloched and covered him over with branches and stones, we set off for the spot where we had left the Killadar some five or six hours before. Just awakened from sleep, he had no idea that we had been away so long, and fancied we were joking when we told him of our sport.

He sent his people, guided by Ponto, to sling the venison on poles and bring it in, and "there was a sound of revelry by night" in his little fortress, for after sending a couple of haunches into cantonment, we divided the rest among his followers. I turned in that night very tired, and considerably bruised with sundry falls, but delighted with the success of my first day's deer-stalking.

On the following morning the Killadar got us up a beat in the ravine where a tiger had been seen some days previously, but it proved "a blank;" and the day after, "our leave being up," we had to bid adieu to our native friends and return to cantonment.

CHAPTER II.

HOG-HUNTING.

The fortress of Golconda.—The Tombs of the Kings.—The gardens.—Persian inscriptions.—The gathering.—Plan of operations.—Reminiscences of the past.—The start.—The rendezvous.—My nag Lal Babba.—A moment of suspense.—The find.—We're away.—The chase.—The first blood.—A purl.—The advantages of being on good terms with one's nag.—The tug of war.—Exciting moments.—The struggle for the spear.—It is won.—The charge.—Mischief ensues.—The death of the boar.—The wounded hog-hunter.—The death of an old friend.—The trysting-tree.—The trophies.—The return to cantonment.

It was evening; the oppressive glare and overpowering heat of the day were gone, and the sun was setting with that gorgeous magnificence which is rarely to be seen except in "land of the cedar and vine." His last expiring rays tinged the whole of the heavens, from the western horizon to the zenith, with indescribably beautiful gold and crimson hues, and striking upon the numerous gilt pinnacles of the mosques and minarets which rose above the castellated walls of the hill-fort of Golconda, formed a contrast with the deep verdure of the mango groves and the lighter foliage of the graceful tamarind, on which the eye rested with delight.

On the one hand lay Golconda, with its lofty rock-built citadel, bastioned walls, and loop-holed battlements; and on the other rose those magnificent structures of ancient days, the tombs of the kings, with their massive domes, gigantic cupolas, towering minarets, and stately piazzas.

Many changes have taken place since the last of the Kootub Shawee dynasty was placed in his regal sepulchre. His kingdom has passed away into the hands of strangers, and his very name is now forgotten in the land where he was once preeminent; still, these time-worn but stately monuments will attest to many succeeding generations the splendour and magnificence of the ancient rulers of Hindostan.

No such works are carried on in the present day; and what makes these buildings more remarkable is, that the immense blocks of granite with which they are constructed have had to be transported from long distances, none being procurable in the immediate vicinity. The stupendous domes of these royal mausoleums were formerly ornamented with inlaid enamel of different colours, forming beautiful arabesques; but time, aided by the depredations of the ignorant, has succeeded in obliterating a great part, and it is only in the more sheltered and out-of-the-way places that this beautiful enamel can be seen in the same freshness of colour as it exhibited when first laid on. The wilful damage these relics of the past have sustained is the more to be regretted, as the very art of making this beautiful enamel has been forgotten. The gray granite walls in the interior are beautifully carved, and in some places the doorways and ornamented niches are of highly-polished black granite.

The largest of the tombs will contain about 8,000 people, it being built in the shape of a square, having a verandah with forty-eight arches all round. Some of the pillars are carved out of single blocks of granite; and I noticed slabs with which the interior is paved upwards of sixty feet in length. Under the centre of the dome is the tomb itself, hewn out of a solid piece of black granite, highly polished as the finest marble, and covered with beautifully carved arabesques, Persian inscriptions, and verses from the Koran.

At each corner of the building is a small archway, and a circular staircase in the thickness of the wall, leading to the tops of the minarets, from the upper galleries of which the Moussins used to call "the faithful" to prayer at five certain times during the day. In capacious vaults below are the tombs of the wives, favourite mistresses, and children of the kings, also of black polished marble, covered with inscriptions. Besides the seven large tombs there are several smaller ones, also numerous Mosques, Eedgahs, Shrines, Tanks,

Baths, Durm-salahs, (almshouses), Caravanserais, and Choultrees, for the accommodation of pilgrims and travellers, which are falling to ruin from neglect.

There is a very tolerably kept up garden round one of the tombs, in which the mangoe, orange, lime, citron, pumelow, fig, jack-fruit, pomegranate, plantain, cocoa-nut, vine, and betel-nut flourish. It is a delightful place, and quite in the Oriental style, having long shaded avenues, with stone borders, numerous fountains, and streams of running water on each side, to irrigate the plants. Parterres of roses and Indian jessamine load the air with the most delicious fragrance, and at intervals are beautiful "*kiosks*" or garden-houses, of the most elaborate and delicately carved Saracenic architecture, profusely ornamented with arabesques and quaint Arabic and Persian inscriptions, some of which I took the trouble of deciphering, and found them to be guzzels, or verses, in which some fair beauty is described "*as having dark, almond-shaped eyes, in which the purity of her heart was reflected: but which committed more destruction among the hearts of men than the double-edged sword of Rustum; whose voice was like the evening song of the Bul-bul, mingled with the distant murmuring of many waters; whose beauty made the rose turn pale with envy, and the passion flower drop to the ground from jealousy; whose gait was graceful as that of the silver moon sailing through the firmament; whose lips were more delicious to taste than the rosy wine of Sheraz: whose smile gladdened the heart of all beholders, which became water in the presence of the lovely one."* Numerous fountains to cool the air, and places for streams of running water, encircled many of these retreats; but the former would not play, and the latter were choked up, from neglect, and falling into ruin.

The large tomb was appointed the rendezvous for a party of hog-hunters, of which I formed one; and the number of cots stowed away in the numerous recesses round the interior of the building, showed that the "meet" would be well attended. Almost under the centre of the cupola, numerous gaily dressed attendants were engaged in laying out a table for dinner, and in the verandah, knots of Anglo-Indian officers, of all ranks, were sitting, with their feet resting against the stone pillars, or on tables, enjoying the comparative coolness of the evening breeze. A light and airy costume, consisting of silk long drawers, shirt sleeves, and slippers, was the order of the day—some of the dandies amongst us indulging their *penchant* by "coming out" in gorgeous smoking caps, fancy muslin shirts, gold or silver kinkob pajamas (loose drawers,) and embroidered papouches (slippers.)

We were a motley gathering of all arms. There were Light Cavalry and Light Bobs, Queen's and Company's, Regulars and Irregulars, old weather-beaten veterans, bearded like the Druids of old, who had passed a quarter of a century in the country; and smooth-faced youngsters, who had not yet passed the first year of their *griffinage;* yet all were in the same state of excitement at the thoughts of the morrow's sport.

As we sat, waiting until dinner was announced, enjoying the murmuring, gurgling melody of our hookahs, or the fragrant weed in the shape of a Manilla or Trichinopoly cheroot, N——, who was the originator of the expedition, proceeded to unfold the programme of the morrow's sport.

We were to partake of an early breakfast at three A.M., and mounting our hacks, were to proceed to the scene of action, near Raneepet, a village about twelve miles distant, where our tents and best cross-country horses had been despatched the day previous. Our shekarries and beaters had marked down several sounders (herds) of hog in a long strip of low jungle contiguous to some tolerable riding ground, and had formed a chain, so as to prevent them making their way back into the denser cover.

As the moon was nearly at the full, and the distance but short, beating was to commence at daylight, and first-rate sport was anticipated, for we had some old hands amongst us—such as D——, S——, N——, C——, and O——, who were well known as the best spears and the boldest riders in the Deccan, where hog-hunting, ever the favourite sport, was carried on in the greatest perfection, so that the first sportsmen of India came from far-off stations to display their skill, and the goodness and courage of their cattle, at these meetings.

As it became dusk, some one sounded the dinner-call on a key-bugle, which had a very fine effect, as the sound was echoed in the dome several times, as also among the other tombs. We sat down, nearly thirty, to table; and after the clattering of knives and forks, and the popping of corks, had subsided, we withdrew to one of the kiosks or pleasure houses in the garden, where songs and brandy panee* passed round freely until a late hour.

Since that night many long years have glided on, and I have wandered over half the globe; still, when I hear those old, familiar airs, the scene often comes before my eyes, and I think I see the well-remembered features of my old associates, in the forest and the field, who used to sing them, although I know that many sleep beneath the sod, having fallen on the field, or been cut off by pestilence in the flower of their years, and the few survivors are scattered, and I have lost sight of most of them. India is not, *perhaps*, a land to live in from choice, still my heart clings to it with a kind of unhallowed love; for it ever appeared to me to possess a peculiarly fascinating charm, which I have found wanting elsewhere. Memory takes me back to those happy days I passed in that glorious land;

* Brandy and water.

and as I look around my boyhood's home, in my native land, (which to me long absence has given a novel freshness,) and see the trophies of many a hard-fought field, and the spoils of my rifle and the spear hanging against the wall, I often think with affectionate regret of my old companions, and dream of the land

> "Where the maidens are soft as the roses they twine,
> And all, save the spirit of man, is divine."

In the morning, at the time appointed, a bugle again rang through the place, and we were soon round the breakfast-table, equipped in leathers and boots. Some of the old hands had also *sambur* (elk) skin jackets, and all wore hunting-caps. We were soon in the saddle, and after a couple of hours' canter by the light of the moon, arrived at our tents, which were pitched under a stately banian, under whose widely spreading arms some sixty Arabs were picketed, each being groomed by his respective syce (horsekeeper.)

Coffee, brandy and soda water, and cheroots, &c., were handed round, and half-an-hour was allowed for the saddling, when a messenger came from the head man of the village (who was with the beaters) to say that the hogs were undisturbed, and that all was in readiness.

The tree under which our encampment was pitched must have been of great age, for underneath were the ruins of a small Hindoo temple, which bore traces of great antiquity. Some of the shoots of the trunk had insinuated themselves amid the masonry, and appeared to grow out of the roof.

The scene around was very picturesque; craggy hills were towering above the sea of forest in every direction, and a beautiful lake lay between us and the village, on which water-fowl of different kinds were distinctly heard. Partridges were calling all around as we mounted, and the first streaks of dawn were visible in the East.

I was mounted on a very favourite chestnut Arab, called Lal Babba, (Lal signifies red, and Babba is a term of endearment, generally used towards children,) full of fire, and who seemed to be as eager for the sport as any of us. He was of a very high caste, of great courage, yet exceedingly docile, having a good mouth—an essential quality in a hog-hunter, and a famous cross-country horse, although small, not being over fourteen hands two inches; but extremely active, very swift, and of great endurance, and I felt, as he bounded under me, that he was in first-rate working condition, and would not disgrace me.

We cantered out to the scene of action, which was about half-a-mile from our tents, mustering twenty-seven well-mounted horsemen, and as soon as we had all taken post, two and two, some short distance from each other, like videttes, in the dry bed of a nullah, or watercourse, the banks of which hid us from view, the signal was given, and the beat commenced.

We waited some twenty minutes without being able to distinguish anything, although we heard the distant sounds of tomtoms (a kind of drum,) and cholera horns, (a huge brass trumpet shaped like the letter S.)

After some time we began to discover, here and there, a long line of men slowly advancing through the bushes, and when they got near enough for us to distinguish their turbans and black faces, the yells and ferocious shouts, together with the wild flourishes of the cholera horn, the rolling of tomtoms, and the constant discharge of matchlocks and rockets, made them appear like some wild horde advancing to attack us, with some slight show of discipline.

As they closed upon us the din became horrid, and their screams and yells were more discordant than ever, when suddenly loud cries were heard along the line of "Soor! soor! (hog! hog!) Kalee janwar!" (black beasts) and each horseman stood up in his stirrups and strained his eyes to ascertain which way the game had broken. It was an anxious moment, and intense excitement was depicted on every face, as we waited impatiently in our hiding-place for the signal bugle which was to announce the start.

At last the long-wished-for note rang forth; each horseman grasped his spear, crushed his hunting-cap firmly on his head, dug in his spurs, and sprang from his cover at speed upon the plain. A sounder of seven hog were seen scouring over the ground at a tolerable pace, some four hundred yards from the cover from which they had broken.

As soon as they heard the tramp of our horses approaching, they increased their speed, and a huge gray boar fell back to the rear, champing his tushes and tearing up the ground in a most threatening manner. As our object was to force them further into the plain, so as to cut them off and prevent their returning into the jungle, we rode slowly for the first quarter of a mile, then our pace increased, and we went fairly in at them. When we approached they separated, and some of the youngsters of our party made after four sows which kept off to our left.

Although the pace was now becoming severe for some time, we appeared to gain but little on the boar, who, with a couple of sows, dashed away in a gallant style, clearing *en route* a nullah, (watercourse,) which brought many of the field to a check.

Lal Babba was doing his work well, although he had become so excited with the chase that I had some little trouble in keeping him in hand. We cleared a yawning chasm which, though not more than nine feet wide, was difficult, as the opposite bank was two feet higher than the near one. Hearing a burst of laughter behind from O——, I turned my head, and saw five or six of our number rolling in the dust, and one seemed *hors de combat.*

Still on we tore, the field becoming more select,

not numbering more than a baker's dozen. We now had a good burst, and one of the sows lagging behind, bit the dust after having twice charged in a most gallant manner. N—— claimed the first blood of the day.

The pace was now becoming tremendous, and the second sow was rolled over by S——, O—— and D——, whose spears were applied several times before we heard the final squeal (the signal of dissolution).

I kept steadily after the boar, and by this diversion gained a couple of lengths ahead, when my horse put his foot on the loose stump of a tree and rolled over, giving me a *header* which made me see a considerable number of stars, and left me rather confused for the moment. On swept the field, which I could see was "tailing off" very considerably; and after I had ascertained that no bones were broken, and Lal Babba had given himself a shake, I sprang into the saddle again, and was once more *en route*.

I was very much thrown out by this spill, and had lost ground, but, as luck would have it, the hog made for a deep ravine, having a drop of more than a dozen feet, which brought our field to a check. The boar managed to scramble down, and running along the bottom of the nullah for some distance, climbed up the opposite bank.

After riding some distance along the edge of the chasm, which was overgrown in places by stunted bush, I found a place which was a little more practicable, though the drop was still about eight feet deep, and the slope of the bank very steep. One more chance, thought I, springing from my horse, taking off the saddle and tying up the bridle—Lal Babba and I were old friends, and he would follow me like a dog—I threw the saddle into the bed of the nullah, and scrambled down afterwards myself. I then called him by name several times, and he came trotting along the bank as if he was seeking a more suitable place to descend. He then returned to that part of the bank down which I had scrambled, and stood pawing the edge hesitatingly. I again called him, and pretended to turn away down the bed of the nullah, when I shall never forget his appearance as he stood cocking his ears and laying his head on one side, as he watched my motions with evident distress. He remained motionless a moment, as if he was considering what was to be done, then gave a loud whinny, sprang, and in a moment was rubbing his nose against my shoulder.

I patted him on the shoulder, and talked to him as I adjusted the saddle, and from his intelligent looks one would have thought he understood every word I said. I then walked along the bed of the nullah for some little distance, and we managed to scramble up the opposite bank, at a place which was not so steep.

I then looked around for the hog, and at length

discovered him jogging along at a very easy pace, about a quarter of a mile off, in the plain. I made after him, having first dipped my pocket-handkerchief in a pool of the nullah, washed the dust from the mouth and nose of Lal Babba, and given him a mouthful of water in my hunting-cap to refresh him; and, in a short time, found myself within fifty yards of the boar, who evidently exhibited signs of distress, for he reeled from side to side, as he ran with his head strained forward, and his flanks heaved and were covered with foam.

I was now joined by N——, O——, S——, D——, C——, and W——, who came up with their horses nearly "pumped," as they had had to ride nearly a mile down the nullah before they could find a place to cross.

We were perceptibly gaining upon our prey, when, with a burst of recovered speed, he swerved off to the left, and in a moment I saw amid a few bushes a break in the ground, about a hundred yards in advance. I knew another "yawner" was ahead, and took a pull of my horse, so as to get him more in hand, and gather him together for the leap. This let N—— and C—— get a couple of lengths ahead, and S—— and T—— were neck and neck, closely followed by O——, D——, and W——.

The hog cleared a deep chasm like a bird, and we all followed except W——, whose horse fell on landing, giving him a heavy fall, and rolling over him. The ground now became firmer, the pace was terrific;

and now came the tug of war for the honour of the spear—suddenly the hog, which was not more than a dozen horses' lengths in advance, disappeared. "What's that?" cried some one behind. "God knows," cried N——, ramming his hunting-cap down over his eyes, and in another moment we had leaped the steep bank of a nullah, (a perpendicular drop of about seven feet,) and were floundering in sand and water.

D—— got an ugly fall, his horse rolling over him, and putting him *hors de combat;* S—— also found his horse sprained in the stifle, and he had also to pull up. N——, C——, O——, and myself, managed to scramble up the opposite bank, and were once more on *terra firma.*

The pace was very severe, and began to tell; and although Lal Babba appeared less distressed than the other horses, I knew he could not last much longer. Still, on we went. I was neck and neck with N——, and C—— and O—— were close behind. We were evidently fast closing with the hog, when we came to another yawning chasm, of which he made "*an in and out.*" "Never say die," cried N——, and over it we both flew, landing safely on the other side, (it was a good thirteen feet from bank to bank.) O——'s horse fell with him, and C——'s was fairly done up to a stand-still, so we left them both behind.

The game now lay between N—— and myself. He rode a splendid large-made Arab, of high caste, called Bidgeley, (lightning,) well known throughout the Deccan as a hog-hunter. My horse was smaller, but I had the advantage in weight of at least a stone, besides which, Lal Babba had been spared the long run down the banks of the ravine, and had not had the lost ground to make up, which told severely on the other horses.

We were now upon a bit of very fair riding ground, and the boar was not more than a couple of spear-lengths ahead. The pace was too good to last long, and I could see it was telling severely on N——'s horse, who was doing all he knew to keep him together. We were neck and neck, and now came the "struggle" for the spear. N—— made a vigorous attempt to hustle his horse, but without avail. Sitting steadily in my saddle, I gained the lead and kept it easily, Lal Babba following every twist and turn of the boar, like a greyhound after a hare. The tusker, now evidently nearly done, was slackening his space, and reeling from side to side as he ran. Another moment, and the point of my spear was among his bristles—a touch of the heel—a lift of the bridle—a chiffney rush—and the victory was won. The blade of my spear was planted deeply into his loins.

With a ferocious grunt, a rolling of the eyes which portended mischief, and a champing of his tushes, he turned short round and charged. I wheeled Lal Babba round on his haunches, just in

The Spear Won.

time to evade his frantic rush; he passed me like a shot on the near side, and attacked N——, who was a couple of lengths behind, who received the charge on the point of his spear; I saw the bamboo shaft bend like a wand, and then fly high up into the air; another second—I heard a crash, and horse and man were rolling in the dust.

In the twinkling of an eye I was alongside the infuriated animal, who was indulging in a series of grunts of defiance, preparatory to another charge, and, watching my opportunity, I buried the blade of my spear behind the shoulder-blade, and drove it out of his breast. He uttered a faint squeal, (the note of departing life,) gave a sudden twist, (his expiring effort,) which wrenched the spear from my hand, struggled a few paces further, fell, and bit the dust, dying game to the last.

I dismounted and drew my hunting-knife across his throat to let out the blood, loosened the girths of my saddle, and then went back to see what had become of N——.

I found him sitting on the ground, with his face buried in his hands, in great distress, for his horse was struggling in the agonies of death a few paces from him. The boar, in charging, had ripped up his belly, his tushes cutting like a knife, and the intestines, also much injured, were protruding from the wound. I saw at a glance that it was a hopeless case, and tapping N—— on the shoulder, I give a significant look to a small pistol that I always carried loaded in my belt on such occasions, in case of accidents.

He understood what was passing in my mind, walked up to his dying *serviteur*, and patted his neck. The poor animal, in spite of his agony, recognised his master, for he raised himself up partly from the ground, and rubbed his nose against his shoulder in a most affectionate manner. N—— kissed his forehead, and, passing his hand across his eyes, rushed into the jungle, saying, "Do not let him linger." When his back was turned, I placed the muzzle of my pistol to the suffering animal's temple, and pulled the trigger—a slight quiver of the body followed the report, and "Bidgeley" was dead. N—— cut off some of the hair of his forelock and tail for a *souvenir*, I slung his saddle and bridle over Lal Babba's back, and we slowly retraced our way towards the tent.

We soon fell in with O—— and C——, who were reclining under a tree, as their horses were quite done up; and in a short time our syces (grooms) came up with fresh mounts. After having directed them where to find the hog, we mounted and rode into camp—a distance of eight miles; the boar having led us a chase of at least seven.

We had a fearfully hot ride, as the sun had risen high above the horizon, and there was not a cloud to intercept his rays; the sultriness was getting more and more oppressive, and we found the wind scorching. To add to our distress, every now and then a "pishash," or whirlwind of dust, came twirling amongst us, filling our eyes and mouths.

At last, as our encampment came in view, we could distinguish six hogs hanging to our trysting-tree; and shortly afterwards the boar was hoisted up alongside of them. He was a huge brute, measuring thirty-eight inches in height at the shoulder, and his tushes were nearly nine inches in length.

We sat down to a substantial breakfast, (pork chops forming one of the items,) and in the cool of the evening we returned to cantonment, some of us with aching bones and curious bumps on the cranium, which would have puzzled Gall or Spurtzheim; others with strips of diachylum plaster on the face; and all of us with cracked lips and sunburnt faces. Our horses, too, showed their work, and "our gayness and our gilt were all besmerched." Still every one was content with the sport, and the incidents of the day afforded us ample topics of conversation when we met at Mess, when N—— was heard consoling himself for his loss, by observing that Bidegley had died as his master hoped to do—"*on the field in the moment of victory.*"

CHAPTER III.

MULKAPOOR.

"Here couch'd the panting tiger on the watch;
Impatient but unmoved, his fire-ball eyes
Made horrid twilight in the sunless jungle
Till on the heedless buffalo he sprang,
Dragg'd the low bellowing monster to his lair,
Crash'd through his ribs into his heart—
Quaff'd the hot blood, and gorged the quivering flesh
Till drunk he lay, as powerless as the carcass."

Our camp.—Mulkapoor.—The Patel.—Good news of shekar.—W———'s family.—Scheme for a Nautch.—The Begum.—Her love of good liquor.—The prescription.—Chineah and my shekar gang.—The doctor's ruse.—News of a man-eater.—Departure of the gang.

It was a fine morning, soon after sunrise, in the month of March, 18—, when I arrived at the little village of Mulkapoor, two days' march from Hydrabad, in the Deccan, in command of some irregular cavalry which, with two companies of native infantry, formed the travelling escort of a begum (a lady of rank) and her daughter, who, with a large suite of followers and attendants of both sexes, was *en route* for the Presidency. The cavalcade consisted of numerous elephants, camels, palanquins, tonjons, hackeries, and vehicles of every description and colour, accompanied by a large body of gaudily-dressed mounted attendants.

The principal personages occupied the public bungalow, round which high canvas walls had been placed, and sentries posted, so as to prevent intrusion, and render it entirely private; besides which numerous black eunuchs guarded the fold, and seemed to take a jealous care

> "That none should pierce the secret bower,
> But those who watch the women's tower."

The troops and camp-followers halted on the open ground in front of the traveller's bungalow, and in a few short moments tents of every description uprose as if by magic; elephants, camels, and horses were eating quietly at their pickets; and in less time than it takes me to write, this little clearing from the surrounding jungle was converted into a busy camp.

The scenery about Mulkapoor is very wild and beautiful. On all sides are ranges of hills, some covered with luxuriant jungle, others presenting bold scarped rocks and naked fantastic peaks, whilst in every direction from amongst the dense foliage noble forest trees towered like giants above the lower waving jungle.

The scene in camp, though of everyday occurrence in India, would appear curious enough to a stranger, and merits description, for the noise of the trumpeting of elephants, the jingling of the camels' bells, the neighing of horses, the lowing of carriage bullocks, the bargaining of sepoys and camp-followers with the bazaar men, was only heightened by the chase of a stray capon, whose errant ways were calling forth the indignation of my maity (cook) "Five minutes," (a cognomen he had acquired from the invariable answer he gave when anything was wanted,) who, joined by half a dozen sepoys, was shying his slippers at this victim devoted to "sudden death" for our breakfast, and venting their spleen by abusing its female relations up to the tenth generation. Three English officers belonging to the detachment of infantry, and a Scotch doctor, who had medical charge of the party, had taken refuge under a large tamarind tree from the rays of the sun, that was rising high on a sky which had not a cloud upon it to intercept his beams, and were discussing brandy panee, tea, and manilla cheroots, waiting until their tents were properly established.

As I joined the group, the old patel, or head man of the village, came up, and having presented the customary lime, performed a series of low salaams to each of the party. He then drew up his hands together in token of respect, and begged us to excuse his not having made more preparations for our reception, stating "that he had only received intimation of our coming the day before, and that, on account of this short notice, he had become '*lachar*' (desperately miserable) when he thought that, perhaps, we might want something that he had not had time to provide."

As the old man had provided plenty of "gram" (beans) and forage for our horses, with a fine table sheep and fat fowls for ourselves, we declared ourselves satisfied, upon which his face brightened up, and stroking down his long gray beard, he exclaimed several times in a very complaisant manner, "Allah talah!" "Al-humda lillah!" (thank God! God be praised!)

"I should much like to halt a few days here," said Mac, the senior subaltern, addressing Captain W——, who commanded the infantry detachment, "for there must be splendid shooting in those dense ravines."

"Yes," answered W——, "it looks quite 'a tigerish spot.' What say you, old man? Have you not plenty of 'shekar'* here?" continued he, addressing the patel.

"Yes, sahib," answered he, "there is plenty of shekar to be found in these jungles. Tigers, bison, bears, panthers, elk, milghau, antelope, and spotted deer are to be found, besides all kinds of small game; but if the 'sahib log' (gentlemen) wish to be successful, they must take some one with them who knows the haunts of the animals; so, with your permission, I will take my leave for the pre-

* "Shekar," *sport.*

sent, and fetch Kistimah the peon (policeman) and Veerepah the dhoby, (washerman,) both of whom are good ('shekarries') hunters, and will be useful to your honours." So saying, he made a profound obeisance, and retired gracefully.

As he strode away, I heard him muttering audibly, though rather *sotto voce*, "Oh, fool of an old man that you are, what have you done? Your face will become black before the sahib log, if neither the peon nor the dhoby are to be found; and if, 'God helping,' they should be at home, still, perhaps, those jungle animals of defiled fathers will not allow themselves to be seen, and again I shall eat dirt. Abah! Abah! Toba!"

"Well, my chickens!" exclaimed W——, "as the old Moslem gives so favourable an account of the place, I think we cannot do better than halt a day or two, provided the old begum raises no objections to the proposition, for I have another strong reason for wishing to remain here a short time, which is, that our supply of liquor will not last the trip, if we get on as fast as we have done, for when it was ordered, I did not think we should have made it quite such thirsty weather. By stopping here a few days, I shall be enabled to send a coolie to the Mess for a couple of chests more of Bass's pale; for, between ourselves, this hot and dusty weather, beer is as necessary to keep one up to the mark, as my grass-cutter's wife's milk is to my bereaved Brinjarry pups, whose canine mother died in convulsions, leaving her orphan progeny to my paternal care, and I, like a good guardian, have turned them over to the care of my grass-cutter's wife, who nurses and suckles all six, with her own little animal; and as they tumble about in her lap, howling, squalling, and caterwauling, I think the father would have some difficulty in swearing as to which was his own. He, however, looks upon his wife's services as a good speculation, as I feed her well, and he pockets an extra pagoda* a month; for the other day the scoundrel came up to me, grinning and showing his teeth, with the request to be permitted to provide another wife to bring up the Poligar greyhound's litter; and when I did not agree to his proposal, he had the impudence to try and persuade me that his wife's family were all growing 'berry handsome' about the face, on account of the good milk."

"Well," answered Jock, "I must say they appear to be a very thriving family, and do credit to their 'bringings up.' But what do you say to my proposal of politely insinuating to the begum, that time hangs heavily on our hands in the evenings, and that a *nautch* (dance) now and then would be much appreciated, for I am quite sure some of her dancing girls would prefer enlivening our spare hours to wasting their sweetness on the desert air. Do you not think a gentle hint, or a polite intimation of the general wish, with our united salaam

* Pagoda—three rupees and a half.

would have the desired effect with the *khanum sahiba* (lady)?"

"Hout awa, mon," put in the doctor; "if that's your game, I should just guess you'd be better leaving the leetle delicate affair to me, as I'm invited to visit her ladyship this morning."

"What? Eh? What's that, Saw-bones?" exclaimed W——. "You going to visit the begum? Why, you old reprobate, you have got the start of us all."

"Yees; and this child intends to keep it, too," replied the doctor, with a knowing grin, and a succession of very audible grunts, which, with him, always denoted intense satisfaction.

"Whatever can be up? Is she ill?" asked Mac.

"No—not vary—that is, I couldna just say that she's doun-right ill," answered the doctor; "but she sent for me last night, after dinner, and made me to understand that she was uneasy about her insides, hinting that she thought she had been struck with the evil eye. Weel, ye must know that I didna just remember what the *vade mecum* prescribes for sich like a disease, and as the medicine chest was made up, an' I didna think it was worth while to unpack it, by way of an experiment, I sent her negresship a good big bottle o' stiff gin toddy, a trifle stronger than I was then imbibing, and I reckon she found this potent remedy so conducive to her feelings, that early this morning she sent that ugly black henchman, of the neuter gender, with a mouthful of compliments, and what I esteemed verra much better, a basket of fine grafted mangoes as a present to your humble servant; and that dark ill-looking functionary informed me, in that queer squeaky voice, peculiar to the third sex, that his mistress was so much better for the clever hackeem's (doctor's) medicine, that she wanted to see him again personally some time during the morning; so ye see, boys, there is some good in the profession after all, for oft-times it gives us the means and ways of ingratiating ourselves wi' the fair sex, e'en though we are not, maybe, just so young and smooth-skinned as we might ha' been. Ugh! ugh! ugh!"

"Well done, Bones," said I. "You have indeed commenced the attack well, but the trail must be closely followed if good is to come of it. Now listen, and I will unfold a plan which must, if properly carried out, ensure success, or I resign all pretensions to strategy in managing old women.

"It is evident, from your account, that your patient has acquired a liking for your resusticating fluid, and has confidence in your *gin*-copathical genius. Taking this for granted, 'Go, thou, oh learned man, at once, and prepare a good quart bottle of the same stiff stuff, taking care to mix it strong enough to make her wince again, and cause her oculars to condense water in the same quantity as Mrs Parasina's did, when her infuriated husband, Azo, ordered his hobstreperous and houdacious 'hofspring,' Mr Hugo, her dewoted lovier, to have his head amputated for a heart complaint, *vide* the Poets. Leave me to write the directions on the label of the bottle in Hindostani, and give the spell time enough to work, which it will do after she has swizzled a few glasses more or less, then you drop in upon her, and if her heart will not have become sufficiently softened to grant you any little request or favour you may have to make —oh, you sly dog, doctor!—call me—too late for dinner."

"Oh, ye bauld chiel o' the deil! ye Irregulars are maist as bad as ranting wild Irishmen!" exclaimed the doctor, when I had concluded my oration; "but I do not just know at present what better to propose, so boy come here, ye ne'er-do-weel, and fetch me the gin."

"Weel, weel!" he continued, as the flask was produced, "that'll do; there's maist two-thirds o' the bottle left, and she'll just fill up the rest wi' strong tea, to disguise it, so that she'll no be suspected o' having only one salubrious concoction in the shop, as that old skinflint, Duncan McQuæ, the auld Glasgow medicaster, where I performed the rudiments at twa and saxpence a week, used to prepare for the poor townsfolk, wha got their ain bottles filled for twopence.

"Ah, gentlemen, you'll hardly believe"—here the doctor made a fearfully wry face—"that this child had when a growing loon, to swallow a good gill of the washings o' a molasses cask, seasoned wi' jalap, every Monday morning of his apprenticeship, to lay the worm in his stomach, and to prevent him from eating too much during the week. Oh! Duncan McQuæ, Duncan McQuæ! I do not wish ye any waur, where ye are noo, than to be swimming in your own 'regimen for all disorders, from elephantiasis to tape-worm.' Oh, the verra recollection makes me feel ill and squeamish. Now," he continued, screwing up his dry old countenance, as he tasted the brew; "come here, and make out a prescription to this effect, in your best Hindostani—'*One glassful to be taken every quarter of an hour, or oftener if required.*' Ugh! ugh! ugh! Let me see—that'll just allow sax glasses, by rule, for the hour and a half I shall be at my breakfast, and that's no allowing for the little requirings. Ugh! ugh! ugh!"

I wrote the label as directed, and the draught was despatched to the begum, with plenty of salaam from the doctor, who grunted and purred like an old tom cat, from extreme satisfaction, until he fell asleep in his chair.

Almost at this moment the patel returned with the two villagers, accompanied by Chineah, my head shekarry or huntsman, with the rest of my gang, which numbered about a dozen at that time.

Chineah was quite a celebrated character in his way, and merits description. He was middle-sized of dark olive colour, rather slightly made, with small quick eyes, placed very much apart, a straggling moustache, and an apology for a beard, in the shape of a few stiff hairs, sticking out like cat's whiskers, from the point of his chin, which he pulled and twisted about most violently whenever he got excited.

He wore an old cast-off green shooting-coat, a dirty brown *langooty* or waistcoat, untanned deerskin gaiters, and soldiers' ammunition boots, which were oftener slung over his shoulders than worn on his feet. His long coarse black hair was twisted round his head, being partially covered with a skull-cap of some strange looking material, of which the kind and quality were perfectly undistinguishable from grease and dirt.

Round his waist was a broad leather belt, hung round with numerous pouches, containing ammunition, a small axe made by the celebrated Arnatchellum of Salem, a huge shekar knife, and a *chuckmuck*, or leather bag, with flint, steel, and tinder. To complete his appearance, a telescope and brandy flask hung from each shoulder, and in his hand he carried my favourite double two-ounce rifle, a masterpiece, by Westley Richards. From his cocky mien and jaunty swagger, our friend evidently thought no "small beer" of himself, and he was, I must own, an invaluable personage in his way, being a first-rate tracker, cool and steady in the time of danger, a wonderful supporter of fatigue, and the most persevering follower after large game, besides being entirely devoted to me. His only fault was his love of *rackee*, (spirit made from the sap of the Palmyra palm, date, or cocoa-nut tree.)

The rest of the gang, who were almost naked, with the exception of the waistcloths, leather skull-caps, and their sandals, carried my other guns and light short bamboo spears. Each had a bill-hook stuck in his waistcloth behind, which they used with great dexterity in cutting their way through the jungle, and two carried large American backwoods-man's axes slung at their back, and another a *mushak* or leather bottle containing water. Both the village shekarries were in similar costume, and each carried a long native matchlock on his shoulder, and a huge knife in his belt.

"Well, Chineah," said I, "what news of shekar have you got?"

"*Boht utcha kubber hy, sahib*" (there is very good news, sir.) "All people tell that, near Botta Singarum, one village two coss* off, there got one *burra bagh* (big tiger,) who kill plenty men, sahib; Kistimah, this man here, he tell, eat one old woman yesterday. *Boht shytan hy, sahib* (he is a great devil, sir,) for though all shekarmen, and village people, plenty, plenty looking, never can find, when all come home, tiger go kill one man. *Wo burra chor hy, sahib* (he is a great thief, sir.) Ah, sahib, this very good shekar country. All *janwars* (beasts)

* A coss is about two miles.

plenty got; suppose master stop here few days, plenty, plenty shooting. This dhoby man, very good shekarry, know all this country, shoot plenty years in this jungle; other day kill one cheeta, now bring master skin, suppose some gentleman want buggy mat."

"Well! that will do," said I; "go all of you to the tent, and Yacoob Khan (my head-servant) may give each of you a glass of *rackee* and some tobacco; after which you will all go to the village of Botta Singarum, and there find out all you can about the haunts of this tiger. Promise the villagers plenty of *bucksheech* (presents) if they assist you, and I will come with Kistimah, the peon, after I have had breakfast. Chineah, take care that no shot is fired at deer or peafowl. Do not loiter on the road, for I shall not be long after you; and keep a bright look out for the tiger's *pugs* (footprints.) Well, gentlemen," continued I, to the other officers, "you have heard the news; who is going after the man-eater with me? I intend starting immediately after breakfast for the village, near which he is said to prowl; then, what steps I may take, will depend upon the information I may there receive."

"Oh! we will all go, except the doctor," exclaimed W——, "and he will take charge of our camp, as he does not shoot, and has an engagement, which as there is a lady in the case, must not on any account be put off. What say you, 'Sawbones,' will you superintend the catering for dinner, and arrange matters about the nautch?"

"Yees, yees," replied the kind-hearted old Scotchman, "gang yere ways, gang yere ways, and tak' ye care and kill the tiger, and dunna let him kill ony o' ye; for though there's not much more use o' sich like folk than a pack of wild Irishmen, I do not want to hae' ony o' ye scragged."

CHAPTER IV.

THE MAN-EATER'S LAIR.

The start.—The man-eater's depredations.—His habits described. —His last victim.—His trail.—We are on his track.—More game.—The scent becomes warm.—The lair.—The remains of many victims discovered.—The plan for the morrow.—A resolution.—W——'s idea of shekar.—We arrive in camp.—The Pill's garden.—The bath.—Dinner.—The doctor's visit to the begum.—Effect of his medicine.—My future husband.—The nautch arranged.

DURING breakfast, sundry modes of proceeding with regard to this tiger were discussed, but no particular plan was settled upon.

When the meal was finished, we donned our *shekar gear*, mounted our nags, and started for Botta Singarum, each followed by a horsekeeper, carrying a gun, rifle, or boar spear. Kistimah led the way, and as we went along, I asked him what he considered the best plan to follow.

He answered in a remarkably shrewd manner that he hardly knew what to advise, as this was no common tiger, or it would have been easy enough to arrange matters; "but," added he, "these *man-*

eaters are so desperately cunning that one can hardly ever be up to their moves. It is of no use picketing bullocks in the places he frequents, for he will not touch them. I have frequently known him to carry off the man who was watching the cattle, and leave the herd untouched. One is never sure of his movements; he is so cunning that he very seldom shows himself, and although after he has carried off some one, I have frequently followed his trail for miles, yet his lair has not yet been discovered, and I believe he never remains two nights in the same place. They say he has killed more than forty people within the last six months; and as I know myself that sixteen post-runners have been missed within that time, I have no doubt but that he has carried them off. The *dauk* * post runners will not go alone now; they carry the *tappal* bags in bands of five or six, armed, and with fire-sticks, and even then so great is the fear inspired by this brute, that they often choose to go by an out-of-the-way road rather than run the chance of meeting him. He would be a lucky man, indeed, who killed this beast, for great rewards are offered for his skin. I have followed his trail many a long day, and once got a sight of him as he was drinking; but when I tried to steal near enough to be certain of my aim, he got wind of

* *Dauk* or *tappal.*—Indian post. The letters being carried in leather bags, on men's shoulders, who are relieved every five miles.

me, and sprang into the thick jungle. I saw him very distinctly, as the sun was fast setting, and he appeared to me to be of a different colour to other tigers, being of a dirty yellow, the stripes not showing."

"Well, Kistimah," said I, "the only way to make sure of the colour of his skin is to bag him; and this is the way I propose setting about it. When we arrive at the village, I shall order the *tassildar* (head police authority) to assemble as many beaters as he can, to be ready at the earliest dawn to-morrow, and we will try and beat him out. To-day we will follow up his trail, and visit some of the places where he has been lately seen; perhaps by good luck we may come across him."

"Well, sahib, your plan is good; you speak like a book, and I have nothing better to propose; still I am not very sanguine of success, for he is a very old and cunning devil; but, *Inshallah,* (please God,) I'll burn his whiskers for him yet. Who is the tiger of defiled fathers, that he should cast dirt on our beards?"

By this time the village appeared in view, and I sent on to Kistimah to warn the head man of our arrival.

He came out to meet us as we entered the village, and we dismounted and seated ourselves under the shade of a large tamarind tree, in front of the *tannah,* or police station.

After the usual compliments and salaams, he proceeded to tell us of the great devastation this man-eater had caused in all the villages round about, and he offered to give every assistance in his power to enable us to find his haunts and destroy him.

Having arranged all about the beaters to be collected from the neighbouring villages, and ordered them to be ready to take the field before dawn the following morning, we went out with a party of villagers to a well, about a hundred and fifty yards from the village near which a woman was said to have been carried off by the tiger the day before, as she was drawing water in the evening about dusk.

I examined the place attentively, and although the marks of the tiger's pugs were effaced near the well from a flock of goats having passed by, yet, near a tamarind tree, some little distance off, they were plainly visible, and even the marks of dried blood, and some long hair were left on the roots.

I also noticed the place behind a bush, where the herbage was pressed down, and the marks still left in the dust showed that the cunning brute had lain for some time on the look out, before he seized his prey.

Here I found Chineah, the dhoby, and the rest of the gang in deep consultation, and was just in time to hear the fag-end of a long string of curses, maledictions, and prophecies, in which it seemed to be allowed, by all parties present, that this tiger's female relations were anything but a chaste lot, and that he would be sure to come to a bad end.

I noticed that the trail of his retreat did not lead in the same direction as that from whence he came, and he seemed to have made the circuit of the village two or three times before he fell in with his victim. I followed the marks of his pugs through some rather open custard-apple jungle, to the dry sandy bed of a nullah, or watercourse, where the trail was very plain; and although there were no marks of blood to be seen, yet I knew that he had still carried his victim, as the pugs of his fore feet were more deeply imprinted in the sand than those of the hind, from the extra weight he carried in his mouth, whereas I have observed that the marks of the hind feet are generally the plainest.

A little further on, I perceived a large patch of dry blood, round which the flies were buzzing, and from the marks in the sand I knew that the brute had lain down the body of his victim for a moment, in order, perhaps, to get a better gripe.

Whilst showing this to W——, I noticed marks in the sand which made me believe that his victim had not been quite dead at this time, for there were impressions as if she had made convulsive clutches with her hands.

I tracked him down this nullah for upwards of a mile, until we came to a pool of water. The banks, which had become steeper and higher, were covered with dense thorny jungle, which waved darkly overhead. Here the pugs of the tiger were much obliterated by the marks of other wild animals, amongst which I noticed those of two bears, a cheeta, and innumerable signs of spotted deer, pig, and jungle sheep.

Near the other side of the pool I observed marks as if he had again laid the body down, whilst he drank, for there were impressions in the sand, round which swarms of flies were buzzing, and although there were no stains of blood to be seen, I knew something must have attracted them; besides which, there were two distinct trails, which showed that he had gone to the water, drank, and returned to the body.

As we continued on trail down the nullah, at times we disturbed herds of spotted deer and "*sounders*" (herds) of pigs, and an old female bear and two half-grown cubs were seen trotting along in front of us; but we let her go undisturbed, for we were after nobler game.

On we went for about two miles further, when we came to a place overgrown with high grass, where the *nullah* divided into two courses for about eighty yards, when it joined again, forming an island, which was covered with long dry grass, reeds, and brushwood.

There the man-eater's trail was crossed by that of a tigress and her two half-grown cubs. We were still enabled to distinguish the pugs of the man-eater from their peculiar form, and continued to follow them for about half-a-mile further, when the trail quitted the nullah, and led us into dense thorny jungle, through which we made our way in Indian file; and as we went along I pointed out to Jock small pieces of rag and long hair sticking on the thorns of a bush, proving that the tiger had brought his victim that way.

"Gentlemen," said I, "as the scent begins to warm, please look to your guns, and be ready in case we may surprise him. W——, I wish you would take the rear, and prevent the people from straggling. Chineah, keep near me with my second gun, and Rungasawmy, do you cut the way in front with as little noise as possible. We may very possibly come across him sleeping somewhere in this thick cover after his feed, so keep a bright look out on all sides, and take care and make as little noise as you can in getting through the bushes."

We were in single file, I leading, with much difficulty, through the thick jungle, which had become very dark from the dense foliage overhead.

The intense silence which reigned around was broken now and again, as we moved slowly on, by the crackling of a twig underfoot, or a low grunt from some one of the gang, as a sharp thorn entered his naked and unprotected shoulder. At times was heard the distant bark of the elk, or a pattering of feet, as a herd of deer or a sounder of pig got scent of us, and skirled away frightened through the thickets, or a peacock rose with a loud cry, scared by our movements.

On we went, the trail still distinctly visible, when

suddenly I fancied I heard a slight noise. I halted the gang, and whispered, or rather made signs to them, to lie quiet, for we were almost on our hands and knees, and laid my ear to the ground to listen. We distinctly heard grating sounds, like the gnawing of bones, accompanied by low snarls and growls. I noticed Chineah's eyes sparkling with excitement, as he lay listening to the ominous noises; and the convulsive grabs he made at the few bristles which adorned the point of his chin told me what was passing in his mind. Not a word was spoken, though I saw the eyes of the gang were following my movements.

I examined the nipples of my rifle to see that the powder was well up, and making signs to Chineah with my spare gun, and Mac, who was next me, to follow, I cautioned the others to be perfectly quiet, until they heard a shot, and stole gently forward on my hands and knees, moving with the greatest caution, and stopping every now and again to reconnoitre.

We made our way with great difficulty through the dense underwood for about a hundred yards, the noise becoming plainer and more distinct as we advanced, until at last we emerged into an open glade, with a large black rock on one side, surrounded with jungle.

Here, looking cautiously around, I found the noise proceeded from two jackals, who were munching and tearing the flesh from some half-stripped human bones. These immediately got wind of us, and slunk away growling into the bush. After examining the place thoroughly, to make sure that the object of our search was not there, I gave a low whistle, which brought up the rest.

This was evidently the hecatomb of the man-eater, for I counted, from skulls and remains of half-eaten bodies, about twenty-three victims of both sexes, as we could see, from the hair, clothes, broken bangles (armlets,) and gold and silver ornaments belonging to native women.

We picked up two massive silver bracelets belonging to his last victim, whose fresh remains exhibited marks of tattooing, which were recognised by one of the villagers who was with us. We also found two gold *teekas*, or neck oraaments, which mark the "*married*" woman, and a knife, which the dhoby assured us he knew as having belonged to a post-runner who had been killed about a month before.

The stench from the decayed animal matter was almost insupportable, and we were glad to leave it and breathe the fresh air once more. I gave orders to the gang to collect the remains, but not to bury them, until they had been seen by the village authorities; as I thought that some would be recognised, and their friends might wish to inter them with their "caste" ceremonies.

"What a fearfully sickening sight it is!" said

Mac. "I declare it has made me feel quite queer, and given me an all-overishness I shall not get over for a week."

"I wish we had brought some beer with us," said W——, with something very nearly approaching to a sigh, "for I want a draught to wash my throat after the tainted air I have been inhaling, which has half suffocated me. Come, Chineah, produce your master's brandy-flask, and let us have a little refreshment after our exertions."

"Poor little woman," exclaimed Jock, "look, here is a long lock of her hair attached to a piece of scalp, that I found sticking to my boot as I came out,—I shall keep it as a souvenir."

"Well," said I, "the only souvenir that I should care to keep, to remind me of this day's scene, would be the skull of the man-eater; and if my right-hand has not forgotten its cunning, and my grooved bore does not fail me—which, all praise to the Bishop of Bond Street and Westley Richards, it never has done yet—that trophy shall yet adorn my domicile, for I do not intend to leave a stone unturned until I bag the brute. My gang shall sleep at Botta Singarum to-night, so as to be ready for work at dawn to-morrow; and I vote we ask for volunteers among the detachment, and allow the steadiest men to take their muskets with them, so as to defend the line of beaters. It must, however, be an understood thing that no one is to fire a shot at any other game until our object is attained, or all chance of finding him is over; when we will finish the day by a general beat, bagging everything."

"Yes," said W——, "you are perfectly right; there must be no firing at deer or hog. That is the only way of doing the thing so as not to lose a chance; but, as it is now getting late, let us go back to the village, caution the police authorities again about the beaters, mount our nags, and be in time for the Doctor's catering—for, between ourselves, I am powerfully peckish. 'By the piper that played before Moses,' it is worth while going out shekar, were it only for the appetite it creates, and the relish it gives one for beer."

On arrival at the village, we arranged all matters with regard to the number of beaters required. The ameldar, or head man of the village, sent to all the neighbouring hamlets to collect men; the gang established themselves for the night in a choultry or caravanserai, after having begged some coin from us to buy sheep and fowls on the plea of sacrifices being necessary to certain "Sawmies" (Hindoo deities) to ensure good luck on the morrow; and mounting our horses amid the "Salams," "Mashallahs," and "Inshallahs" of the villagers, we rode back to camp—the scene we had that day witnessed, our hopes of the morrow, and sundry hazardous speculations as to the doctor's success with the begum, forming the chief topics of our conversation *en route*.

We arrived in camp just before sunset, and were

delighted to see the old Pill carefully watering what, to the uninitiated, must have appeared like a garden of straw, but we knew that a goodly store of "*long corks*" (claret) and "Bass's" nectar, "may his shadow never be less," was cooling in the wind for our evening repast.

We all adjourned to our different tents to enjoy our bath, which the day's fag rendered particularly refreshing. In no part of the world is the real luxury of a bath so appreciated as it is in India. There you bathe the first thing you get up in the morning; again, when you come back tired after a hot morning parade; again, before you sit down to dinner; and, in the hot weather, if you want to sleep well, you will plunge into your bath just before you turn in for the night. Are you overcome and oppressed by the hot weather? Take a bath. Do you return tired to your tent after a hard day's fag under a hot sun? nothing in the world serves sooner to dispel fatigue and lassitude, than a few chatties (earthen pots) of cold water thrown over the body. Trust an old soldier, my gentle reader, there is some truth in the cold water cure.

Refreshed and enlivened by our ablutions, we all met at dinner, "hungry as hunters," and the doctor's catering met with our universal approbation. After the clattering of dishes and the popping of bottles had somewhat subsided, Mac astonished the doctor's weak nerves with an account of the tiger's lair, and at last worked up the old Scotchman to such a state of excitement that he jumped up, gave his thigh a tremendous slap with the palm of his hand, and exclaimed, "Dom, but this child will gang wi' ye in the morn just to ha' a crack at the bluid-thirsty auld cannibal!"

"Bravo, doctor! We shall be most happy to have your company," answered I; "but, old Sly Boots, what about the visit to the begum? How fared you there? Eh?" continued I, giving him a sharp dig in the ribs with my forefinger, which made him grunt again.

"Yes; out with it, doctor!" cried W——. "Don't mince matters, but give us a full account."

"Husht your whisht, and I'll tell ye all about it," replied the doctor. "You must know that I went to the bungalow about two hours after you left camp, and that black gentleman of no sex, who had evidently previously received his instructions, conducted me at once into the centre room, where I saw a figure, closely veiled in a chedder (cloth) which concealed everything but a pair of sparkling eyes, sitting tailor-fashion on a carpet, wi' two or three decent-looking lasses attending her.

"When I entered, and she saw who it was, she waved her hand, inviting me very graciously to seat myself near her, which I did. She sent the other women away, and then, with a knowing wink, pulling the cloth away from her face, passed me the hubble-bubble she was smoking when I first went in. I found her to be a guid '*auld has-been*,' that is, the remains of a fine woman, with a very pleasing and comfortable cast of countenance. As I was puffing away, with my understandings twisted in such a knot that I started the seams of my galligaskins, she kept smiling and nodding in such a way at your humble servant, that I fairly thought that I should ha' had to cut and run, for she seemed to ha' made a dead set at me, so I just told her I was a married man, wi' fourteen sma' bairns at hame; but even the prospect o' sae mony incumbrances did not seem to discourage her—she was as sweet on me as ever, and presented me with betel-nut and some sweetmeats, both of which I refused. She then offered me the identical flask I had sent her in the morning, which I took, and just to show her that I was no' afraid o' my ain drugs, I raised the bottle to my lips, lifted it higher and higher, but de'il a drop o' the creature was there in it. 'Twas as dry as a bone. I gave the old lady a look from the corner of my eye, but what was my astonishment when I saw her apparently in a fit, on the broad o' her back, almost bursting wi' laughter. When she came to herself and could speak, she gave me a gentle hint that a full bottle was better than an empty one, and that the stuff was good, and agreed with her constitution; so I couldna do less than promise her more.

"We then got talking together quite familiar-like, and she told me that her daughter was as beautiful as a peri, and was about to be married to the Nawab of ——, at the same time asking me if I had ever seen her intended son-in-law. Determined to pay out the daughter, whom I heard joking at my expense wi' the ither lasses, behind a purdah (screen) in the next room, and commenting on my personal appearance in no verra flattering terms, I pretended to be intimately acquainted wi' the gentleman in question, whom I described to be rather less in stature than myself and not nearly so good-looking. I also said he was much to be pitied, for he had the misfortune to have a curious-shaped lump (sometimes running) in the middle of his face, with a great black patch o' hair underneath, and I never heard tell that any doctor had been bold enough to offer to remove it.

"As I said this, the giggling behind the curtain ceased suddenly, and I knew the shot had gone home, from a faint cry of horror, which I conclude came from the affianced bride. The black factotum seemed to be very grievously affected at my recital; he cocked his head on one side, winked both eyes, screwed up his blubber lips, wrung his hands, and then, as if he could not contain himself, burst into a loud yell, threw himself his whole length on the floor at the begum's feet, and in great agitation and trembling began, in a voice something like the higher notes of a jackal's howl, broken by frequent bursts of sobs and great overflow of tears, which actually drenched his face, to inform her that he, the most miserable of her slaves, had once seen an individual labouring under a similar misfortune; that he was always fearfully vicious and cranky, especially at certain times of the day when the pain from the tumour drove him mad; and he conjured his mistress not to send her faithful servant to the harem of such a terrible bud-surut (ugly man,) who would make him eat dirt all the rest of his miserable existence.

"The old lady, herself, did not seem to care much about it, the potion had done its work, and she continued to smile very benignantly on her humble servant, so I gave her a gentle hint that time hung very heavily on our hands in the evenings, and that a nautch, now and then, would much enliven us; upon which she desired me to invite you all over to the bungalow to-morrow evening, and, at the same time, clapping her hands, her servants entered and she gave them orders to prepare a grand 'tamasha' (entertainment.) I then took my 'rooksut' (permission to depart,) and, as soon as I got back to the tent, despatched a flask of gin with 'bohc salam' (many compliments.")

"Why, you old reprobate!" said W——, "whatever did you mean to insinuate about the Nawab having a lump, and hair in the middle of his face? I have seen him scores of times, and never observed it."

"Weel! You ha' na' guid eyesight," answered the doctor, "that's certain, for the last time I saw him he wore both a nose and a moustache, and I dunna ken hoo I've exaggerated onything in my description o' his personal appearance. Can I help it if the young lady chooses to take it in a wrong light? Sarve her weel right too. Did I no' hear her jeering at me as I first came in the room, and telling the other lasses that the Fehringees (Europeans) were a clever and wise people, for they always choose the smallest and ugliest old men to make doctors of, as then there was no fear of the women falling in love wi' them? Ugh! Ugh! Ugh! But I paid her out in her own coin." And the doctor's grunts reminded me of a cat well-pleased.

"Bravo! doctor," I exclaimed, "you have done remarkably well, and deserve a leather medal for your gallantry in the attack; as, besides getting us the nautch, you have done your best to disgust the young lady with the thoughts of her future husband, which perhaps may prove to our advantage, for she may now feel disposed to take a more favourable view of mankind in general, as up to the present time she has certainly been, like the flower, 'doomed to blush unseen,' and waste her sweetness upon such disgusting lumps of humanity as the begum's blubber-lipp'd guardians of the fold."

"Yes," said Jock, "I think old 'Bones' has played his game with a great deal of management, and shown that, although he is perhaps a rum one to look at, he is a good one to go. So here's your health! Stick to your present mode of treatment, and I'll warrant you'll soon gain the patronage of the whole sex."

It was now late, and, as we should have to be in the saddle some time before dawn, the party broke up, each retiring to his tent.

CHAPTER V.

A BATTUE.

Preliminary arrangements for the beat.—The doctor's great appearance.—His famous feat.—W—— falls in with tigers.—Fatal accident.—The death of a tiger.—The game warms.—The battue.—Another tiger dies.—The bag of the day.—The doctor again.—The ceremonies of my gang.

THE next morning we all assembled in my tent an hour before the slightest appearance of dawn, and after having partaken of a hurried collation which my invaluable servant, "Five minutes," always managed to have ready at the proper time, we mustered about eighty sepoys and troopers with their muskets and carbines, and about twice that number of villagers, well supplied with matchlocks, tomtoms, and dubties,* cholera-horns, and other melodious instruments of music of that description; and mounting our nags, preceded by masaltjees or torch-bearers, we started for Botta Singarum.

* Dubties—native drums.

As we approached the tannah, or police-station, we found all the head men of the surrounding villages waiting for us, each attended by several of his people, armed with matchlocks, swords, spears, clubs, or any weapons they could lay hands upon, As we approached the entrance, the crowd of villagers surrounding the building made way for us, and I proceeded to explain to them the arrangements for the battue; which were that a large half circle of four miles in diameter was to be formed, having for its base the river, which was broad and deep, and along the opposite banks of which I had the evening before given directions that a chain of matchlock-men should be posted, to observe and be prepared to resist the tiger should he attempt to swim over. The nullah, or watercourse, and the lair we visited the day before were enclosed, and I distributed the armed sepoys and the village authorities among the beaters to see that the line was properly kept; sending the other officers (with the exception of the doctor, who chose to remain with me) to different places, where I thought they would have a good chance when the game broke.

One of my gang accompanied each; the rest, with most of my suwars, or irregular cavalry troopers, remained with me, and I chose my place in the part of the line that would pass over the nullah and the lair we had seen the day before.

As it was almost impossible to beat that part of the forest, on account of the dense underwood, I had provided my troopers with two hundred rockets in order to drive the game into the more open jungle.

In an hour I received intelligence that the line was formed ready to advance, and, it being now broad daylight, I gave the signal to move on by a ferocious flourish of cholera-horns, which sound was immediately taken up by all the tomtoms, horns, and dubties; and this discordant music was only surpassed by the unearthly howling and shouting of the beaters, who seemed to outvie with each other as to who could utter the most fiendish yells.

The doctor, who kept near me, was armed with a heavy single four-ounce rifle which he had taken from one of the gang; and as he marched along he shouted at the top of his voice, in a most ferocious and threatening manner, something that appeared to me to be some very ancient Gallic war-cry, until his breath failed him. His route was perfectly well marked by strips of his old blue regimental frock-coat, which were left hanging on the thorns of the bushes as he passed.

As we advanced, sudden crashes every now and again in the jungle let us know that the game was a-foot. Now a herd of deer, or a sounder of hog were visible for a moment, as they bounded through the thicket in front of us. Sometimes a flock of peafowl passed over our heads, or a swarm of monkeys went jabbering away in the trees above us, shrieking and making faces at us as we passed, and, perhaps, thinking the Millennium was at hand, from the terrific noise made by the beaters.

Suddenly, cries were heard along the line of "Reech, Reech!" "Yellago bunte!" (a bear, a bear!) And almost immediately a large female bear and her two cubs came rolling along the line of beaters towards us.

The doctor gave a fiendish yell, and, unable to restrain his impetuosity, let drive and hit one of the cubs which passed within six paces of him—the recoil of the piece, for which he was not prepared, knocking him down on the broad of his back. The enraged mother charged right at him, overturning a beater in her course, and in a moment more she would have given him a severe mauling, if I had not tumbled her over, dead, with a ball behind the shoulder, as she was in full career towards her fallen enemy. Bones picked himself up, and, though considerably shaken by his fall, rushed frantically to secure his prize, which was struggling in the agonies of death. The other cub was caught alive by one of the beaters.

I reloaded my rifle, and then took the doctor to task for firing on the lesser game; but it was of no use talking to him, he evidently considered he had performed a great feat, and, although tears ran down his good-natured old face as he wrung my hand and thanked me over and over again for my lucky shot, still he felt he was quite a hero, and shouted at the top of his voice for the rest to hear him, "I've killed a bar! I've killed a bar! Jock, mon, do ye hear? I've killed a bar!" After much difficulty, I persuaded him to relinquish his much-esteemed trophy to the charge of a beater, and Chineah having reloaded his gun, the line moved on.

The old man went along, delighted as a child; and amid a succession of grunts, which with him denoted satisfaction, I heard him muttering something about preserving the skeleton, tanning the skin to make a muff, and boiling down the fat to be sent to an old sister, &c., although the wild animal he had killed was but little larger than a sucking-pig. He strode along perfectly happy, as if he had done his work.

Very shortly afterwards we heard several successive shots on the right, where I knew W—— was posted, and almost immediately a beater came running up with the news that three tigers were afoot, and that W—— had wounded one severely, but that it had taken refuge in the high grass we had passed through yesterday.

Ordering the line to halt, and taking three troopers with me, loaded with rockets, to drive them out, should it be necessary, I went to join W——, who had just reloaded his guns as I came up.

He told me that he had seen three tigers, one of which he had wounded, after having fired five shots as they were bounding through the long grass and brushwood.

I examined the pugs and found them to be the

same as those that had crossed the trail of the man-eater the day before, and which I had supposed to have belonged to a tigress and her two cubs. Several of the beaters saw the wounded tiger linger after the others, and had marked it take refuge in the small island caused by the dividing of the nullah.

It was a kind of bank, raised about three feet above the bed of the watercourse, and, perhaps, eighty yards long, by thirty wide, being covered with grass and reeds about five feet high, and so overgrown with low bushes, and tangled underwood, that it would have been impossible for the beaters to have made their way through it.

I posted the doctor, W——, and some of the gang, with fire-arms, so as to command a view on all sides, cautioning each how to fire so as not to hit any of the rest, and when all was ready Chineah struck a light with his flint and steel, and standing to windward, fired the high grass, which was as dry as tinder from the long drought, and blazed up, roaring and crackling, in an instant.

I then took post by a hole in the bank, where the grass bore traces of having been recently disturbed and trodden down, it being, I thought, a likely place for the tiger to break.

Everything promised well; we were all ready with our arms, and waited with impatience for the appearance of the tigers.

The devouring element had burnt half through the patch; still we could perceive no signs of their presence, or, indeed, any movement in the grass. The fire roared and crackled like the file-firing of musketry, dark and dense volumes of smoke rose in a huge column against the cloudless sky, and I began to be afraid that the beaters had been mistaken in supposing the brute to have taken refuge in the cover, when suddenly the air resounded with a fearful roar, and immediately a magnificent tigress and a half-grown cub sprang into the sandy bed of the nullah, from a place close to where the fire had reached. I heard a simultaneous discharge of half-a-dozen shots, and through the smoke I just discerned the brute make a second spring, which was immediately followed by a piercing yell. I knew that some calamity had taken place, and sprang forward just in time to see the infuriated brute tear away the flesh from the thigh to the knee of W——'s poor horsekeeper, who was lying motionless. The tigress, who appeared wounded, was stretched half-leaning over her victim; she turned her head as I approached, and couched, as if to make a spring; I raised my rifle slowly, fearing to injure the poor fellow, and then let drive. The ball went crashing into her brain, and she fell dead on her side, the blood streaming from her mouth aud nostrils.

The poor horsekeeper did not appear quite dead, though I saw at once that there was no hope for him; for the whole back part of his head was carried away by the first blow from the paw, which, at the same time, had torn down the flesh from the back of the neck between the shoulders as if it had been done with an iron rake. The hands were beating the ground with a nervous, palpitating motion, and two or three tremulous shudders passed over the whole body; but soon all was over, and I gave orders to a couple of coolies to carry the corpse to the village for burial.

One of the shekarries had killed the cub with his matchlock, and the remains of the other was found partially burnt by the fire, W—— having wounded it so severely in the hind-quarters, as to prevent it being able to move away on the approach of the line of fire; and the tigress appeared to have remained with her offspring until the fire had actually reached her, for I afterwards remarked that the skin was much singed and burnt in places.

W—— was much affected at the loss of his horsekeeper, for he had been in his service for some years, and had always proved himself a faithful servant. However, as nothing could be done, we retook our station in the line, and the *battue* was continued.

On approaching the lair discovered the day before, we discharged several rockets into it, and a fine bull-neilghau and two cows charged boldly against the line of beaters. Mac broke the shoulder of the bull with a well-directed shot, which stopped him in his mad career, and, stepping up, despatched him with the second barrel as he lay upon the ground before he could pick himself up. He was a very fine specimen, with a long, flowing mane. The two cows broke through the line of beaters and escaped, though one of them appeared severely wounded by a volley from the beaters. A young cheetah was killed by the dhoby, as he attempted to sneak away through the bushes.

We had now driven the game into a large patch of jungle running along the river, on one side of which was a piece of tolerably open ground, and here we posted ourselves behind trees or rocks, in the most favourable places when the game broke. I also formed a second chain of men armed with muskets and matchlocks, as I knew that an immense quantity of game had been driven into that patch of jungle, and that some of it might escape our first line of guns.

When we were all ready I gave the signal, and the beaters began to drive the game towards us. Sounders of pig and herds of elk and spotted deer burst several times to the edge of the jungle, but always broke back again, as if they dreaded danger in the open ground and feared to cross it.

At last a sturdy bear showed the way into the plain, and was rolled over by Mac with a single ball. Soon afterwards a herd of sambur (elk) and a sounder of hog broke; and a fine buck, two does, and a sow bit the dust from the united volley poured in from all sides.

Then two cheetahs came bounding into the plain

followed by another bear; and one of the former fell by a ball from Kistimah's matchlock, and the other was badly wounded by one of my troopers, and afterwards despatched by the matchlock-men on the second line. The bear was killed by Jock, having made several ferocious charges after he had been wounded, in one of which a cooly was slightly mauled by his claws. Then another cheetah broke, and charged through our line scathless, though several shots were fired at him.

The beaters were now heard approaching very near, and I thought everything in the shape of large game must have been driven out of the inclosed patch of jungle, when suddenly I heard a cry of "Bagh! Bagh!" (a tiger! a tiger!) from one of my troopers, and almost immediately I saw a magnificent full-grown tiger stealing quietly across a little open glade or break in the jungle.

He was almost broadside on to me, but I was afraid of firing as I saw a group of my people were beyond him in the line of fire. I let him go on a little, threw up my rifle, and took a steady aim just behind his shoulder, pulling the trigger just as he moved his fore arm whilst walking.

When the smoke cleared away a little, I had the pleasure of seeing him stretched lifeless on his side; my ball having passed through his heart, death was instantaneous. He was a fine, full-grown male tiger whose beautifully marked skin measured eleven feet four inches from the tip of the nose to the end of the tail. I got another shot at a buck spotted deer, which I wounded in the hind quarters, paralysing them, and W—— finished him for me.

The beaters now made their appearance; they had killed four deer, three pigs, and a bear, and reported that two other tigers, some neilghau, and several herds of deer and hog had burst through their line.

One of their number was severely wounded in the thigh by a huge boar, which charged and knocked him down after he had been wounded. The flesh of the thigh was cut as clean as if it had been done with a knife, so we bandaged it up as well as we could, the doctor devoting a certain part of his nether clothing for the business, which performance caused us no little amusement, as we could not for some time make out what the old gentleman was after.

Constructing a litter with the branches of trees was the work of a few minutes, and we sent him to the village carried by coolies. Although he must have suffered a good deal of pain, he kept up his spirits in a remarkable manner, and seemed quite satisfied when he saw his antagonist brought in dead. We halted by the side of the river, where we bathed whilst the beaters were collecting the game, of which the following is the list:—Two tigers and two cubs, three cheetahs and one cub, three bears and two cubs (one taken alive,) five elk, four spotted deer, four pig (four small squeakers, taken alive,) one porcupine, and one bull-neilghau—total, thirty-two head of game.

I then despatched the gang to cut some stout poles, which, being thrust through the back sinews of the game, the coolies were enabled to carry it away slung on their shoulders, after having disembowelled the neilghau and deer. The total weight of our bag may be fancied, as over two hundred stout coolies were employed to carry it, and even then they went but slowly, had to rest often, and were frequently relieved by their comrades.

My gang went in front with their bill-hooks and axes, cutting down the branches so as to enable the loaded coolies to pass, and as the jungle was thick in some places our course was necessarily slow.

As we approached the village of Botta Singarum all the cholera horns, tomtoms, and dubties, forming up in procession, poured forth their notes of triumph; and, joined by the voices of the united company of beaters, bearers, coolies, servants, sepoys, and villagers, the row was something fearful, and better to be imagined than heard. When we came near our camp the procession was re-formed; my gang and some of the sepoys amused themselves by dancing in front of the dead tigers, before which our guns were carried decked out with flowers, and singing an extemporary song, the burden of which was something to this effect: —"That great and gallant deeds had been performed that day; that four tigers of burnt fathers having eaten dirt, and the brave and generous gentlemen being satisfied with their day's sport, plenty of buksheesh and inam (rewards and presents) would, as a matter of course, fall to the lot of their well-wishing followers, whose mouths were watering and stomachs panting with the thoughts of how they would be filled by the sheep which the well-known charitable and generously-minded gentlemen would certainly distribute." The chorus, being taken up by the whole party, was something deafening.

The game was laid down on the open space of ground in front of the bungalow, and the ceremony of breaking up was commenced by the oldest shekarry present burning the whiskers of the dead tiger, whilst he sang a monotonous song, in which he abused the whole race, and finished by spitting on his face and right paw.

The begum, who, it appears, was watching the performance with great interest from the bungalow, sent one of her followers to me with plenty of salaam, and a request that I would send her a tiger's heart and liver, with some of the blood, for medicine: which I did, to her great satisfaction.

The game being now all broken up and cut into pieces, a fine haunch of venison was sent to our tents, and a young doe, which, when wounded, had been properly "*hollolled*" by a Mussulman, (that is to say, had its throat cut whilst the operator muttered a certain text of the Koran, asking a blessing on the meat,) sent for the acceptance of the begum; the rest was divided among the whole number of troopers, sepoys, beaters, and camp-followers.

We also made a subscription amongst us, which was divided as buksheesh, and every one went to his home satisfied and happy.

CHAPTER VI.

THE GANG.

The begum's invitation accepted.—My shekar gang.—Googooloo's history and the discovery of the Yanadi caste.—Googooloo's gifts.—Insinuations.

As I was standing superintending the preparation of the skins, which my gang were pegging down tightly on the ground and rubbing with cocoa-nut oil and turmeric to preserve them, the black aide-de-camp of the begum came up, and, with many compliments on the part of his mistress, informed me that she would only be too happy if we would do her the honour of attending a nautch that evening.

I accepted the invitation on the part of us all, bidding him tell the Khanum sahiba "that her kindness had made a deep and lasting impression on our hearts, and that, ere the evening gun boomed through the camp, our shadows would cross her hospitable threshold," and then joined the other officers, who were sitting smoking in front of my tent and discussing the sports of the day.

"Do you think, Harry," asked W——, as I came up, "that the tiger you killed to-day was the man-eater who has committed all these depredations lately?"

"No," I replied, "Kistimah assures me that it is not; and I have no reason to doubt his assertion, as tigers are common enough in this part of the country. I shall, however, again try for him, for I hear we shall be detained here three or four days longer, as the begum expects some one coming from Hydrabad. You are aware that I have sent the best of my gang to follow up his trail, so we have not heard the last of him; for if Googooloo and Naga are at fault and cannot find out his whereabouts, I do not believe that there is a man between this and Cape Comorin who can."

"I readily believe you," answered W——. "There is not such another shekar-gang in the country, and Googooloo is certain as a bloodhound if he once gets on trail; I have seen him track a bear over rocky ground when I could not observe the mark of a single pug—it must be innate instinct."

"Yes," said Jock, "he is a wonderful fellow. But what astonishes me most is the extraordinary manner in which he watches his master's eye, as if he could there read what was required of him; and when he speaks I can only understand a word or two now and then, although I have a tolerable knowledge of the different lingos."

"You must give us a history of the gang after dinner, Harry," said W——, "for we have not time now, as the first bugle has sounded some time."

"Yees," put in the doctor, who just joined us, "and ye had all better be quick, too, as my stomach has been crying cupboard this long time, an' this child will no be answerable for his actions 'gin ye come not soon after the viands are placed on the table. Ugh! ugh! ugh!"

So we all rose and returned to our tents, and after a refreshing bath again met at the table. We were in good appetite for our dinner after the day's fag, and "Five Minutes," whose ordinary colour was a bright black, assumed quite a greenish tinge, as he blushed at the praise his *cuisine* called forth.

The old doctor was in great spirits, and became actually uproarious when Mac, alluding to his feat with the bear, proposed his health as a sportsman who that day had made his *début*, and he actually crowed and purred again when I advised him now to adopt a bear for his crest, with the motto, "Ursus Vinci."

"Now, Harry," said W——, when dinner was over and cheroots and brandy panee (water) circulated, "you must give us the history of the gang."

"Yes, yes!" vociferated the rest, "let us have it."

"Very well, gentlemen," said I, drawing in a long pull at my hookah; "I shall begin with Chineah, my head shekarry. He is the son of my old waterman, and has been in my service since he was quite a boy, when he used to carry my powder and shot, and act as a beater when I went after snipe. I found him very clever in marking down birds, and he seemed to take such an intense delight in going out with me that I bred him up to the work, and taught him to clean and look after my guns, which you know he does now to perfection. This is seven years ago, and now I should hardly know what to do without him.

"He is devoted to my interests, very cool and steady in time of danger, a first-rate hand in picking up news of game, and never so happy as when out in the deep jungle. His only fault is, that he is at times too fond of rackee (spirits,) and has too large an establishment of the fair sex, who are always squabbling and fighting for him in the servants' outhouses."

"Oh, yes," said W——, "I know him of old; but tell me about Googooloo, and let us hear where you picked him up."

"Googooloo's history is a strange one," I answered, "and I came across him in an extraordinary way. You may all perhaps remember poor old M—— of the —th, the kindest-hearted fellow, the best shot, and the coolest sportsman who ever pulled trigger, and who came to such an unfortunate end. We were great chums, and were always out together in the jungle; and to his intuition I must attribute my knowledge of forest life, for, although always fond of sport, I must confess I was but a griffin until he took me in hand. Well, we were out together in the Chettagunta jungles, about five years ago, in the very hottest weather, and had fagged for three days with very little success. There was no possibility of 'stalking,' for, in consequence of the great drought, the leaves and twigs on the ground had become so very dry and brittle that every step we took they cracked underfoot so loudly that the game always took the alarm before we could get within shot. On account of the great heat, we had been expecting the monsoon to break every day, and M—— had observed that it was that day the 6th of June, and that for several years past the hospital register showed the monsoon had broken between the 6th and the 10th. As there was not a cloud to be seen on the deep cerulean sky, I stated my opinion that we should have no change of weather that day, and away we went far into the deep jungle, where we intended to sit up at night by a pool of water, near which a tiger was said to lurk, and where bison often drank. We had come into a beautiful open glade in the jungle, in the centre of which, on a rising ground, stood a magnificent 'banian,' whilst clumps of huge forest trees were scattered about in groups here and there, giving the place much the appearance of a gentleman's park in England. In a 'jheel' or swamp, which was nearly dry, orchideous plants of every form and hue formed such a parterre that Chiswick itself could hardly equal; and never did I behold such luxurious vegetation. Yet this was in the centre of dark and almost impenetrable jungle, and at least twenty miles from the nearest habitation we knew of. Whilst we were remarking on the extreme beauty of the scene, suddenly I observed that the sky had become overcast, and thunder was heard rumbling in the distant hills. Presently large drops fell, and we had every indication of a heavy fall of rain. I gave orders to my people to pitch a small hill-tent we had with us as soon as possible, so that at any rate we might keep the guns and ammunition dry, and in the meantime we took shelter under the banian tree, where the people were employed in cutting tent-pegs and gathering firewood. M—— was reclining smoking on a carpet, close to the main trunk of the tree, when suddenly we thought we heard a rustling above our heads, about ten feet from the ground, just where the branches and arms began to shoot, and almost immediately we heard an extraordinary kind of sneeze coming from the same quarter. We started up and seized our guns, but could see nothing, for the whole fork of the tree was covered with masses of various kinds of parasitical plants 'Look out, Harry!' cried M——, 'there is some beast in that tree; most likely a leopard lying in wait for deer.' Having warned our people to move out of the way we walked carefully round, trying to discover where the brute lay hid; but all was now still, and we could see nothing from below. I got up one of the many branches thrown out by the parent stem, and looked carefully among the mass of vegetation which rested on the fork of the tree, still I could perceive nothing. I then got down and climbed upon the shoulders of a stout cooly, with a couple of men holding me by the calves of my legs, so as to keep me steady, and rifle in hand I made them walk up close to the foot of the tree, M—— standing near ready to cover me with his fire should any beast make a spring. Still I could see nothing. Bidding one of the coolies hand me up some stones, I threw them in the thickest parts of the masses of creepers, when I distinctly heard a low grunting. I desired the coolies to go to that part from whence the noise appeared to proceed, and, after a careful investigation, I thought I saw a pair of bright eyes twinkle, and something black moving about, which at first sight looked like the hair of a bear. I put up my gun and covered the object, but did not like to fire, as I was afraid of only slightly wounding the beast. M——, who saw the motion I made with my gun, asked me what I saw. I told him I thought a bear was concealed in the tree, as I could distinctly see some long black hair. 'A bear,' said he, 'perhaps it is; these gentry often climb trees on the look-out for honey, yet I think it is much more likely to be a black monkey. Fire at it, however, whatever it is, I am ready to look out for squalls, and perhaps it may be a black panther.' With any other man than M—— I should have hesitated to fire, considering the awkward position I was in, perched on the shoulders of a man who I knew would bolt at the first sign of danger, and expose me not only to a nasty fall, but also to the mercy of a wounded brute. But with M—— I felt quite safe, knowing his extreme coolness in time of danger, and the fatal accuracy of his aim. Again I raised the rifle to my shoulder and was about to pull trigger, when I bethought me that if it was only a bear he could not spring on me, and that I could fire with more fatal effect from the tree itself. I accordingly got on to the fork of the tree, and as soon as I got a steady footing I raised my rifle to fire. Again I put it down, thinking that I might only slightly wound the brute by firing in this way, so I gave the black mass of hair a poke with the end of the barrel of my gun in order to stir it up. Imagine my astonishment when I saw the upper part of a human face and a pair of eyes bob up and then go down again! To hang my rifle on a broken branch and whip out my shekar knife was the work of a moment, and thus armed I clutched the supposed animal by the hair, and shouted to M—— and the rest to come up; when the thing I was holding began to moan and struggle, and shortly a curious kind of paws, with huge claws, emerged from below and fastened on my hand, and it was only by frequent blows with the handle of my knife that I could prevent them from tearing the flesh. At that moment I was not sure whether I had not got hold of some kind of chimpanzee or ourang-outang, and I shouted out lustily for help. M——, the shekarries, and coolies soon got up into the tree, and with their assistance I dragged up from a hollow in the trunk two most extraordinary creatures in human shape. One was old and wrinkled, the other quite a child, and both belonged to the weaker sex, but whether of the genus 'man' or 'monkey' I was not at all sure. They were of a dark olive colour, and the tallest was nothing like four feet high. She just was a beauty, without a stitch of clothing except a piece of creeper tied round her hair to keep it out of her eyes, which were small and very piercing when she opened them, but she kept them shut, just taking a peep now and then like a frightened ape. She grunted very hard, and I saw a couple of tears rolling down her weather-beaten and wrinkled cheeks as the gang tied her by the leg to the root of the tree to prevent her running away. The child hung close to the mother, keeping its face hid in her lap, and I had a dog-chain passed round its ancle, and fastened with a padlock to a root also. We looked at them for a long time before we were quite sure whether they were human. I fancied at first that they were some kind of *hybrid*, for I never beheld such strange objects. The nose was nearly flat, the mouth most capacious, and full of large yellow teeth.

The arms were long, attenuated, and wizened ; and may Jove defend me from such nails as were attatched to the extremities of the digits, which resembled more the claws of a huge vulture, both in colour and form, than anything else. M—— said that the existence of these wild people of the forest had been often questioned, but that he had always believed that there were such tribes, having come across their traces in the dense forests to the south of the Neilgherri Mountains.

" A heavy shower of rain fell in the afternoon, but towards evening the weather cleared up again, and we pitched our tent, built a hut of branches for the people, and lit a huge fire, round which all were assembled, preparing the evening repast. One of the shekarries brought a piece of hard wood with a sharp point, and three or four wild jungle yams, which he said these wild people must have dug up just before we surprised them, as they were quite fresh. I gave the yams to the child, who, after a little hesitation began to eat, in which operation the mother assisted. I then sent for some raw potatoes, which both ate with great relish, though they still evinced great fear of us, and watched with suspicion every movement we made, with their little twinkling eyes. When our dinner was served we threw them bits of meat and some boiled rice, which seeing us eat, they followed our example. When we took our coffee after dinner I gave them some sugar, at which they evinced their satisfaction by clapping their hands on their thighs as they sat on their heels, smacking their lips and uttering some curious grunting sentences to each other, which neither M——, myself, nor any of our people could understand. Towards evening they appeared to have gained more confidence, and I made one of the servants unfasten the old woman. He had hardly done so, when, finding herself at liberty, she gave herself a shake like a dog on coming out of the water, and with a grunt and a yell sprang into the jungle before any of our people could stop her. Finding, however, that the child which was still fastened, did not follow her, she returned, and again crouched down by its side. I made the people take no further notice of them, and gave her more sugar, which she took and ate without hesitation. She now seemed to have made up her mind that we did not intend to do her any harm, for she began to examine us more closely, and even to finger our clothes, which she must have imagined to be of Nature's own providing, for she slunk back alarmed when she saw M—— pull off his cap, as if she thought his head would have followed, At dusk we were all sitting round an immense log-fire. The usual glass of rackee and allowance of tobacco had been distributed to each of the gang, and we were discussing the prospect of the morrow's sport, for we were not inclined to sit up for game that night, when suddenly M—— sprung up and shouted in Hindostani, 'Look out, men! those *jungle wallahs* are about.' I seized my rifle, and listened attentively, but could hear nothing. M—— said, 'I am sure they are near at hand, for I distinctly heard the chirping of a squirrel, which sound, you know, is never heard after nightfall, and I noticed the old woman's eye glisten as she caught up the sound.' He was right, for almost immediately four or five arrows fell about our fire, though without hurting any one. I took one to the old woman, and, giving her a lump of sugar and some raw potatoes, told Chincah to lead her towards that part of the jungle from whence the arrows appeared to come, I following at some little distance with my gun and one or two of my people, to protect him should it be necessary. When we got out of sight of the fire she made a queer noise, like the cooing of the imperial pigeon, which sound was almost immediately taken up in two places from behind some clumps of bushes. Again she uttered a curious note, and shortly afterwards I saw other figures join her in the gloom. At first I felt rather apprehensive for Chineah's safety, but, as they did not seem inclined to offer him any violence, I did not join their party, fearing to give them alarm. After a consultation, which seemed to last nearly a quarter of an hour, between the old woman and her people, they followed her towards our fire. When I came up I found the group consisted of three men, two women, and a child, all in the same state of nature as those we had discovered in the tree. The men were but little over four feet, and the women considerably shorter, and they all wore their hair tied with a piece of creeper at the back of their head, and spreading out behind like a peacock's tail. They had short bamboo bows, the strings of which were formed of the sinews of some animal, and the arrows were reeds hardened by fire, and tipped with the quills of pea-fowls. They were in great fear when we first approached, but seemed to get over it by degrees, and ate sugar, raw potatoes, and rice with great relish. They held a long communication with the old woman, in a strange guttural language which none of us could understand; and she must have allayed their fears, for they all laid down by the fire and slept, or rather pretended to sleep, for every now and then I saw one or the other open his eyes and look suspiciously round. Some of my gang kept watch during the night, and I still kept the first child chained by the leg. In the morning when I got up, I found them squatting on their hams in deep consultation. I showed them the skin of a bear which M—— had killed a few days before, and they evidently knew what the animal was at once, for they imitated the noise of his grunting exactly. I pointed out the bullet-holes in the skin, and showed them my gun, which, much to their consternation, I fired against a tree; and, when their fright had a little subsided, I showed them the hole in the trunk which the bullet had made, and one of my people cut it out with an axe. This instrument seemed to surprise them more than anything else. They could not understand it at all at first; but, after they had seen it used a few times, nothing would please them so much as to set them to work chopping up firewood. They amused themselves thus for hours together watching the chips fly, laughing and grunting to each other, and conversing in their curious guttural language.

"I shot in those jungles nearly a month, and then it was that I found what invaluable shekarries the Yanadi tribe make; for as trackers none equal them. Day by day they acquired more confidence in us, and in a short time they began to fall into our ways, and joined my gang. Googooloo attached himself to me like a dog, and has been with me ever since; the others are still in their old haunts. We speak a jargon of our own that no one understands but ourselves; it is a medley of Hindostani, Malabar, Tellegoo, and his own peculiar grunts. He can, however, now make himself tolerably understood by my people, though we are sometimes at a loss to know what he means. Chineah and he are great friends, and each in their way are unequalled as shekarries. Googooloo used to look upon me as a superior being for some time, but now I think his adoration has been transferred to my huge bone-smasher, (a six-ounce rifle,) to which he has frequently been seen to salaam and pray, laying the choicest flowers before it, much to my gardener's indignation. I have since heard that these aborigines of the forest have been found in all the deepest jungles throughout India, and are called Yanadi, Crumbers, Mulchers, Yaks, Carders, Morats, and Coons. They live upon roots, fruit, and any small animal they can catch in the jungle having no habitations of any kind, but generally living in trees or caves. From constant practice, their senses of seeing, hearing, and smelling are developed in an extraordinary way. Googooloo has the eye of a hawk, the car of a hare, and the nose of a hound. Often, whilst going along in the jungle, have I seen him suddenly halt, stand a moment with his nostrils dilated, as if he was snuffing the air, and then, drawing his axe, rush into the jungle, from which he would presently return with a honeycomb, which he had discovered in some hollow tree by the scent alone. He is wonderful in this way, and you may fancy what a useful follower he is in the deep jungle."

"I can, indeed," said W——, "but your fellows are all the same; they seem to consider you and everything belonging to you as part and parcel of themselves, and when anything is required they go to work with a will. You never seem to have any trouble in looking after them, yet your horses are always in the best condition, your dogs are well cared for, your guns are kept so clean that one might rub them with a cambric handkerchief without soiling it; your cob, saddles, and harness are always in first-rate order, and you always sit down to a comfortable table. I cannot imagine how you get everything done, exactly as it should be, without giving any orders or directions; I am always changing my servants, and still never get any to suit me."

"Just the very reason why you are always unsettled and uncomfortable," I replied. "I have had almost all my servants for a long time. My head boy has been with me ever since I arrived in the country, and knows all my ways; the same with my hooka-badar, (pipe-bearer,) and Abdulla, my horse-keeper. My dressing boy is the grandson of an old native officer, who fought at Assaye and Seringapatam under Wellesley Bahadoor, (the brave;) and "Five Minutes," my cook, Chincah, Googooloo, Naga, and sundry other of my retinue, have been with me for years, and will, I think, stop until the end of the chapter. They all required some little teaching and breaking in at first, but now they know what is to be done. I have very little trouble with them."

"You are somewhat right there," said the doctor, "and ye certainly have a weel managed household; but there's mair in it than a' that. Flunkies are somewhat like the brute bastes of the field; they know right well when they are kindly treated, and they are easier led than driven, but from certain strange coincidences, this child is of opinion that there is a third party behind the scenes who rules the roast. Tell me, oh, ye Irregular! have ye not a pair o' bright eyes, belonging to some gentle Lallbee,

Amirbee, or Zenobee, who has taken a kindly interest in the management o' your affairs for the sake o' the master? or what are ye doing wi' palanquins and covered carts in a bachelor's establishment, when you belong to a moss-trooping order, 'whose word is snaffle, spur, and spear'? Ugh! ugh! ugh!"

"Spare Hal's blushes, and let us adjourn to the begum's nautch, for I hear the sound of native music in that direction, and I suppose they are only waiting for our attendance to begin," said W——, rising from his chair.

CHAPTER VII.

THE NAUTCH.

The nautch: its fascinations.—Indian dancing-girls.—Oriental eyes.—Their dress and jewels.—Soaping the begum.—Indian jugglers and their tricks.—The celebrated mango-tree.—The sacrifice to Bowain.—Explanation.—The doctor's wonder.

"No treacherous powder bids conjecture quake,
No stiff starch'd stays make meddling fingers ache;
No damsel faints when rather closely press'd,
But more caressing seems when most caress'd."

—BYRON.

As we entered the garden or compound round the bungalow we found great preparations had been made for the nautch. The verandah was enclosed all round with fine mat tatties or screens, behind which the begum and her attendants sat, and through which they could see the performance without being exposed to the gaze of the public. In front were placed about a dozen chairs, the centre ones being left vacant for us, and the others occupied by the native officers of the detachment. In the centre of a large circle of troopers, sepoys, camp-followers villagers, and attendants, who were seated in rows on mats placed on the ground, was stretched a large carpet, round which several huge brass candelabra were placed. Overhead a large red and white chamiana was stretched, sheltering the spectators from any dew that might fall; and in the rear was placed an open tent, containing the musicians, who were about twenty in number.

The instruments consisted of sarindas, (a kind of guitar,) clarionets, several queer-shaped fiddles, cholera horns, (trumpets about five feet long, shaped like an S,) hautboys, tomtoms, dubties, dolkies, and drums of every size and shape; besides small bells, which were used as castanets.

Large brass and wooden trays piled with betel-nut, pawn-leaves, mangoes, oranges, figs, plantains, limes, grapes, melons, pomegranates, custard-apples, and every kind of fruit of the country, were scattered all round, besides cakes and sweetmeats, which were served up *ad lib.* to the spectators.

As we entered the music struck up, and the whole company rose and saluted us, remaining standing until we were seated, and the begum's black aide-de-camp paid us many compliments on the part of his mistress.

The tinkling of the bangles and gungroos * was now heard, and about forty handsomely-dressed dancing-girls entered the circle, and salaamed gracefully to the company. Half-a-dozen of the young-

* Feet-ornaments, and strings of small bells of various tones, worn round the ankles when dancing.

est and prettiest then stepped forward and placed garlands of double jessamine flowers round our necks, at the same time presenting each of us with a lime and a curiously-fashioned bouquet, tied to a short stick of sandal wood. They then deluged us with rose water, and scented us with otto of roses and oil of sandal, and tripped away to the rest of the performers in the centre of the circle.

The music, which up to this time had been rather monotonous, now broke forth into that extremely beautiful Persian air, by the immortal Hafiz, "Taza ba Taza, Now ba Now," and each of the fair minstrels, taking up the words of the song one by one, it gradually swelled into a full chorus; so, in a like manner, one by one they commenced their graceful and voluptuous measure until all were in movement, and at last their beautiful sylph-like forms seemed to flit before us as in a vision.

As I reclined upon the sedan, inhaling the fragrant narcotic from my hookah, which at the same time soothes and exhilarates, and drank in the words of the songs, I felt a strange delightfully ravishing sensation stealing gently over my senses, such as I never before experienced; and as I gazed on the graceful, fawn-like carriage of the exquisite figures, cast in the purest mould of elegance, before me, I thought of the prophet's seventh heaven, and the green-kerchiefed damsels who ever attend "*the Faithful*" in Paradise.

Their regular features, soft skins, and full swimming eyes glancing through their glossy raven hair, gave them, in my eyes, an interest which the colder beauties of northern climates have never raised. Gentle reader, have you ever visited the land of the sun? If so, you, too, must have marked that languid, expressive voluptuousness issuing forth from the gazelle-like eyes of her daughters, which you seek for in vain in other less favoured lands. You, too, may have been captivated by some one of the many fair maidens of Hind; and, perhaps, as you have gazed intensely into the depths of her dark and ever-changing eyes, which, sparkling with their brightness, lovingly refracted back your own, you have felt they spoke a language your heart has well understood; and perhaps at such a time, as you have gently put away those thick jet-black and glossy tresses from her fair brow, you have whispered softly in her ear, "Mera Jan, tera waste mera dil panee ho gia!" (My life! on account of you my heart has become water;) and when her fond, expressive glance has met your gaze, and she has twined her snow-white arms around your neck, you have "ta'en her answer from her murmuring lips," and felt, as you pressed her delicate and yielding form the closer to your bosom, that e'en the much lauded beauty of your own loved though far-distant land was cold and tame compared to hers. But I am wandering, and bygone scenes and happy days passed long ago in those fair lands "flit o'er my mind like blissful summer's dreams," and as my thoughts veer back to days of yore and long-lost friends, I feel those bright recollections stealing vividly back to memory like sunny spots and pleasant oases in my varied life's career.

Mais revenons à nos moutons. The ordinary dancing of the kunchnees (or dancing girls) consists more of different changes of position than any defined step or figure; and in the elegant attitudes and graceful postures with which they advance and retire, the arms, hands, feet, neck, and eyes, moving in unison with the music; and I think they ought rather to be called singing than dancing girls, for it has always appeared to me that their dancing is only a graceful and expletic accompaniment to their songs, which, treating, as they generally do, of love, often assume rather a lascivious character. The interior edges of the eyelids are darkened with "soormah," a preparation of antimony, which heightens their beauty, and gives them a peculiarly fascinating and bewitching appearance.

The nautch has charms which possess a powerful and almost irresistible influence on the affections and passions of the inhabitants of the East, and forms the principal recreation and amusement both with high and low. The European stranger who does not understand the language, and is unacquainted with the habits and customs of the country, may look upon a nautch as a monotonous and unmeaning performance; but to one who can understand and appreciate the beauties of Sadi and Hafiz, it has an inexplicable and alluring charm, and many a live-long night have I passed most delightfully, whilst my regiment was quartered in the Nizam's dominions, in the kiosk (or garden house) of one of my native friends—an Emir of Hydrabad, where, lulled by the sounds of gurgling waters and flowing fountains, which cooled the air, deliciously impregnated with the fragrance of groves of roses and jessamines, I have remained until gray dawn broke, listening with rapture to the flowery language of the Persian poets, and gazing on the elf-like forms that flitted before me.

The ordinary costume of the Moosulmaunee dancing-girls consists of a "cholee" or boddice, fitting tight to the form, and cut low in front down the breast, with short sleeves. It is generally made of bright-coloured silk, richly embroidered with gold, and is supposed to answer the purpose of stays, corsets, and all such abominable gear with which European damsels are in the habit of distorting their form into what they call shape, and which must, *I fancy,* (I am not a Benedict,) prove a considerable obstruction towards their lover's advances; for clasping one of those stiff, whalebone-sided damsels round the waist must give one nearly the same sensations as embracing a lamp-post or a mile-stone.

The "loonga," similar to the Persian "peshuajh," a richly-embroidered petticoat, is gathered round the waist, and seldom falls far below the knee, showing the graceful swell of the leg and beautifully-turned and slender ankles. Oh! ye fair maidens of the North, with what envy would you behold the delicate forms of the daughters of "the Faithful," whose full-flowing garments are confined round their naturally taper waists by a silver or gold zone, of less than eighteen inches in circumference. The "kurtnee," a vest of the finest and most transparent muslin, without sleeves, with the edges richly embroidered, is worn over the "cholee," reaching to the waist. Over all is the "sarree," a bright gauze scarf, often of gold or silver thread, which is passed round the waist, having one end thrown gracefully over the shoulder.

The hair, which is almost always very long and silky, and of raven black, is worn in the Madonna fashion in front, but gathered up in long plaits behind, often falling to the ankles.

The edge of the hair from the centre of the forehead to the back of the head is often adorned with a fringe of seed-pearls, or small gold chains, which hangs parallel to the arch of the eyebrows, and has a beautiful effect on their clear skin. This ornament is also worn to this day by the Jewish women of Constantinople and Syria, and many of their other jewels are of great antiquity, and resemble those described by the prophet Isaiah as having belonged to the daughters of Zion; more particularly "the tinkling ornaments about their feet, and the round tires like the moon, the nose jewels"—which latter ornament is called the "boolaq," and is generally a golden crescent, set with rubies, diamonds, or emeralds, and worn in the cartilage of the nose, through which a hole is bored, falling to the upper lip with very pretty effect.

Round the ankles, heavy massive silver or gold "gungroos" are worn, of curious construction, resembling three double curb-chains, to which rows of small fuschia-shaped bells are attached, of different tones, which jingle as they walk, and with which they keep time to the music when they dance.

Ear-rings are worn all round the ears, but from the lobes hang beautifully-formed bell-shaped drops, fringed round with seed-pearls.

The neck and arms are covered with all kinds of necklaces, bracelets, armlets, bangles, and silver or gold rings, besides numerous charms and amulets, which are supposed to shield the wearer from misfortune, and to avert the influence of the Evil Eye.

The fingers and even the toes are ornamented with rings, and the nails of both are stained a bright red with "maindee," or the juice of the "henna,"

During the nautch several curious feats requiring great suppleness of body were performed. For instance, a row of girls stood fronting us, standing with their feet about six inches apart, between which was placed a rupee or a needle with the point upright; they then all bent backwards together, and introducing their hands between their feet, picked up the money with their lips, or the needle with their eyelids, regaining their standing position without having moved their feet.

Various kinds of fruit and sweetmeats were handed round to us, the latter having been expressly prepared for us by the begum herself, as her factotum informed us. As they were really famous in their way, I broke out in a rhapsody, in which I declared "that the Nawab with the lump on his face was indeed born under a lucky star, and was much to be envied, in spite of the misfortune with which Allah had afflicted him. Was he not to get into his harem the same day a young wife, beautiful as a peri, and a mother-in-law who must have made her studies of the *cuisine* in heaven. The only thing that astonished me was that the chobadar or gatekeeper ever allowed her to leave the abode of the blessed."

The begum, her daughter, and female attendants, could hear everything I said, they being seated on the raised verandah just behind our sedan, a fine mat screen preventing them from being seen; and the old lady took the whole of the compliment to herself, and warmly reproved her followers for tittering at my speech, assuring them all in a very grave manner, "that the Mogli sirdar (Mogul officer) with the long black beard (meaning myself) was a very respectable man, and knew what was what; and that when a man was hungry, a group of peris from heaven would be but a poor exchange for one good cook."

On hearing this I drew in my breath, gave a deep sigh, and declared "that the gifted woman who was hid from my sight by the cruel screen spoke like a book; and that although pretty women were as numerous as the hairs of one's beard, yet an observant man might travel from country to country until his hair was white without finding or even hearing of such a paragon of perfection as she whose hospitality we were then enjoying."

Just at this moment two jugglers entered the circle, during an interval between the dances; and one of them placed before him a large earthen jar, over the mouth of which a piece of skin was tightly stretched, so as to form a kind of drum, which he beat with two small sticks, keeping time to a curious monotonous song, in which he exhorted his companion to display the utmost of his talents, so as to amuse the noble gentlemen, if he did not wish to eat dirt and have his face blackened.

The other replied that, Fate helping him, he would receive great presents from the truly charitable gentlemen on account of the great feats he would perform; and, after having beaten his breasts and uttered sundry cabalistic incantations, he rummaged in a bag containing the implements of his profession and produced a queer-shaped doll, which, when touched with his wand, appeared to utter curious squeaks and groans.

This he designated Madras Ramasawmy, and he proceeded to inform us that it was by means of his aid that he was going to amuse us, for that he was a great jadoo-wallah, (magician.) I noticed, however, that, during the course of the performance, he (the doll) received several cuffs if some of the feats of skill did not succeed the first time.

The juggler then passed round a common-looking white stone for our inspection, and then gave it to a pretty little dancing-girl who was sitting close to me. She closed her hand on it, and, after he had touched her with his wand, he told her to open it, and it was found full of white sand.

He then called a very black musician, and removing his turban, made him sit down near him; then taking a pinch of the sand, rubbed it down his forehead, leaving a bright yellow mark. A second pinch produced a blue, a third a red, and so on, every pinch producing a different colour. He then told the girl to close her hand, which he again touched with his wand, and the sand was turned into a small live snake, which the little woman threw down with a loud cry, which awoke the Doctor, who had fallen asleep on his chair near me, and caused him to stretch his legs and arms, and rub his eyes for some time before he knew where he was. "Ugh! ugh! ugh!" he exclaimed, starting to his feet with a grunt of amazement, "I must surely ha' been dreaming, for I thought that auld vixen of a bear was after me, and, ugh! but she was no just a cannie customer, coming tearing and rampaging after a puir body wi' her lugs in th' air an' her jaws open like a bluid-thirsty cannibal, looking for a' the world, as if she thought no more o' swallowing ane o' the faculty than a blue pill. Och, the varmint! but what can you expect when one o' the profession goes blackguarding about the country wi' a real gun in the company of the likes o' ye Irregulars? Ugh! ugh! ugh!"

The juggler then caught the snake, and tapping it with his wand appeared to turn it into a stone again, which, after having passed round for examination, he swallowed. Then, stroking his stomach, he made us understand that this hard living did not agree with his constitution, but that, with the proceeds of the generosity of the sahib log, (gentlemen,) he hoped to live well in future, and not to be obliged to make such meals as he had done that morning, the nature and quality of which he proceeded to show us; for, striking his chin with his wand, and opening his mouth, he produced some pounds' weight of pebbles, followed up by a quantity of small shells, then long strings of paper of different colours, and finishing off by ejecting a huge black scorpion all alive, round which he danced, testifying his joy, as he proceeded gravely to explain to us that this bold reptile having got into his stomach in some water which he had drunk from a well on which the Evil Eye had fallen, he had had no peace ever since, as it devoured all the food he put into his stomach, and prevented his appetite ever being satisfied.

He now handed round for our inspection a dry mangoe-stone, which he afterwards buried in the ground, muttering imprecations against all evil spirits as he did so, and pouring a little water over the spot, which he assured us came from the blessed Ganges.

He then produced a small stone image of the goddess Bowanee,* to which he prayed that he might live to eat of the fruit of the tree of which he had just planted the seed. Immediately afterwards he dug up the stone, and finding it in the same state as when he had buried it, pretended to be in a great rage, and commenced abusing the goddess in not very measured terms, revealing certain antecedents to her memory, which, if true, did not speak much in favour of the general morality of the Hindoo divinities. His ire even led him to forget common politeness to the sex, for he struck her repeatedly with his wand, but finished off by promising to break cocoa-nuts in her name, provided she assisted him to please the gentlemen; and after having effected a reconciliation, he again dug up the seed and showed it to us, with little white germs growing out of one end.

He again buried it, and recommenced coaxing the image to assist him, promising to sacrifice a cock to her, provided she listened graciously to his prayer, then covering the spot with a basket, to

* Bowanee or Kalee—the Hindoo goddess of destruction, the deity of the Thugs.

prevent the influence of any evil spirit from interfering with the working of his spell; in the meantime he showed us some very clever sleight-of-hand tricks with cups and small cloth-balls, something like thimble-rig.

When this was over he removed the basket and showed us a young mangoe-plant growing, it having put forward the two first leaves; and at our request he dug it up from the ground and showed us the roots with the stone still adhering to them. This he again planted and covered it over with the basket, after which he showed us some very clever juggling with knives and balls.

When he again uncovered the plant it was covered with blossom, which we examined carefully before the basket was replaced.

He then showed us a very interesting feat, in which there was really no deception. He made his comrade lie down on his back, and placed on his bare stomach a double betel-leaf; then, taking a sharp sword, he made a ferocious drawing cut, entirely dividing the leaf and making a line on the man's stomach, yet not dividing the skin. He then placed a lime on the palm of a man's hand, and cut it in two with a stroke, so that both halves fell on the ground, making a mark with the edge of the sword on the man's hand, yet not cutting the skin.

When this feat was ended he asked the Doctor to remove the basket, and when he did so, lo! and behold, the tree was bending from the weight of five fine mangoes, which were plucked and offered for our inspection.

The performance was deservedly much applauded, but the operator was looked upon with much distrust and suspicion by the natives, who imagined he did everything by supernatural agency; for when I cut the mangoe he presented to me and offered half of it to the little Mussulmannee girl who sat at my feet, she actually shuddered as she put it away from her, begging me in the name of Allah not to eat any of it, as it could not be otherwise than bad, coming from such a source.

I however ate it, and found it very good, though I could not persuade any of the natives to taste it.

The next trick was also exceedingly good, and merits description. He crouched down before the stone image of the goddess, and, making a most profound obeisance, thanked her for the favour he had found in the eyes of the honourable company then assembled, and declared himself her most humble votary from that moment; and in confirmation of which solemn vow he declared that he would immediately sacrifice his only daughter, and henceforward devote himself to her service. He told his intentions to a beautiful little girl, about six years old, who was sitting near, and she began to cry and struggle in a most natural manner; but he seized her, and, after stripping off all her jewels and upper clothing, and loosening her long black hair, which fell over her little naked breast and shoulders, deliberately bound her hands and feet, covering her with a thick black veil.

He then swept the ground, on which he sprinkled some of the holy Ganges water, and laying her down covered her with the basket he had used with the mangoe trick, spreading a white cloth over all. He then commenced a prayer to the goddess Bowanee, prostrating himself before the stone image and invoking its aid, and finished by breaking a cocoa-nut as a sacrifice, and placing the pieces before it.

Then breaking out into a long wild cry, he rolled his eyes, foamed at the mouth like a maniac, and seizing a double-edged sword, plunged it into the centre of the cloth, through the basket under which he had placed his child, repeating the stroke twice in different places. Dark streams of blood were seen running from underneath the cloth, the sword being also stained; and at each blow shrieks and groans appeared to rise from under the basket. For a moment all was still, and every face transfixed with horror at the supposed crime; loud murmurs were heard among the men, and cries of alarm arose among the females, who rushed wildly about screaming and beating their breasts; then the juggler coolly made an obeisance to the idol, and lifting up the bloody cloth and basket, displayed to the excited spectators only the veil pierced in three places, and the cord with which the child was bound. The child had vanished.

All were thunderstruck, and some of the bystanders seized the juggler and threatened him with their vengeance if he did not restore the child he had spirited away by magic. He shook them off, and bowing again to the image, called thrice the name of Chandbee, and the little girl came tripping in from somewhere outside the circle and embraced her father. Our applause was long and loud, and when the little maid went round with the plate, the numerous donations placed upon it announced the satisfaction of all the spectators.

The old Doctor, who had been rubbing his eyes and twisting himself uncomfortably in his chair for some time, now burst out into a dolorous grunt, and with a serio-comic expression of countenance exclaimed, "Ugh! ugh! ugh! Weel! weel! Dinna ye believe in the de'il and a' his works noo, as yere catechism says? but I reckon that was no a part o' the bringing up o' the likes o' ye. But, oh! dear mon, was it no just a fearfu' sight? This chiel felt his e'en maist greeting, an' his temples bursting, when the auld heathen streck'd his gullie wi' sic a like thud into his sonsie little bairn as coolly as if he was opening a haggis, and she just felt as if she couldna thole it; for brimstane smelt right strong, as the auld bleezin' hornie went down on his marrow-banes to the little ne'er-do-well stane kelpie; and whilst the carle was in that position this half-scared infant just peeped twice at his nether end so as to mak' sure there was no dark, ill-looking appendage attached or hid in the folds o' his cloth."

"It was a magnificent trick," said W——, "for though I knew what was to follow, having seen it before, and studiously watched every motion, I have not gained the slightest clue towards finding it out, and I cannot understand it at all."

"It was certainly an extraordinary deception," I replied, "but the mangoe-trick puzzles me most. I have a shrewd suspicion that I know how the child vanished from under the basket, although I must confess that I did not see it move; but do you not remember that, when he struck the first blow through the cloth and drew out the sword reeking with blood, several women rushed frantically round with shrieks and cries of horror, causing some confusion: well, I imagine that at this time the child must have crept from under the basket, and slipped away concealed under the flowing drapery of a female accomplice. I remember I fancied the outrageous grief of one old Mussulmannee woman was got up for the occasion to divert our attention, for I noticed that, although she was wailing and beating her breasts most vehemently, no tears fell, and she raised her hand and put a piece of betel-nut and a paun leaf into her mouth, which action impressed me with the idea that she was a confederate, and that her grief was 'all my eye.'"

"It must have been as you say," says Jock, "if Sawbone's friend 'Old Hornie' did not play a part in the performance, which, in my eyes, at first bordered on the supernatural, I must confess."

The jugglers then withdrew, and the nautch continued until the gray of the morning, when our rising from our seats was the signal for the sports to cease, and the spectators to retire.

We, the European officers, having distributed our largess to the dancing-girls, proceeded to a tent close by, where a handsome native supper was served in the Mussulman style of cooking, and here we remained chatting and smoking our hookahs until intimation was given us that the sun had risen, when each retired to his tent.

CHAPTER VIII.

THE DEATH OF THE MAN-EATER.

News of the man-eater again.—We are once more on his trail.—The scent lost.—Googooloo gives tongue.—It warms.—My plan. — Preparation. — Execution. — A ticklish moment. — Death of the man-eater.—Ceremonies of the shekarries.

As I was preparing to turn in for an hour or two, my head shekarry, Chineah, came up grinning, and told me that the patel of the village of Botta Singarum had sent to say that the tiger had been seen skulking near the outskirts of the village a short time after our return to camp.

I immediately sent for the dhoby and Kistimah, and despatched them, with Chineah and the gang with my guns, to the village, to find out all the particulars; and, having questioned the villager who brought the message rather closely, for I had some doubts as to the truth of the report, I appointed a place of meeting, and after a couple of hours' repose, a bath, and a hurried breakfast, I mounted my nag without disturbing the other officers, who were still sleeping, and joined my people at the Botta Singarum police-station.

Without dismounting, I went, guided by a villager, to the place where the tiger had been seen the evening before, and there I found unmistakable signs of his presence, as the pugs were plainly visible.

I sent my horse back to the village, and, accompanied by the gang, followed his track through a narrow ravine densely wooded.

Here the trail became exceedingly difficult to follow, as the brute had evidently been walking about backwards and forwards in the bed and along the banks of a dry nullah, and we could not distinguish his last trail.

I caused the band to separate, and for half-an-hour or so we were wandering about as if in a maze, for the cunning brute had been describing circles, and often, by following the trail, we arrived at the place we started from.

Whilst we were all at a loss, suddenly I heard a low "Coo" twice repeated, and I knew that Googooloo, who was seldom at fault, was now on warm scent, and from his call I was as certain that the game was afoot as any master of hounds would have been, while breaking cover, to hear his favourite dog give tongue.

The gang closed up, and, guided by the sound, we made our way through thick bush to where Googooloo was standing by a pool of water in the bed of the nullah.

Here were unmistakable marks of his having

quenched his thirst quite lately, for when we came up the water was still flowing into the deeply-imprinted pugs of his forefeet, which were close to the edge of the pool, and I noticed that the water had still the appearance of having been disturbed and troubled.

After having drunk, the brute had made his way to some very thick jungle, much overgrown with creepers, through which we could not follow without the aid of our axes.

Thus, stalking with any hope of success was out of the question, so I held a solemn consultation with Kistimah, Chineah, Googooloo, and the dhoby, as to the best means of proceeding.

I felt convinced that the brute was still lurking somewhere near at hand in the jungle, for, besides the very recent trail we were on, I fancied I heard the yelling of a swarm of monkeys, which I attributed to their having been frightened by his appearance; besides, this was just the kind of place that a tiger would be likely to remain in during the heat of the day, as it afforded cool shade from the sun, and water.

All the gang were of my opinion, and Kistimah observed that, on two different occasions, after a post-runner had been carried off, he had remarked that the trail of the tiger led from this part of the jungle to a bend in the road, where he had been known frequently to lie in wait for his prey.

"These man-eaters," added he, "are great devils,

and very cunning, and I should not at all wonder if even now he was watching us from some dark thicket."

As he said this I carefully examined the caps of my rifle, and I observed some of the gang close up with a strange shudder, for this brute had inspired them all with a wholesome fear, and prevented their straggling. Two or three spoke almost in whispers, as if they were afraid of his really being sufficiently near to hear them conspiring for his destruction.

At length Kistimah said that he had been thinking of a plan which, though dangerous in the execution, might be attended with success. It was for me to go, with a man dressed as a runner, down the main road at sunset, being the time the tiger generally carried off his victims, and to run the chance of getting a shot.

At this proposition sundry interjectional expressions, such as "Abah!" "Arrez!" "Toba!" "Toba!" escaped from the lips of the by-standers, and, from sundry shaking of heads and other unmistakable signs, I could see that it had not found much favour in their eyes. Chineah, the dhoby, and one or two of the gang, however, approved of the plan, and Kistimah offered to accompany me as the post-runner.

This, however, I objected to, for I thought that I should have a better chance of meeting the tiger if I went alone than in company; besides, I preferred having only myself to look after. The plan of action once settled, I returned to the village and obtained from the patel the bamboo on which the tappal-runners sling the mail-bags over their shoulders. To the end of this is an iron ring with a number of small pieces of metal attached, making a jingling noise as the man runs, which gives warning of the coming of the post to any crowd that might be obstructing the path, allowing them time to get out of his way. Having broken off the ring, I fastened it to my belt, so as to allow it to jingle as I walked; and, arming myself with a short double rifle by Westley Richards, a brace of pistols and a huge shekar knife, I made Kistimah lead the way down the road towards the place where the man-eater was said to lurk.

About a mile from the village I made the gang and the villagers who accompanied me halt, and went on with Kistimah, Chineah, and Googooloo to reconnoitre the ground.

The road was intersected by a narrow valley or ravine, along the bottom of which was a dry, sandy watercourse, the banks of which were overgrown with high rank grass and reeds, intermixed with low scrubby thorn-bushes. To the left was a low, rocky hill, in some places bare and in others covered with thick jungle, with wild date or custard-apple clumps here and there.

Kistimah pointed me out a clump of rather thick jungle to the right of the road, where, he said, the tiger often lurked whilst on the look-out for his prey, and here we saw two or three old trails. He also showed me a rock from behind which the brute had sprung on a post-runner some weeks before, but we saw no signs of his having been there lately.

It was, however, quite what an Indian sportsman would have termed "a tigerish spot," for bold scarped rocks and naked fantastic peaks rose in every direction from amongst the dense foliage of the surrounding jungle. Here and there noble forest trees towered like giant patriarchs above the lower verdure of every shade and colour.

Not a breath of air was stirring, nor a leaf moving; and as the sun was still high up, without a cloud to be seen to intercept his rays, the heat was most oppressive, and respiration even was becoming difficult, on account of a peculiar closeness arising from the decayed vegetation underfoot, and the overpowering perfume of the blossoms of certain jungle plants.

After having reconnoitred the country I felt rather overcome with lassitude, and returned to the rest of the gang, whom I found sleeping in a clump of deep jungle, a little off the roadside. Here I laid down to rest, protected from the piercing rays of the sun by the shade of a beautiful natural bower formed by two trees, which were bent down with the weight of an immense mass of various kinds of parasitical plants, in addition to their own foliage.

The mournful silence and strange stillness that reigned was only broken at times by the distant scream of peafowl, or the shrill crowing of a jungle-cock, who, unsuspicious of our presence, was scratching up the ground and clacking to his hens in an adjoining thicket. The shrill and peculiarly wild notes of these birds seem as if they were ordained by nature to accord with the calm, still solitude, and sublime grandeur of scenery of "the deep jungle." They inhabit that deep jungle of which Ferishta says truly, "That death dwells in the water, and poison in the breeze; where the grass is tough as the teeth of serpents, and the air fetid as the breath of dragons." For so it is: the deadliest fevers lurk in these places most beautiful to the eye, the air being poisoned and impregnated by the exhalations of decayed leaves and other decomposed vegetable matter.

I must have slept several hours, for when I awoke I found the sun sinking low in the horizon; however, I got up considerably refreshed for my nap, and, giving myself a shake, prepared for the task I had undertaken.

I carefully examined my arms, and having ascertained that nothing had been seen by any of my gang, some of whom had kept a look-out, I told my people to listen for the sound of my gun, which, if they heard, they might come up, otherwise that they were to remain quiet, until my return.

I ordered Chineah, Kistimah, Googooloo, and the dhoby to accompany me down the road with spare guns, in case I might want them, and when I arrived at a spot which commanded a view of the ravine, I sent them to climb different trees.

Kistimah begged hard to be allowed to accompany me, as he said this tiger never attacked a man in front, but always from behind; but I would not permit him, as I thought that two people would perhaps scare the animal, and his footsteps might prevent me from hearing any sound, intimating his approach.

The sun had almost set as I proceeded slowly down the road, and, although I was perfectly cool and as steady as possible, I felt cold drops of perspiration start from my forehead as I approached the spot where so many victims had been sacrificed. I passed the rock, keeping well on the look-out, listening carefully for the slightest sound, and I remember feeling considerably annoyed by the chirping made by a couple of little bulbuls, (Indian nightingales,) that were fighting in a bush close to the roadside. Partridges were calling loudly all around, and as I passed the watercourse I saw a jackal skulking along its bed. I stopped, shook my jingling affair, and listened several times as I went along, but to no purpose.

Whilst ascending the opposite side of the ravine I heard a slight noise like the crackling of a dry leaf: I paused, and turning to the left, fronted the spot from whence I thought the noise proceeded. I distinctly saw a movement or waving in the high grass, as if something was making its way towards me: then I heard a loud purring sound, and saw something twitching backwards and forwards behind a clump of low bush and long grass, about eight or ten paces from me, and a little in the rear. It was a ticklish moment, but I felt prepared. I stepped back a couple of paces, in order to get a better view, which action probably saved my life, for immediately the brute sprang into the middle of the road, alighting about six feet from the place where I was standing. I fired a hurried shot ere he could gather himself up for another spring, and when the smoke cleared away I saw him rolling over and over in the dusty road, writhing in his death agony, for my shot had entered the neck and gone downwards into his chest. I stepped on one side and gave him my second barrel behind the ear, when dark blood rushed from his nostrils, a slight tremor passed over all his limbs, and all was still. The man-eater was dead, and his victims avenged.

My gang, attracted by the sound of my shots, came rushing up almost breathless, and long and loud were the rejoicings when the tiger was recognised by Kistimah as the cunning man-eater who had been the scourge of the surrounding country for months.

He was covered with mange, and had but little hair left on his skin, which was of a reddish brown colour, and not worth taking. I made Chineah

cut off the right paw with his axe, and sent a post-runner into camp with it to announce my success. A bullock-cart was then fetched from the village, on which the carcass was with much difficulty hoisted, and dragged off in triumph by the villagers, for the bullocks were so frightened by his smell that they would not allow themselves to be harnessed to the cart; all force and coaxing being in vain to get them sufficiently near to place the yokes on their necks.

All the villagers turned out to witness our entry, poojahs (religious ceremonies) were performed, sheep and cocks sacrificed, and prayers offered up to sundry Sawmies (Hindoo gods) in my name. I was the centre of attraction of all the young girls of the village, whose dark sparkling eyes flashed kindly on me as they stood waving their hands on either side of the road. As for the old women, I really had some difficulty to get out of their clutches; they kissed the hem of my old green baize shooting-coat, cracked their knuckles over my forehead for luck, stroked my face and beard, patted me on the back, and at last became so vehement in their attentions that I had to beg of my gang to keep them off.

All the men in the village turned out with torches and firesticks to escort me home to camp. Rockets and fireworks were burnt, matchlocks discharged, and tomtoms, dubties, and cholera horns poured forth their notes of triumph before the dead tiger, whose head was carried in the front on a spear.

My gang marched at the head of the procession, and five ancient dancing-girls from the village were pirouetting before the cart, howling and yelling as they whirled on the "light fantastic," in such a manner that they reminded one strongly of the witch scene in Macbeth. The whole camp turned out to view the carcass of the man-eater, and many were the congratulations I received from all parties that evening.

I gave a few sheep and fowls to my gang, with some rackee, and throughout the night "there was a sound of revelry." The next day the mutilated carcass was paraded on a cart in all the neighbouring villages by Kistimah and the dhoby, who, by levying contributions either in coin or kind, realised a little fortune for themselves.

I have killed many tigers both before and since, but I never met with such a determined enemy to mankind, for he was supposed to have carried off more than a hundred individuals. He fully exemplified an old Indian saying, "that when a tiger has once tasted human blood he will never follow other game, men proving an easier prey." On the spot where the tiger was killed a large mausoleum now stands, caused by the passers-by each throwing a stone until a large heap is formed. Since that day many a traveller who has passed that way has been entertained by the old pensioned sepoy who is in charge of the public bungalow, with a long account of the death of the celebrated Admee Khanna-wallah, (Man-eater,) and old friends have told me that many anxious and kind inquiries have been made as to the health and welfare of the black-bearded cavalry officer who slew him.

SECTION II.—SOUTHERN INDIA.

CHAPTER IX.

TRICHINOPOLY.

Trichinopoly.—The evil influence of caste in India.—The return of Chineah, and our prospects of sport.—My shooting-cart and battery described.—Preparations for a start.

I WAS quartered for some time at Trichinopoly, one of the dullest of our military stations in Southern India, which city certain learned authorities aver has only a single sheet of brown paper between it and the infernal regions. Every Anglo-Indian will tell you that it is famous for three things—viz., magnificent snipe-shooting, unrivalled cheroots, and delicate and exquisitely wrought gold chains.

Trichy, (short for Trichinopoly,) like most other Indian cities, possesses a stone citadel, formerly an old pagoda, built on an almost inaccessible rock, which rises isolated out of the plain and commands the neighbouring country. This is surrounded by a pettah or native town, fortified by double bastioned walls of solid masonry, a deep ditch, (which can be filled from the Cauvery, that flows at a short distance from the northern face,) a covert-way and glacis. This place was the scene of some severe fighting in the year 1753, when the French attempted to assault the place by surprise, without success. Within the walls are the ruins of a handsome palace, which was formerly the habitation of Ameer al Oomra, also several Mussulman mosques, and Hindoo pagodas, dedicated to divers Sawmies (images) of uncouth appearance and very questionable character, if we are to believe the history of their lives, which is generally carved on the exterior of their temples. The mainguard, commanded by a European officer, is in one of the principal gateways of the fort, which also contains an arsenal, (formerly an old pagoda,) barracks, magazines, storehouses, and a well-stocked bazaar, in which everything may be bought, from a handspike to an elephant. Outside of the walls are extensive suburbs, and at a short distance is the military cantonment, where are quartered a European regiment of foot, either of Her Majesty's or the East India Company's service; a regiment of Native Light Cavalry, some Artillery, and three battalions of Native Infantry.

Trichinopoly is situated on the south bank of the river Cauvery, and is considered a holy city by Hindoos, being to the Madras Presidency what Benares is to the Bengal. Almost opposite the town, upon an island formed by the division of the stream, is the celebrated temple of Seringam, the outside wall of which contains an area of more than a mile square. It is the very hotbed of Brahminism, and here congregate from all parts of the south of India those fat, lazy, greasy cumberers of the earth, who live upon clover, by the sweat of other men's brows, and thrive and grow rich upon the offerings which they wring from poor deluded Hindoo pilgrims by working upon their credulity and superstitious fears.

It was in the latter end of the month of April, and our old stagers declared they had never felt anything like the heat. We were all nearly baked, and, as old Paddy S——, of the —th, used to say, "looked like carefully dried resuscitated mummies;" for our faces were burnt almost coffee-colour from constant exposure to the sun whilst out snipe-shooting.

I felt thoroughly disgusted and worn out with the changeless monotony of an Indian garrison life, and was heartily sick of parades, drills, guard-mountings, inspections, courts-martial, courts of inquest, inquiry, request, committees, meetings, and boards of every kind. Mainguard and regimental duty seemed to come round oftener than usual, and nothing was stirring except the mosquitos, which are one of the plagues of India, and those of Trichy are celebrated as galleynippers.

I was sitting, after dinner one evening, in the verandah of the mess-house, conversing with three or four of my brother-officers, listening to the regimental band, and cogitating upon the vapid life I was leading, when suddenly my chochra (a young Mussulman lad, whose office it was to assist me to dress and wait at table) rushed up with frantic haste, exclaiming, "Sahib, sahib, Chineah iya hy!" (Sir, sir, Chineah has come!) Now Chineah was my head shekarry or huntsman, who had been out on a reconnoitring expedition after large game, and a great man in my establishment.

"Let us have him in at once," said B——, "and hear where he has been, and what shekar-khubber (hunting news) he has brought."

So Chineah was sent for, and in a few minutes was salaaming before us.

"Well, Chineah," said I, "what great news have you brought, that you have been away so long? From not having heard from you, I have been expecting you back every day for the last fortnight, and at last began to imagine that some accident had happened, for three or four of your women came up to me declaring that they had heard in the bazaar that you had been eaten by a tiger."

"Women no good, master," answered he, "tell plenty lies, go too much to the bazaar; plenty, plenty talking, never do any work. I go away nearly two months, then come home, find no cloth in go-down,* no rice, no nuffin. To-morrow make plenty bobbery, (noise), plenty floggee. Ah, sahib!

* Go-down—servants' quarters, generally out-offices.

karree log kuch fida na, (Ah, sir! womenkind are of no good.")

"Never mind them," replied I, "let us hear what news of game you have brought, for B—— sahib and I are going out on a shekar trip in the course of a few days, and we want to hear what our chances are."

"Well, sahib, master knows very well I went to Putchee Mullah and Koolee Mullah Hills, where I only see a few chetel, (spotted deer,) so I went on to Salem, and on the sides of the Sheveroy Hills I saw some sambur, chetel, and old trail of jungle bice, (bison.) I stop at Mulliarry village, five, six days, and there I meet one man, Naga, very good shekarry, so I bring with me; suppose master want other shekar man. This man tell me that there plenty shekar got in Bowani Jungle, so I go there with him, and all over the Combei Jungle, where I see plenty janwars, (wild beasts.) There got tigers, panthers, bears, bison, elk, spotted deer, and antelopes, and near the Hassanoor Pass I saw plenty old marks of elephant and some neilghau, (literally blue cow.) Suppose master go to Bowani, get plenty good shekar. Naga knows that jungle very well; and I tell all Mulcher men (a jungle tribe) that master coming soon; and suppose master get plenty shooting, Mulcher men get plenty, plenty buckshcesh, (presents.")

"Well, Chineah," said I, "you have done your work very well, and in the course of a few days,

Inshallah, (please God,) we shall try our luck in that part of the country. Now go to Yacoob-Khan, and tell him to give you a gold mohur (about 30s.) for yourself and the gang to make merry with, but take care none of you get into trouble; for if any of you find your way into *chokee* (quod) and are brought up before the gora sahib, (white gentleman, a name often given to the European magistrate,) I shall ask him not to fine you, but to take the change out of your backs."

"Me nebber want to see that gentleman till me goes to 'Jehanum,'"* exclaimed Chineah, as he withdrew, grinning and showing his teeth—"him no good."

"Well, B——," said I, "I do not think we can do better than try the Bowani Jungle, for I anticipate good sport from Chineah's account of the country, which you may rely upon is correct, as he has been with me a long time, and I have never yet found him deceive me. I shall go at once to H——, and ask him to forward my application for two months' leave of absence, and I will then ask the general to give me permission to start at once in anticipation of leave from army head-quarters."

I found Major H——, who was then commanding the regiment, in conversation with old S—— of the Commissariat, and he consented at once to forward my application, at the same time tell-

* Jehanum—"the infernal regions."

ing me that he had no doubt but that it would be granted.

The next three days were devoted to preparations for my sporting campaign, which I shall describe for the benefit of the uninitiated.

I had constructed, according to my own plan and fancy, what I should advise every Indian sportsman to possess—that is, a very comfortable teak-wood bullock-cart, on springs, and fitted up for travelling. Mine was seven feet long by four broad, and contained three large watertight boxes or compartments, to hold my kit and comestibles *en route*, with a fourth, copper-lined and fitted with a screw-top, which fastened with a lock, for my ammunition, besides a rack for eight guns. The wooden sides were about two feet and a half in height, and from them sprang six bamboo hoops, on which the white painted canvas top was extended; the whole of which gear was movable, and could be cleared away at a moment's notice. The bottom of the cart was slightly bevelled off round, caulked and sheathed with copper, so that, by taking out the linchpins and putting the wheels into the cart, my trap served me as a boat to transfer myself and goods across rivers otherwise impassable. When in cantonment I took out the pole and bullock-yoke, and fitted in a pair of shafts; and although it was not a very light vehicle, an old Australian mare I had used to trot along with it with great ease. The whole length of the bottom of the cart was fitted with a hair mattress, and the sides were well padded, so that I managed, when travelling, to get along pretty comfortably.

With posted bullocks I could generally average about four miles an hour; and as I halted only during the heat of the day, I managed to get over the ground pretty quickly for India.

My battery, on which I prided myself very much, consisted of a brace of ten-gauge rifles by Purdey; a double rifle and two smooth-bores eight-gauge by Westley Richards; a double rifle by Burrows of Preston; two fowling-pieces, sixteen-bore; a Purday and a long Joe Manton, both clipping shot-guns; a long four-bore duck-gun by Fullard, (after a single discharge of which I have picked up seventeen duck and teal;) and a German pea-rifle.

A large Yankee backwoodsman's axe, a couple of bill-hooks, an adze, and other tools, were fitted against the side of my cart, so as to be ready at hand in case of a break-down, which is an event of frequent occurrence in Indian travelling. An obstreperous bullock or a careless driver is very liable to smash a pole or a yoke *en route;* and, in many parts of the country where game abounds, village smiths are difficult to be met with, and I have often been saved hours, and even days' delay, by having the means of repairing them at hand.

A well-supplied medicine-chest, in which the quinine bottle loomed very large, was carefully stowed away in one of the compartments—a very necessary precaution in a country where disease makes such rapid progress. Besides having often found this chest extremely useful, the mere fact of having it with me inspired my people with confidence, and overcame their fear of the malaria of the dense jungle.

My supplies consisted chiefly of tea, coffee, sugar, spices, curry stuff, brandy, tobacco, biscuits, and kiln-dried flour, (country flour will not keep.) As bread soon gets dry and spoils in a hot climate, I used to prepare a kind of rusk for travelling, by cutting up loaves in small pieces, and having them baked until they became of a light brown colour. Prepared in this way, if they are carefully kept in tin cases, they remain fresh and palatable for many weeks, and are a great improvement upon Indian biscuits for breakfast.

My boy was very clever in preparing chapaties or hoppers, which are a kind of girdle-cake baked on an iron plate, and generally made of rice-flour. The materials being always to be procured, even in the smallest village, these cakes are much used in India as a substitute for bread.

My time for three days was occupied in preparing for the trip, hiring coolies, and superintending the casting of bullets for my different guns. In case of meeting with elephants I had some brass bullets cast, besides others, which I now infinitely prefer, made of a mixture of lead and zinc. Bullets of this material are much heavier than if they were made of brass, and are sufficiently hard for any purpose. I generally put in one-third of zinc to two of lead; and often, when I could not get zinc, I have used tin in the same proportion, which I found equally good.

For my large smooth-bores I used round balls, and generally put a couple in my second barrel; for, although I have frequently heard people animadvert upon this practice as dangerous, I never found any evil effects resulting from it: nor are the guns shaken, although I have used them upwards of a dozen years, generally firing from four to five drachms of powder. For close shooting (when I have a gun by a maker whom I can depend upon) I prefer to have a brace of balls in my second barrel; and although I do not advocate this as a principle, I have found it more effectual in stopping the charge of an infuriated wounded animal.

I may, however, observe that I go to a good gunmaker, pay a fair price, and see that I get a first-class article for my money. I have always found it cheaper in the end to have a first-class arm, and I think that success in the field often depends upon the degree of confidence which is placed in the guns.

Having given some account of my shooting-cart and battery, I shall go on to describe the rest of my equipment, as perhaps a few wrinkles on the proper dress for a sportsman might be useful to young hands.

The first great rule to be observed is to have all your dress as nearly as possible of the same colour as the general aspect of the country you are going to shoot over. Thus, when you are deer-stalking or tracking large game in woods before the leaf has fallen, green is the best colour; when the trees are bare, dark brown—the colour of the trunk and branches; are you after antelope on the plain or ibex among the rocks, drab is the best colour. Should you be waging war against the grisly bear or ibex in the snow, you would be able to get much nearer to your game unobserved if you, as I have done, wore a shirt outside. Even in duck-shooting on the coast of England, in winter, you stand a much better chance of making a heavy bag if you follow this plan of dressing.

The second rule is, having all your clothes made to fit well. The most convenient costume for large-game shooting is a long jacket, reaching a little over the hips, with pockets outside, and sleeves like a shirt, fastening at the wrist with a couple of buttons. It should be loosely made, so as to allow the greatest ease and freedom to the limbs. A long waistcoat, with pockets, and breeches fitting loosely over the knee but rather tightly over the calf.

The gaiters, which I like to fasten with leather buttons down the outside, should fit tightly to the leg and well over the boots. The best material to have them made from is corduroy, fustian, or moleskin, when you cannot get properly dressed deerskin.

I always found laced-up ankle-boots of deerskin the most comfortable wear for hard fagging, and I prefer substantial single soles, double ones being too heavy to run in.

A leather hunting-cap is the best protection to the head for large-game shooting in the jungles of India, and I prefer to have peaks both before and behind, as the one saves the eyes and face from thorns, and the other prevents anything from falling down the back of your neck. In jungles where the tree-leech abounds this is a great consideration, for those animals often drop from the branches as you shake them in passing and alight upon your person, when they seem all to make for the back of your neck by instinct. When in such jungles it is absolutely necessary to wear leech-gaiters, or long closely-woven cotton stockings, over your socks, (which should be of lambswool,) under your boots and gaiters, and over your breeches, as far as they will go. Even with this safeguard I have sometimes found my boots and stockings drenched with blood in the evening, though I could not ascertain how they got in.

I found velveteen, corduroy, or moleskin, the most comfortable for wear whilst out after large game, and I had entire suits made of different colours, so as to suit the ground I was going to shoot over.

Round my waist I always wore a stout, broad leather-belt, with an iron ring substantially fastened at the back, to which I could fasten a strong silk cord. This I found of great use as a safeguard in case of having to descend any steep slope or narrow ledge of rock when in the pursuit of game.

In my belt I carried a small double-barrelled pistol, (a revolver would have been preferable,) a double field-glass, a small-pouch for ammunition, a leather case containing flint, steel, and tinder, and a straight double-edged hunting-knife, which, with the glass and pistol, had small rings attached, so as to enable me to fasten them by thin cords to my belt, to prevent their being lost.

In my pocket I carried a pricker, a nipple wrench, turnscrew, spare nipples, and a little instrument for filling the nipples with fresh powder.

Chineah, my head shekarry, carried a telescope, by Dollond, and a brandy flask slung over his shoulders, a shekar knife, and small axe in his belt, and my favourite rifle, with its ammunition. Besides which, he always managed to stow away for me a pair of clean socks, which I found a great luxury after a severe fag.

Googooloo, who was my best tracker, always kept at my heels, with my second gun, and carried in his belt a knife, a bill-hook for cutting the way through thick jungle, and a few rounds of ammunition.

Mootoo, (short for Choury Moottoo,) Veerapah, Narinah, and Rungasawmy, trackers, each carried a spare gun with its ammunition, and a knife with a saw, bill-hook, or axe in his belt.

Ramasawmy (a preparer of skins) carried a large

backwoodsman's axe, as well as the implements of his profession, and Perriatumbee, who usually went by the abbreviation of "the Gooroo," on account of his having some pretensions to priestcraft, carried a large leather "*mushuk*" or skin containing water.

To Naga, the Mulliary whom Chineah had enlisted in his late reconnaissance, I entrusted a gun, and furnished him with the bill-hook and short spear, with which weapons all my people were armed, as they served not only as a protection, in case any of them were detached, but also as a kind of badge which showed they belonged to the shekar gang. Besides my own regular shekarries, I engaged four coolies to carry my traps through jungle-paths where carts or ponies could not go.

I had given orders to my head servant to see that every man was provided with a new pair of "chupples" or sandals, a dark "langooty" or waist-cloth, and a "combley jule" or country blanket, made of coarse wool, as I could not afford to have any of them laid up with sore feet or illness; and the day before they were to start I had an inspection parade, at which each man appeared in his new tog, equipped for the road.

B—— did the same with his followers, and we had our tents pitched, our horses and dogs picketed, and our coolies, baggage-ponies, and bullocks examined, so that we might be certain that nothing requisite was left behind, and everything in order.

We had a large double tent for ourselves, whilst

en route, fitted with cuscus-grass tatties, a hill-tent and a bachoba (a tent without pole) for jungle work, two bell-tents for our people, and a large "shamiana" or canvas screen, to sling between trees or fasten on poles, so as to shelter our horses from the intense heat of the midday sun.

My stud consisted of two Arabs, (first-rate horses for cross country after hog,) "Gooty," a Mahratta shooting-pony, who could do everything but speak, and an Australian mare, which I generally rode on the march, and sometimes, when the road was good, drove in the cart. B—— had two horses and two ponies, and we had besides hired four baggage-tattoos and four carriage-bullocks for our tents and baggage.

My servants, who were almost all Mussulmans, consisted of Yacoob Khan, my head man, "Five Minutes," my cook, Hassan, a hooka-badar, Cassim Bey, and Lall Khan, two youngsters who waited at table and helped me to dress, a waterman, a tent-Lascar, four "syces" or grooms, four grass-cutters, two dog-boys, and two soldiers, who, in cantonment, were supposed to keep my regimentals in order, but when on a shekar expedition made themselves generally useful.

B——'s followers numbered more than a dozen, so that altogether the gang, our servants, coolies, and camp-followers, amounted to about forty individuals.

They all paraded in marching trim, to receive a

small advance of pay to be left with their families, and I gave them a trifle to be expended in making caste ceremonies, and offering Poojahs to their favourite deities, so that each might propitiate his Sawmy for good luck on the expedition.

The Gooroo rendered himself very conspicuous by killing a sheep in front on an image of Cajasouramardanam, (the god of Hunting,) who is represented with four arms, having a lance in two hands and curious reptiles in the others, clad in a tiger's skin, and seated upon that of an elephant.

CHAPTER X.

THE SHEVEROYS.

Departure of the gang.—Our start.—The journey.—Salem.—The Sheveroy hills, and our reception.—Anglo-Indian hospitality.—Claret cup.—News of bison and bears.—Googooloo on trail.—We follow.—A bull-bison lost.—The news of bears confirmed.—Their habits described.

ALL were in good spirits, and it would have been a curious sight for a stranger from Europe to have witnessed the departure of our party as they filed through the gateway in front of my bungalow, singing an extemporary song descriptive of the great sporting feats they were going to perform.

First came our eight horses in their head-stalls and jules, (stable - clothing,) with their saddles loosely girthed, each led by his respective syce or groom and followed by the grass-cutter, who carried the head and heel ropes, gram, (a kind of bean,) and cooking-pots, &c. Then came my two dog-boys, one with a couple of Anglo-Persian grey-hounds, and the other with four huge creatures of the Poligar breed, famous animals to lay after a wounded deer, or to bring a bear or hog to bay. These were followed by the gang, with Chineah at their head, each carrying a gun or rifle and short spear, and numbering with B——'s followers close upon a dozen strong and wiry fellows, fit for any kind of work. Baggage-ponies, bullocks, and coolies, laden with tents, boxes, &c., with a troop of servants and hangers-on, brought up the rear.

Our people were all going on three marches in advance to the village of Totteyum, (about thirty-five miles from Trichy, on the Salem road,) where they were to await our arrival, as, our leave not having yet appeared in orders, we were unable to quit cantonments until the next day. The police authorities had been previously warned to have carriage-bullocks posted for us every five or six miles, as we determined to lose no time on the road. The next day being the 1st of May, we attended a muster parade, and, after paying a few visits P.P.C. to the ladies of our acquaintance, and bidding adieu to some "of the kindliest men who ever drew sword," at about 3 P.M. we attired ourselves in the light and airy costume of muslin shirts, silk long-drawers, and slippers, and stepping into my cart, in a few moments we were rolling along at the rate of five or six miles an hour on the northern road leading to Salem.

For some time we amused ourselves by chaffing and poking fun at the wayfarers, particularly with some pilgrims who were carrying two encased chatties (earthen pots) of Ganges water,* which we taxed them with having taken from some tank on the road, and which at last they avowed.

When it grew dark we lighted our lamp, and chess and *écarté* served to pass away the time until we grew sleepy, when we rolled ourselves in the coverlids, and were soon in the arms of Morpheus.

About 2 A.M. we were awoke by the flashing of torches and the sound of voices, and found ourselves halted in front of the Travellers' Bungalow at Totteyum, surrounded by our people, who had arrived the evening before. After hastily swallowing a cup of coffee, and lighting cheroots, fresh bullocks were yoked, and we were soon again *en route*, surrounded by the gang, our tents and baggage having gone on before.

At about 8 A.M. we arrived at the Travellers' Bungalow of Namkul, (distance twenty miles,) where we found our servants, a bath, and breakfast awaiting us. After having arranged these preliminaries to our satisfaction, we strolled out with our guns, shot a few teal and snipe under the bund or embankment of a tank, and visited a fine old hill-fort, which is close to the town, and which was built by the inhabitants in former years as a refuge

* The water of the Ganges, being considered holy, is much used by the Hindoos in the performance of their "caste ceremonies," and is an article of commerce in the south of India.

against the Mahratta hordes and other predatory bands which then ravaged the country.

As our people had not yet got quite into marching trim, we slept at Namkul, starting the next morning for Moonoo-Choudy, distance fifteen miles, where we remained during the heat of the day, going on in the cool of the evening to Malloor, distance eleven miles, in which place we passed the night, and rode into Salem the following morning, putting up with Captain S——, who was commanding the detachment of native veterans which garrisoned the station.

After breakfast we visited the shop of the celebrated Arnatchellum, whose well-balanced boar-spears, axes, and hunting-knives are renowned throughout India for the temper of the steel and the superior finish of the workmanship. He charges European prices for everything, and I found him as overreaching a rogue as any other nigger.

Salem, though a large and densely-populated town, possesses very few attractions, and as the weather was fearfully hot, and cholera was carrying off great numbers of natives daily, I did not care about exposing my people to it more than necessary, so I sent them off at once with the baggage to Bowani, there to await our arrival.

I kept "Five Minutes," Googooloo, a couple of servants, and the pony with me, together with one of B——'s horses and the cart, and directed Chineah and the rest of the gang to try and gain all the information they could about the country round about Bowani.

As soon as we had seen them *en route* we made preparations for ascending the Sheveroy Hills, which rise from the plains about five miles to the northward of the town of Salem, and are about six thousand feet above the level of the sea.

The magistrates, judges, and collectors reside here during the greater part of the year, and we were fortunate enough to be able to engage a furnished bungalow belonging to Mr B——, a coffee-planter, where we resolved to stay for a few days, as B—— had been ailing, on account of the excessive heat.

A short time before sunset we began to ascend the ghaut, (pass,) by a rather steep winding road cut through the jungle, so that it was almost dark by the time we got to the top. The air was delightfully cool, and we appeared to inhale quite a different atmosphere to that we had lately left in the low country. We found a very comfortable bungalow prepared for us, and, being rather tired, we turned in early, and enjoyed a most refreshing night's rest, the first we had had for some time, as in the very hot weather, unless the "punkah" (fan) is kept going over the bed unceasingly, but little sleep is obtainable—one tosses about from side to side all night, and gets up in the morning exhausted, and overcome with lassitude and languor.

I rose quite a new man the next morning, and finding B—— still asleep, strolled out into the garden to enjoy the fresh air, which was mild and cool, as on a May-day in England.

The cottage we occupied is built on a little hill or knoll, and surrounded by beautifully kept coffee-plantations. The sides and roof were literally covered with odoriferous creepers, among which I noticed the woodbine, honeysuckle, jessamine, passion-flower, and a tall climbing fuchsia with very large scarlet bloom. Flowers which I never saw in the low country appeared to grow indigenous. I noticed the primroses, violets, and crocus in the parterres round the house, besides lilies, roses, and geraniums, of all kinds and colours. The kitchen-garden was full of European vegetables, and the cabbages, cauliflowers, turnips, carrots, lettuces, peas, artichokes, radishes, and mustard and cress forcibly recalled to mind my boyhood's home in Old England.

B—— joined me in the garden, and we were engaged in gathering the materials for a salad for breakfast (which in India is considered a great luxury) when we heard the clattering of horses' hoofs on the road, and almost immediately two coffee-planters, D—— and B——, rode up to the cottage-door, and introduced themselves.

In no part of the world, and I have travelled over a good deal of it, have I met with that free courtesy and affable urbanity which is invariably to be found among the British residents in India. A stranger passing through the country meets with the most generous and open-handed hospitality wherever he goes, and the supposed characteristics of an Englishman—"stiffness and cold hauteur of manner"—are rarely to be met with in the East. On the arrival of a stranger at an up-country station, it is the custom for all the residents (whatever may be their rank) to call upon him; hence arises that kind and friendly intercourse which exists everywhere in Anglo-Indian society, and is rarely to be met with elsewhere.

"We heard you had come up," said D——, a fine specimen of an open-hearted, good-tempered Englishman, "and not knowing whether you had thought of laying in a supply of provisions from the low country, as you can procure nothing here, I have taken the liberty of bringing you half a sheep of my own breeding, a few fattened fowls and ducks, some eggs and cream, a leash of hares, and a few brace of partridges, which ought to eat tender, as they were killed nearly a week ago."

"Thanks old fellow!" said B——. "They will indeed prove a treat, for we have been obliged to eat mutton and fowls almost immediately after they have been killed, lately, as nothing will keep throughout the day in the low country this weather. Here, Harry, do you concoct for us one of your insinuating 'claret cups,' whilst I see 'Five Minutes' about the breakfast, for I think we shall be six, as I expect R—— the collector, and the sub-judge, their horse-keepers having already arrived."

Whilst he was speaking they rode up, and in a few moments we were all sitting in the porch discussing the brew; which was so highly approved of by all parties that I will give the recipe, for the benefit of my readers, as it was prepared by the factotum of the late Brigadier of Hydrabad, Arab Mac, (a celebrated old Indian general, of great racing and sporting notoriety,) who gloried in having the finest stud and the best kitchen in India:—"To a bottle of claret add three wine-glasses of cognac, a couple of large tablespoons of sugar, the rind of a lime cut thin, a dozen cloves, the seeds of three cardamum-pods, a quarter of a nutmeg, one green chili, a small sprig of burrage, a dozen leaves of mint, and a threatening of lime-juice, or, what is perhaps better, a lime cut into thin slices. Let it stand for twenty minutes, and then add three bottles of cooled soda-water, stirring it up well, and serving it out with a ladel whilst in a state of effervescence."

After breakfast, at which sundry shekar projects were discussed, D—— and I rode out to a Mulliarry village, followed by our horse-keepers and Googooloo carrying guns, in order to hold a consultation with two men who were said to know the country well.

On the road I shot a brace of spur-fowl and a

hare weighing nearly ten pounds—almost twice the size of the ordinary Indian species, which rarely averages more than six. I also enjoyed the wild raspberries, which grew in the woods in great abundance.

On arriving at the village we soon found the men we were looking for, and learnt that bison had been seen the day before in the jungle on the side of the hills. I accordingly sent Googooloo and one of the Mulliarries to follow their trail, and find out if they were there still; and accompanied by the other, we went to a second village, where a man resided who knew some hill full of caves which were inhabited by several bears.

From the account he gave, we determined to try our chance the day after; and after having waited some time for Googooloo, who did not make his appearance, we returned to our cottage.

Whilst we were at dinner he came in and told me that he had tracked a herd of fine bison (a bull and four cows) to a small detached hill, a short distance from the foot of the Sheveroys, where he came up to them whilst they were feeding, and, after watching them for some time, he retired without disturbing them.

As this was not very far from the place where the bears were said to be, B——, D——, and myself agreed to start early the following morning to try and beat the bison out. The collector sent some of his "peons" (police) to prepare beaters, and D——

sent down a small tent to a village where we intended to sleep the following night.

The next morning we started at daybreak; descended the ghaut, and wound round the base of the Sheveroys for a distance of nearly seven miles, when Googooloo pointed us out the place where he had come up with the bison. Had I been alone, I should undoubtedly have preferred to try stalking rather than beating, but with three (and one a green hand, D——) it was out of the question.

We found the peons had collected about forty Coollies and villagers, whom I sent with Googooloo to the further side of the hill, as I felt convinced the herd, if it was still there, would endeavour to make for the thick jungle on the sides of the Sheveroys.

There were two likely-looking places for the bison to break, at one of which B—— posted himself, and D—— and myself took the other. Both places were by a broad stony watercourse that wound along the valley which separated the hill where the bison were said to be, from the Sheveroy range, and the herd would have to cross it in order to gain the opposite jungle.

D—— was very anxious to kill a bison, and I promised to give him the shot should the herd break into the open near us. He annoyed me very much, however, by his fidgety movements, for he could not sit quiet a moment, and kept handling the lock of an old rifle, until I made up my mind that he would either shoot me or some of the half-a-dozen people whom, in spite of my remonstrance, he would have sitting near us, to my intense disgust; for my olfactory organs received a shock they did not get over for some time, from the offensive smell that was emitted by the exhalation from their bodies, the cocoa-nut oil in their hair, and the garlic and sour rice they had been eating.

At last the bison broke, and a fine bull came tearing down right in front of us, and, when about twenty paces distant, D—— put up his piece; but being an old and unserviceable piece of goods, it snicked, and away went the quarry in the thick jungle on the other side the watercourse.

I caught a glimpse of his hinder quarters as he was tearing along the rising ground on the opposite side of the ravine, and I let drive with my rifle, hoping to stop him by a chance shot. I heard the "thud" of the ball as it struck him, and doubled him up for the moment, but he was not hit in a vital place, and I heard him bellowing as he tore through the dense jungle that covers the sides of the hills.

Both D—— and I tracked him for some distance, and in some places large gouts of blood were visible; but on coming to a watercourse, which bore the marks of his having cleared at a bound, I gave over the pursuit, and went in search of B——, whom we heard fire a double shot. We found him taking out the offal of a doe spotted-deer he had killed, and preparing it for carriage. He had seen three bison break, but they were out of range of his rifle.

The beaters now made their appearance, and, slinging the deer on long poles, which they carried over their shoulders, took it to the place where we had left our horses. I chose a dozen of the most intelligent-looking of the number to accompany us, and dismissed the rest with a bucksheesh, telling them they would be well paid if they brought us news of large game. Then mounting our horses, we rode off to the village where our tent had been sent, which was about six miles further, and found "Five Minutes" anxiously expecting our arrival, dinner being nearly ready.

We had a most refreshing bathe in a tank, on the bund or stone embankment of which our tent was pitched, under the shade of a beautiful banian-tree, and afterwards did ample justice to his entertainment. Poor D—— was in a dreadful way about his old piece, and I spared him the roasting I had fully intended to have given him for the nervous agitation he had shown whilst waiting for the bison to break.

After dinner was over I sent for the head man of the village, and told him our intention of setting out very early the next morning after bears, and we were agreeably surprised to find he had already prepared people who knew their haunts to accompany us.

We assembled all our people in a circle, distributed the usual allowance of grog and tobacco, and afterwards heard all they had to say about the game to be found in the country, and the most effective manner of pursuing it. After I heard all their opinions, I made up my mind to start an hour before the first appearance of dawn for the hill where the bears were said to be, which was about a coss, or two miles, from the village, and to await their returning to their caves; as in this part of the country, during the hot weather, bears roam about the jungle in search of food all the night and return to their caves in the morning, where they remain during the intense heat of the day, issuing forth again at sunset. They live chiefly upon the wild fruits of the jungle and white ants, which latter insect they devour in thousands, by scraping a hole with their claws, and sucking them out of their nests. They are also passionately fond of honey, and show themselves wonderfully sharp in finding out wild bees' nests, climbing lofty trees in search of them.

gooloo, the Mulliarry, and two villagers who knew the bears' caves.

Although the hill was not more than 800 feet in height it was very steep, and the ascent was the more difficult on account of numberless rocky crags which were entwined with thick bush. At last we managed to climb up the dry bed of a watercourse, in which we noticed the fresh traces of bears in many places, and after a good deal of scrambling and climbing up ledges of rock, we arrived at the summit, which was a small table-land covered with tufts of coarse grass and large boulders of rock.

As we were going along Googooloo suddenly stopped, gave his usual grunt to attract attention, and tapping me on the shoulder, pointed me out two bears at the foot of the hill. With the aid of my glass I could see they were very busily engaged in digging up the earth; so, setting the Mulliarry to watch their movements, I went on to the caves, and, after a careful examination, found seven entrances, five of which bore marks of being inhabited by bears.

I sent one of the villagers and Googooloo to bring up the rest of the party as quietly as possible, so as not to disturb the game we knew was afoot, and by the time they arrived, I and the other villagers had managed to block up the two smallest entrances (which did not seem to have been frequented of late) with stones and pieces of rock.

I posted B—— on a rock which commanded the

CHAPTER XI.

BEAR-HUNTING.

We start for the Bear Hill.—The reconnaissance.—Bears afoot. —Their strongholds invested.—A foraging party surprised.— Two bears die.—Three more afoot.—Another couple yield their spoils.—Desperate encounter with an enraged vixen, who almost proved a Tartar.—"The Old Shekarry" in a fix for a time, but wins the game at last.—The bag of the day.— The return.

THE next morning we are all up and equipped for sport by 2 A.M., and, after a substantial feed, started for the Bear Hill on foot, as the villagers said the route was difficult for horses.

At this season of the year the night is not at any time dark, and we managed to get along very well in Indian file, although the path was very narrow, and in some places we had to crawl along on our hands and knees. We arrived at the foot of the hill some time before sunrise, and here I halted the party, which numbered about twenty coolies and villagers, and telling B—— to prevent any of them from straying, and to keep as quiet as possible, I went forward to reconnoitre, accompanied by Goo-

two entrances of the largest cave, and D—— by another. The other two I guarded by some of the villagers who were armed with matchlocks, and I despatched half-a-dozen others to different elevated peaks, from which they could survey all the surrounding country.

When all were in their places I went with Googooloo to the Mulliarry, who was watching the two bears, and he pointed them out to me in the same place we had first seen them.

Accompanied by Googooloo, carrying my second gun, (an eight smooth-bore,) I stole down the hill as gently as I could, making for a large rock which appeared to me to be within a short distance of the place where I had seen the bears.

I was some time before I could make my way to it, as the bush and underwood were thick, and we had to make our way through dense masses of entangled creepers. At last we gained the rock, and Googooloo's quick eye soon discovered our friends still hard at work scraping up the earth of the ant-hill.

We stole gently up, seeking the cover of rocks and bushes, until I got within fifteen paces of them, still undiscovered. Watching their movements until I got a fair opportunity, I planted a rifle-ball behind the shoulder of one, which rolled over and over on the ground in the agonies of death, and then gave the other the contents of my second barrel, which took effect about the small ribs, tumbling her over for the moment. She, however, soon got up again, raised herself on her haunches, uttering a peculiarly melancholy cry, and looked round in a most woe-begone manner. This position offered me a splendid shot, and I finished her career with a ball from my second gun.

Having ascertained that both were dead, Googooloo climbed a large tree that was near, and fastened the Mulliarry's turban-cloth, like a streamer, to one of the highest branches, in order to serve as a landmark for the coolies when they came to collect the game. He also cut off a claw from the right fore-paw of each bear, so as to mark it as mine, a precaution the gang always took, in consequence of an individual having obtained a deer which I had undoubtedly shot at a battue some time previously, and, to the intense disgust of all my people, allowed him to appropriate and carry off.

As we were leisurely returning up the watercourse towards the caves where B—— and D—— were posted, I heard a rolling of stones and a curious grunting noise close behind us. I jumped on a large boulder of rock, and saw three bears making their way slowly up the watercourse in the same direction we were going. I immediately made signs to Googooloo and the Mulliarry to hide, and I crouched behind the rock until they were past, as I wished my friends to get a shot, and they were evidently bound their way.

These three had hardly passed when Googooloo

pointed me out two others making their way up the hill by the same route. Standing behind a rock so as not to alarm them, I let drive right and left as they passed within a few paces of me. They were both badly hit behind the shoulder, and each must have imagined the other was the cause of his injury, for with a ferocious noise they immediately attacked each other, and closing in a hug, rolled down the hill some short distance. I followed with my second gun, and found one dead and the other leaning over him in a very deplorable condition. He was too far gone to take any notice of my approach, although he continued to make a fearful moaning, which I put a stop to by giving him a quietus in the shape of a pill behind the ear, which finished his career.

I had just commenced reloading, when I heard a loud straggling volley from the top of the hill where my friends were posted, and almost immediately it was followed by a shriek from the Mulliarry, whom I saw make a spring into the jungle just in time to avoid the charge of a huge female bear who came rushing down the watercourse in a most ferocious manner. I was directly in her path, and with a roar she made right at me; I let drive at her head with my only barrel that had not been discharged, but it failed to stop her, and she had knocked me down and was on me in the twinkling of an eye.

The slope of the hill was steep, and we both of us rolled over and over several times; I was almost breathless, when Googooloo rushed on her with his bill-hook and endeavoured to attract her attention. Luckily she could not bite at all, as my shot had smashed her snout and lower jaw to pieces; but she kept me locked in her embrace, and squeezed me more roughly than affectionately.

My head was well protected with a bison-skin cap; and getting a tight grasp of her fur on each side, with my arms underneath hers, so that she could not do me much injury with her claws, I regularly wrestled with her for some time; and although I brought my science to play, and threw her on her back several times "by giving her the leg," she never let go her hug, and I was almost suffocated with the quantity of blood and froth that came from her wound and covered my face, beard, and chest.

Googooloo made frantic hits at her from time to time with his bill-hook, (the only weapon he had, having lent D—— his knife,) but I ordered him to desist, as his blows did not appear to do the bear much harm, and I was afraid of catching one. At last Bruin appeared to be getting weaker, and I saw her wounds and loss of blood were telling; and after a little trouble I managed to draw my knife, and drove it up to the hilt in her body under the armpits. She gave me an ugly hug, and fell over on her side, pulling me with her. It was her last effort, and I picked myself up quite out of puff, but not much injured, having only received a slight claw on the loins and another rather more severe on the instep. I drew my pistol, which I could not manage to get at before, to give her a settler, but it was not required—the game was over, my antagonist was dead.

Being covered with blood and dust from head to foot, I must have presented a comical appearance to B—— and D——, who came rushing down in pursuit of the bear, which D—— had slightly wounded before she fell in with me. They had met the Mulliarry *en route,* who said that he had seen me killed; and no sooner did Googooloo get sight of this individual, than he sprang on him like a tiger for his cowardice in running away, and we had some difficulty to prevent him from strangling him and in releasing him from his clutches.

One of the coolies brought me the water-skin, and I washed the blood away from my person and threw off a part of my soiled clothes. I then tore off a part of my shirt and bandaged up my loins and foot, which latter bled considerably, and was very painful when I walked, as the claws had penetrated gaiter, boot, and stocking, entering the flesh to the depth of half an inch. Having arranged matters as I best could, I managed to scramble up the hill, though I had some difficulty in doing so, as the back of my head and my arms, shoulders, and knees were considerably bruised; and I felt rather shaken and tired after my encounter.

When I arrived at the caves I found B—— had

killed the two bears, and D—— had caught a young one alive. We remained there about half an hour longer, when another female and two half-grown cubs came rolling along, all of whom bit the dust before our united volley. D—— also went after two others which were seen coming up the hill, but were deterred from coming near the caves, having taken alarm at the firing. He killed one and severely wounded the other, but somehow or another managed to lose it.

The sun had now risen high above the horizon; the breeze had died away, and not a breath of air was stirring; a mirage was seen spread over the plain, out of which the wooded hills rose like distant islands. The sultriness was getting more and more oppressive, and it was piping hot before our coolies had managed to collect the game at the foot of the hill, which consisted of four male bears, five females, two half-grown cubs, and a very young one caught alive.

A number of village people, hearing of our sport, came to carry the game in; and my servant thoughtfully brought my pony, which I was glad of, as my foot gave me considerable pain.

I superintended the preparation of the skins, (as my own man who usually did that kind of work was with the gang at Bowani,) by seeing them stretched tightly and pegged down on the ground, exposed to the heat of the sun, whilst wood-ashes, cocoa-nut oil, hulde, (turmeric,) and arsenical soap were rubbed in.

Finding myself rather stiff and sore from my bruises, I mounted my pony "Gooty" and rode back to our bungalow at the top of the Sheveroy Hill, where I arrived late in the evening, leaving B—— and D—— to continue their sport with the bears a few days longer, whilst I had my foot looked at by the doctor, and got fit for work again.

CHAPTER XII.

BOWANI.

Sankerrydroog.—An adventure with hyenas.—Bowani.—Alligator-fishing.—We start for Andior.—"Gooty," my shooting pony: his pedigree and achievements.—Small-game shooting.—Antelope stalking.—Andior.—The monkeys and the Brahmins.—Murrel-fishing.

A FEW days after our encounter with the bears, I received a note from B—— telling me that he had heard of rare sport near Bowani, and begging me to join him at the public bungalow at Sankerrydroog, which is two marches from Salem, and about half-way between that place and Bowani. As the wound in my foot was not quite healed I borrowed a palanquin from the collector, and starting the next evening at 4, arrived at Sankerrydroog at 6 A.M., distance thirty-five miles, having stopped a couple of hours for refreshments at M'Donald's choultry.

I found that the trophies of two bears and a fine buck spotted-deer had been taken during my absence, and B—— informed me that a large cheeta had been seen prowling about the old hill-fort for some days previous, and that at last, after some trouble, it had been tracked (the evening before) by some of the villagers to a cave, half-way up the hill, and large stones had been placed at the entrance, so as to prevent its coming out.

After breakfast we began to ascend the hill, B—— and D—— on foot, armed with rifles, and I mounted on my favourite little nag "Gooty," with a boar-spear and my famous dogs "Ali" and "Hassan," which were half Poligar, half bloodhound. We soon came to the entrance of the cave, which was about four feet in diameter, and, after a fruitless examination for pugs and trails, some of the villagers who were with us pulled down the stones built up at the mouth, and D——, B——, and a massauljee with a couple of lighted torches entered, but were almost immediately obliged to return on account of the foul air and stench within. We then placed a bundle of straw inside, and set fire to it, hoping to drive the brute out with the smoke, but no good result was obtained, although B—— thought he heard a moaning kind of noise inside. We also fired off several rockets and crackers, which had the effect of dislodging some of the inhabitants, for hundreds of curious little four-eared bats came out.

Finding that none of these annoyances would bring out the cheeta, I sent in my two dogs, and immediately knew that game was a-foot, as Ali gave tongue the moment he entered, and very shortly afterwards dismal howls and strange rumbling noises were heard issuing from the bowels of the earth, and I began to be alarmed for the dogs, when suddenly I heard a row, and saw my poor friend D—— (who in spite of my remonstrances would stand right in front of the mouth of the cave) knocked over on the broad of his back by a huge male hyena, whilst in the twinkling of an eye the female, a couple of cubs, and my two dogs passed over him as he lay almost helpless on the ground, and made the best of their way down the hill and across some cultivated fields; B—— let drive a couple of shots as they passed, and doubled up the female, and I descended the hill as well as I could, and after a burst of a few minutes, Gooty brought me alongside of the male, who was vainly struggling to get away from my two dogs, one of whom had hold of him by the ear, and the other on the opposite side by the throat. As I did not wish to run the chance of having either of them mauled or bitten, I drove my spear home between the shoulders, and finished the game, after which I went to look after poor D——, whom I found much shaken with the fall, his chin and throat being considerably damaged by the claws of the brutes as they passed over him.

We returned to the bungalow, convinced that the villagers had mistaken the hyena for a cheeta; and after D—— had washed, and plastered up his face, we all three got into my bullock-cart, and arrived at Bowani soon after sunset, where we found Mother Garrow and her dusky train of dancing nymphs from the Pagoda awaiting our arrival at the public bungalow, which is very pleasantly situated on the ruins of an old fort, which, with a large and rather celebrated pagoda dedicated to the worship of the Goddess Bowani, (the deity of the Thugs,) is built at the sungum or conflux of the rivers Cauvery and Bowani.

Chineah and the gang were delighted with the place, and described the Andior and Samungalum jungle as being alive with game of all kinds.

The next morning we strolled along the banks of the river with our rifles, as Chineah had seen several alligators basking in the sun on a sandbank the day before; and although we saw plenty of marks of their huge claws imprinted in the sand near the edge of the water, none were to be seen.

In spite of Dr Johnson's reflections on anglers, I determined to try a piscatorial experiment, so I returned to the village, and got the "lohar" (blacksmith) to forge two large barbed hooks on the ends of a couple of strong English dog-chains, which I made fast to the storm-ropes of my tent, attaching large logs of very light mangoe-wood as floats. I then got a village "chucklar," (shoemaker,) a Pariah of the lowest caste, to accompany me with a couple of young pigs, and my servant brought a quantity of raw mutton to serve as bait. Having made all my arrangements, I returned to the spot where I had left B—— and D——, couched behind bushes waiting for the chance of a shot, and explained my intentions; then passing the ropes over the forks of trees, so as to give me additional purchase, I baited my hooks and flung them into the river. The "chucklar" soon caught up my idea, and by chewing the end of the pigs' tails he elicited the most melodious music, which soon had the desired effect, and attracted the alligators to that part of the river. I threw several pieces of mutton into the stream, and in a very short time there were upwards of a dozen of these immense brutes splashing about and scrambling with each other for the meat.

At last one of my floats gave a bob, (it was more than a nibble,) and then disappeared under water. My gang and a number of villagers seized the rope, and with some difficulty we hauled the brute to the bank of the river, when he began rolling about in the sand, trying to disgorge the bait, and knocking about with his tail, so that I began to be afraid he would cut the rope and escape.

I ran down with my rifle, and with some difficulty slipped a bowline knot over his head, and in a few moments the gang had fastened up his mouth with a roll of strong cord, and doubled his legs over his back, and in this manner he was dragged along in triumph.

In less than two hours we had caught four more, the largest being a little over eleven feet in length. We afterwards let them loose on the plain, and, mounting our horses, killed them with our boar-spears, which entered the throat behind the shoulders and the under parts of the body easily enough; and we found that a hardened rifle-ball would enter any part of the back or head, which have been stated to be shot-proof by some writers. In the evening we had another nautch, which was prolonged until the "short hours," when we distributed our "largess" to the votaries of Terpsichore and turned in.

On the morrow we started for Andior *en route* for Combie Jungles, and as the distance was not much over twelve miles, and small game was said to be abundant, we determined to shoot our way, having our horses following in case any of us being tired.

My little nag "Gooty" was a thoroughly broken shooting-pony, and, although the Rarian system had not then come out, a perfect understanding existed between us: he would come at my call or whistle; stand perfectly quiet when ordered; allow me to fire from between his ears, without flinching; would take the water like a duck; was famous in a scramble across country; had no fear, and could almost do everything but speak. He came into my hands in a strange way; I was encamped outside the village of Nandeir, being *en route* from Hydrabad to Seetabuldee, and tired and overcome with lassitude, having ridden from Mudnoor, a distance of fifty-two miles, in the heat of the day; I was lounging on a carpet stretched in front of my tent, enjoying the soothing fragrance of my hookah, and amusing myself with talking to some handsome Mussulmauni damsels who constantly passed to and fro, as they went to draw water from a ghaut on the Godavery river, when a venerable-looking old man with a huge silver beard rolling down his chest, and clad in a fakeer's or dervish's garb, came up leading a chestnut mare, and accosting me with the usual salutation, begged "Aallah ka nam se" (in the name of Allah) that I would assist him. He evidently took me to be one of the "Faithful," for besides speaking the language fluently, I wore a native dress, consisting of a muslin ungreka, embroidered silk long-drawers and turban, and my naturally dark complexion was considerably deepened by constant exposure to the sun. He told me that he had given up the world, *i.e.*, his wives and family, and had devoted the remainder of his days to the service of Mohammed, but that lately "*dark clouds had been hanging over the garden of his fate, and the blossoms of hope were almost withered.*" He was *en route* from Boregaum on the Wurdah river to Hydrabad, in order to be present at the Mohrum festival in that famous Mussulman capital, but he had been detained by illness on the road, his cash was nearly gone, and moreover, the back of his mare, which had been presented to him by the Oomraootee Nawab, on the occasion of his son's recovery from illness, was so galled that he could not ride her, and did not know how to proceed on his journey.

His mare was a blood-looking little creature of the Mahratta caste, with a running sore on her withers nearly the size of the palm of my hand; and although at the time I thought the wound was incurable, and she would never again be fit for work, I offered ten rupees for her, which the old man very gladly accepted. I had an old Arab syce who was famous for his knowledge of herbs, and under his care she got rapidly well, doing me good service for several years. "Gooty" was one of her progeny by "Chunda lal," (the Red Moon,) formerly the property of the late celebrated Dewan of the Deckan, of that name, a magnificent chestnut Arab of remarkably pure caste, well known in the Nizam's dominions as the winner of the great Moul Alli steeple-chase.

Gooty proved a "chip of the old block," and commenced his career by carrying off the pony races, Galloway stakes, and hurdle-race (weight for inches) at Hydrabad, under the name of the "Red Rover," afterwards beating General W——'s celebrated black pony "D. I. O." in two matches, and distinguishing himself at Bellary and Bangalore, where he put a good many gold mohurs in the pocket of his master, ever proving a thorough good one. His greatest achievement was, however, performed at Gooty (which name he has since borne,) where he carried his master safely up the steep rocky scarp of that celebrated hill-fort to the round-house on the extreme summit, and down again; a feat which, although it has often been attempted, was never accomplished in the memory of the oldest inhabitant, or of the old Nawab who had been confined there as a state-prisoner for upwards of five-and-twenty years. A gallant officer of the 48th had a brass plate fixed on a rock about half way up, to commemorate his having ridden a horse named "Firefly" up to that point.

"Gooty," although he measured barely thirteen hands two inches, was famous in difficult country, and would follow a boar *con amore*, doubling like a greyhound after a hare. "*Mais revenons à nos moutons.*" We passed through a good deal of low brush jungle and rumnah grass, alive with small game; for in less than four hours we were satiated with our sport, having killed three couple and a half of "florikin," (or lesser bustard,) the finest bird for the table in India, thirteen leash of hares, nine brace of gray partridge, and three of gray quail; and as the sun's rays were burning intensely powerful, and our beaters began to show unmistakable signs of distress, we adjourned to the shade of a widely-spreading peepul-tree, and were enjoying our "kieff," (a Turkish word signifying a state of dreamy existence, when the body is motionless, all the senses are at rest, and the mind dormant,) and discussing cheroots and brandy-panee, when a villager who was passing by informed us that he had just seen a large herd of antelope on a "maidaun" or plain about two miles further on.

We loaded our rifles, and after a few minutes' canter arrived at the place indicated, where we saw a herd consisting of about sixty does and seven or eight bucks, which were easily distinguishable, on account of their long spiral horns and much darker colour. They caught sight of us almost immediately, and our sudden appearance caused some consternation; for the does collected in a body behind the bucks, who stood as if on sentry, carefully watching our movements, although we were at least six hundred yards distant. I saw at once that they were very wild, and that the utmost caution would be necessary in stalking so as to get within shot: we therefore rode slowly away, until I could see by my field-glass that they had ceased to take any notice of us.

I then directed B—— and D—— where to take post under cover of some bushes, whilst I undertook to stalk the leader, a fine black buck with a beautiful pair of antlers, and to draw the herd if possible towards their ambuscade. I divested myself of my white pith hunting-cap, substituting a head-dress formed of creepers, and cutting a number of pliable twigs I interwove them into a kind of basketwork screen, in which I fastened green boughs, so as to make it resemble a bush as much as possible, leaving an opening through which I could point my rifle. When this was completed I sallied forth, taking care to get to leeward, and seeking any cover I could find, either behind bushes or from any slight undulations of the ground, until I got to within five hundred yards of the herd, who were quietly browsing, unconscious of danger.

Here I lay for some time at full length on the ground behind my screen so as to give my companions time to get posted, and taking out my telescope I surveyed the herd for some time before I could make out the position of the leader, whom at last I twigged lying down and chewing the cud, under the shade of a bauble-bush, some short distance from the others. I stole gently forwards, sometimes stooping and walking, and at others creeping on my hands and knees, (which is extremely laborious work,) until I got within two hundred yards of him, when, feeling out of breath and rather unsteady, I rested for some time. As soon as I had recovered my breath, I slowly commenced my onward progress until I got within a hundred and twenty yards, when, from the motion of the herd, I saw that my walking bush had excited some suspicion, for they began to close up, and crane their necks in my direction; which movement was immediately perceived and understood by their leader, who sprang on his feet, stamped, and advanced some five or six paces towards me, snuffing the air as if to reconnoitre. This position offered me a fair shot—I raised my rifle and pulled the trigger just as a low bark escaped him, (the signal of alarm to the herd.) It was his last warning, for my grooved-bore was true—the bullet sped, and entered his heart; he sprang high into the air and fell dead. I fired my second barrel at the herd, which was in full retreat, bringing down a doe, my ball entering the small ribs near the spine, and paralysing her hind-quarters; and, after drawing my knife across her throat, I jumped on Gooty, who was brought up by my syce, and followed the herd, driving it towards the spot where B—— and D—— were posted. Both got shots. B—— rolled over a young buck at a long distance; and D—— bagged a doe, missing two other fair shots.

We collected the game, tied it up in front of our saddles, and then made the best of our way towards Andior, where we found our tents pitched under the shade of a beautiful mangoe tope, in front of which was a large square tank, full of water-lilies, and an old dilapidated pagoda, on the walls of which some scores of the common green-tufted monkey sat grinning, jabbering, and making mouths at us as we passed.

A curious tale is told of a detachment of the —th Native Infantry having made a colony of these monkeys revenge an insult which was offered them by the inhabitants of Trippasore, the greater part of whom consist of Brahmins. It appears that the military were *en route* to the Presidency, escorting treasure, and the Bunnias, or grain-sellers, raised the price of rice very considerably the day before they passed through their town, which conduct aroused Jack Sepoy's indignation, who, however, smothered his resentment until his return from Madras, when each man filled his haversack with rice and *dhal*, (a kind of sweet bean,) and on re-passing through the town he threw it on the roofs of all the tiled houses, on which lived hundreds of monkeys, occasioning a most ludicrous scene—for immediately the tiles were seen flying in clouds into the streets, until the greater part of the town was unroofed; for the monkeys, finding the grains slip under the tiles, lifted them up, and threw them into the street, and as they took one up the rice slipped under the next, and so on, until a good roof was demolished in a few minutes, to the utter disgust and mortification of the Brahmins, who dare not molest the monkeys, considering these animals sacred, as being the incarnation of their powerful god, Hanimann.

After we had imbibed some cooled Bass, the best beverage for India, B——, who was a fisherman, went down to the tank with his rod, and in the course of half an hour landed over a dozen fine murrel, (a voracious kind of fish, somewhat resembling the jack,) from four to eight pounds in weight. On cutting them open we found the inside full of leeches, so we declined having them put upon our table, to the great satisfaction of Chineah and the gang, who pronounced them delicious.

CHAPTER XIII.

THE COMBEI JUNGLE.

Early rising.—" Tiger's milk."—A sloth-bear started.—Combei. —Our encampment.—A salt-lick.—Great bag of deer by night.—Ding-ding.—A strange rencontre whilst pea-fowl stalking.—Leg-bail.—The death of the tiger.—B——'s sport. —A glorious chase.—The bull-nilghau.—The bag.—A black panther.—Strange mode of catching deer.—Return to Bowani. —Finale.

GETTING up early in the morning, after a hard fag the day previous, is at all times a painful operation, more especially during the intensely sultry weather preceding the downfall of the monsoon in India; when sleep, balmy sleep, is banished from the couch of the weary one, and he tosses and rolls about, feverish and restless, in an irritable state of mind, with aching bones, overcome with lassitude and fatigue, the whole night long, unable to obtain even a doze until the cool refreshing breeze of the morning sets in, when to be awoke suddenly is indeed a martyrdom, and to arouse a man without a cause at such a time is to render him unaccountable for his actions.

My servant, "Five Minutes," upon whom the task of getting us up in the morning usually devolved, was well aware that at this period "sahib-log" (masters) are somewhat in the same humour as "bears with sore heads;" for many a boot, candlestick, and empty soda-water bottle had he dodged in his time whilst attempting to rouse some heavy sleeping "sub" for parade after a public night at mess; and, being a wide-awake nigger, he now never exposed himself in this somewhat perilous undertaking without having first provided himself with some emollient and resuscitating mixture calculated to better the human feelings, such as well-cooled claret-cup, soda and brandy, or "tiger's milk," which served better than any "soft words," the nigger knew, "to allay wrath." As the latter concoction was considered the most effective, I give the recipe; and if ladies with surly husbands would only try "Five Minutes's" dodge, of administering a dose of "tiger's milk" before they asked for "the needful" to settle the little account of crinoline, &c., they would find it acted upon the milk of human kindness far better than all the wheedling and soft sawder which husbands (too soon, alas!) get accustomed to. Recipe—Beat up the yolks of three eggs well with half a pint of brandy, a wine-glass of sugar, a bit of lemon-peel cut thin, and a dozen cloves and cardamums; add a quart of new milk, mix well, grate in the third of a nutmeg, and serve it in a tankard, of which the bottom should be seen before it is removed from the lips.

When "Five Minutes" thought his master was tired overnight, and would be reluctant to move in the morning, he would carefully prepare a bowl of this insinuating mixture, and, creeping with noiseless steps to the head of the bed, would there remain, bowl in hand, whilst the "cochra," or dressing-boy, turned up the coverlid, put on the unconscious sleeper's socks and boots, and shampooed his limbs until he awoke, when, as soon as he began to rub his eyes, the soothing draught was applied; and its kindly effects would almost immediately demonstrate themselves, for he would allow himself to be dressed "like a good child," and after a cheroot was as mild as new milk.

Antelope-stalking the day before had somewhat knocked me up, and I felt rather stiff on first rising; but after my matin cup, a plunge in the tank of the pagoda, and a few whiffs of the "fragrant narcotic weed," the lassitude wore off, and we all three mounted our nags and started for Combei, distant from Andior fourteen miles, where we intended to sojourn for a few days, as a herd of bison was said to be in the neighbourhood.

As we rode along, D—— twigged a female sloth-bear climbing leisurely up the side of a rocky hill; so slipping the two Poligar dogs, Ali and Hassan, we gave chase with our boar-spears, but the old vixen was close to her cave, and gave us the slip, to D——'s intense disgust.

On arrival at Combei, which we found to be a small deserted village, abandoned by its original inhabitants on account of fever, and occupied only by four families of the Mulcher caste, (a jungle tribe,) things did not appear very promising, so we pitched our camp under a large peepul-tree by a beautifully clear stream full of fish.

When all was arranged to our satisfaction, we strolled out in different directions to look out for bison. D—— and B—— came across fresh trails, but returned immediately, as it was too late to follow them up. I was not so fortunate, although I killed a young spotted-deer, and found out a salt-lick, where there were innumerable fresh marks of elk, spotted-deer, jungle-sheep, and some old ones of bison. These animals come for miles round about to eat the earth which they find here and there in the jungle, strongly impregnated with salt, of which they are extremely fond.

At dinner I mentioned the salt-lick I had discovered, and, as it was not more than half a mile from our tents, we resolved to try the Burmese experiment of shooting deer by aid of an artificial light, as the moon did not favour us. Accordingly, Chineah made a lamp with pieces of rag, and a quantity of fat, oil, and tar, which he got from the cook, and fastened it to a bamboo pole about fifteen feet in height; then, providing ourselves with several guns, a carpet, brandy-panee, &c., we went to the salt-lick, a little before dusk, and, having erected a kind of screen with bushes and branches, comfortably established ourselves in front and to leeward of an open space of ground, which was covered with the footprints of different kinds of deer. Our pole was planted in the ground some half dozen paces in front, and when it got dark the lamp was lighted, and a piece of bright tin (the lid of a cowrie-box) placed behind, to serve as a reflector, and also to prevent the light from revealing our ambuscade.

We waited for nearly an hour without hearing or seeing anything, when suddenly I thought I saw a pair of bright eyes shining like stars from the thicket in front of the light, and in a moment a low bark informed me that my plan had succeeded, and that a buck-elk was at hand. I whispered to the others not to fire until I gave the signal—for I knew, from the cry of the buck, that the herd was at hand; and in a few moments he stepped forward, barking, stamping his hoofs, scratching his back with his antlers, and staring at the light; and almost immediately he was followed by the rest of the herd, which must have numbered nearly twenty. The light engrossed all their attention, and they came to within a dozen paces of it before I gave the signal to fire by a low "Coo." B——, D——, Chineah, and myself let drive double shots, and our volley threw the herd into such confusion that some of us had time to make use of second guns before those that were unwounded could get away.

When the smoke had cleared, we found five dead, and four others wounded, which we despatched. Both B—— and myself felt that it was a poaching kind of game, so we did not care to continue it, and returned to the tent; but D—— and Chineah remained in the ambuscade all night, and managed to bag another buck-elk and four spotted-deer, besides which the gang, with the dogs' assistance, next morning brought in five other deer, which they found dead or wounded some distance off in the jungle. The game proved very acceptable to the Mulcher tribes who roam about these jungles; and the gang jerked a considerable quantity of venison, or rather converted it into what they term "Ding-ding," by cutting the meat into long strips, which they rub with salt, ground spices, and dry in the sun, until it becomes as hard as a board. When required for use, it is allowed to soak in water for a couple of hours to soften, and is then broiled over embers, when it is not at all unpalatable, and often constitutes the principal part of a Shekarry's fare whilst on trail.

During the next three days, although we constantly made long excursions into the jungle, we were very unsuccessful in meeting with large game, only killing a few deer for food. One evening, as I was returning towards the tent after a long weary fag, during which I had not pulled trigger, Chineah and one or two of the gang who were with me asked me to shoot a peacock for them that was screaming in a thicket close by. I bid them remain perfectly quiet where they were, whilst I followed it up, guided by the cry, and at last I got so near that I could hear the old birds scratching up the ground, and the young ones chirping or rather whistling; but the underwood was so dense that I could not get sight of them, although they must have been within a few paces from me. I clambered down the dry sandy bed of a nullah, and was peering between the trees in the expectation of getting a glimpse of the brood, when, turning stealthily round a large jummona-bush, (a kind of willow,) I suddenly came face to face upon an immense tiger, who had evidently been taking his "*siesta*" under the cool shade of the shelving bank, for when I first caught sight of him he was stretching himself and yawning as if only just awake. Doubtless it was a mutual surprise, but I was the first to recover my self-possession, for without a moment's hesitation I swung round, and notwithstanding we were barely six feet apart, and my gun (a double eight-guage by Westley Richards) was only loaded with No. 4 shot, I let drive right and left full into his face. Before the smoke cleared away, the tiger, uttering an appalling shriek of rage, sprang clear over my head, and fell with a crash against the opposite bank: whilst I, without waiting to watch his further movements, gave "leg bail," and ran in a contrary direction down the nullah. Finding that I was not pursued, I reloaded with ball, and "Richard was himself again," for I must own my serenity of mind was somewhat disturbed at such an unlooked-for rencontre. Chincah, attracted by the double report, now came up, and, having taken my pet rifle from him, I slung the smooth-bore over my shoulder, directed him to remain quiet in a tree, and again made my way to the scene of action. I soon came across the tiger's pugs, and followed them up to a pool of water where there were marks of his having quenched his thirst a few moments before.

The double charge of shot I administered at such close quarters had evidently taken effect, for the trail was marked with large crimson drops, and I knew that his sight was partially if not entirely destroyed, as from time to time he had struck his head against the steep banks on each side of the nullah, leaving large gouts of blood behind him. In a few minutes I heard sundry strange noises in a patch of reeds and corinda-bushes by the side of the nullah, and from the "swearing" of a troop of monkeys in the trees overhead on each bank I knew what to expect. I clambered up a boulder of rock, from whence I could see the tiger going round and round evidently quite blind, for every now and then he knocked his head against stones and bushes, when he would give a short angry roar, tear up the ground, and bite at everything within his reach. I saw at a glance how matters were, so stealing gently up I aimed just behind the shoulder, and the ball passing through the heart immediately put him out of his misery, for he sprang high into the air and dropped stone dead. On examination I found the whole of the upper part of the face was blown to pieces, and both eyes destroyed with the effect of my first shots; indeed, the head was a mass of congealed blood, none of the features being distinguishable; however, such is the tenacity of life in the feline race, that he managed even in this condition to make his way for upwards of half a mile, although totally blind.

A whistle brought up my followers, and we immediately commenced denuding the tiger of his spoils, in which operation we were overtaken by darkness, but by lighting a huge fire we managed to accomplish our purpose, and afterwards made the best of our way to the tents, where I found B—— and D—— deeply interested in exploring the interior of a huge marrow-pie, the former having that morning killed a fine nilghau within a few hundred paces of our encampment. After dinner we superintended the pegging down of the skins, and retired early to rest, as the Mulchers had tracked up the herd of nilghau, and we determined if possible to drive them into the more open country on the morrow, and ride them down with our boar-spears.

I sounded the "*reveille*" through the camp an hour before dawn, and after having fortified the "inner man" and partaken of a "stirrup cup," we lighted our cheerots, mounted our nags, and under the guidance of the Mulchers set out for the cover in

N

which the game had been marked. It was a glorious morning, and we were all in the best of spirits. As we rode along, accompanied by the gang and the greater part of our followers, who were to act as beaters, every now and then we put up coveys of quail, partridge, or rock-pigeon, and once or twice we caught sight of troops of antelope and spotted-deer bounding through the more open jungle. After a cursory survey of the country, which was anything but fair riding-ground, being covered with low scrub jungle and intersected with innumerable nullahs and gullies, we took our post some little distance from each other, whilst our people extended themselves in a large semicircle, and advanced slowly, shouting and beating tom-toms. In the course of a few minutes a tremendous yell informed us that the game was afoot, a crashing of underwood was heard, and a herd of nine nilghau, consisting of two bulls and seven cows, broke into the plain.

We immediately laid the dogs into them, and, after a smart burst of about a mile, two of the hindermost cows were brought to a stand-still, Hassan and Slogee pursuing one, whilst Bran and Ali fastened on the other; the greyhounds yelping and giving tongue, but not having the pluck to lay hold. Leaving the fallen to the care of D——, who, being but indifferently mounted, was pounding along in the rear, B—— and I each selected a bull, and after sundry purls and divers charges, in which we were often the pursued, both of us managed to "bring our game to grass." The one I was after charged repeatedly, and, notwithstanding I was admirably mounted on my pet hog-hunter, Lall Babba, it was not until we had covered a good four miles of ground that I managed at last, when the quarry was swerving about from side to side, breathless and exhausted, to drive my spear in behind the shoulder and out of the chest, when he succumbed and bit the dust.

The bull-nilghau (from the Hindostani *nil*, *blue*, and *ghau*, *cow*) is about the height of a galloway and somewhat resembles what a hybrid would be between a deer and a cow; he has curved pointed horns, a short mane, but hardly any dewlap. The cow is smaller, and of a dun fawn-colour. Both have beautiful black eyes, like those of the deer.

On rejoining the gang we found that D—— had despatched the two cows seized by the dogs, and wounded a third with his rifle, which latter the dogs were still chasing. We accordingly loosened the saddles of our nags, and reclined under a tree whilst our syces rubbed them down; and after some time D—— returned, having killed the third cow, when, as the sun was extremely powerful, we remounted and made the best of our way to the tents, leaving the gang to break up the deer and bring in the skins. The flesh of the nilghau somewhat resembles venison, but is coarser; the hump, however, when salted and spiced is not to be despised, and the marrow is one of the greatest delicacies to be had in India.

In the evening, just as we were going to sit down to dinner, one of our people, who had been bathing in the stream a short distance below our camp, came running in with the information that he had seen two bears drinking, close to. We immediately sallied forth in pursuit, and B—— had the luck to fall in with them, killing one outright with the first shot, and disabling the other, which Chineah despatched. After this little episode we dined, and sat round the camp-fire discussing the events of the day until a late hour, when we turned in, highly satisfied with our sport, for slaying a bull-nilghau single-handed with the spear is not an everyday occurrence, even in an Indian sportsman's career.

The next day we moved on to Raupoor, distance nine miles, where we pitched our tents, having heard that a herd of elephants had been seen by some Mulchers a few days before; but after a couple of days' search, during which we found no fresh trails, we advanced to Dewara, where, as we were beating a very thick and likely cover, a black panther started up from a cleft in the ground close under my feet, and I had the good fortune to roll him over with a single ball, which took effect just behind the ear. The skin was magnificent, the spots being distinctly visible when held up to the light, appearing of a deeper black than the rest. The gang declared that the black panther was a much more dangerous animal than the ordinary species; and as I had on a previous occasion seen one, that Walter M—— had wounded, charge most desperately several times, perhaps their assertion is correct. The one I killed certainly was a most formidable-looking customer, having great yellow eyes and long black whiskers, but the fur was soft and silky as velvet. The next four days afforded us no sport except an old she-bear, which was killed by B—— and D—— whilst engaged in eating the fruit of the "mowra" tree; but I was very much struck with the singular and ingenious manner in which the Mulchers of this part of the jungle catch spotted-deer and antelope. They cut strong pieces of the creeping-bamboo about a quarter of an inch in diameter and four inches in length, leaving the curved sharp-pointed stout thorn that grows out of the joint. In the other end of this is a notch, in which is fastened a piece of strong fibre made from the aloe, about eighteen inches in length, to the end of which is attached a small round pebble by a hole drilled in the centre. In some parts of the jungle is found a small sweet-tasted gourd, somewhat shaped like a cucumber, and of this both spotted-deer and antelope are particularly fond. The natives, being aware of the fact, bait a number of these hooks with this fruit and throw them in the runs; the deer unsuspiciously begin to eat them, and finding the string and pebble knocking about, they bend down their head and attempt to break it off by treading on it with their fore feet, or striking it with the hind. In either case, the chances are that the cord gets between the division in the hoof, and, being arrested by the stone, they are irretrievably caught, as the hook fastens in the mouth or throat, and the more they struggle the firmer they are held. They generally struggle so violently that death from exhaustion follows in a very short time, although I have seen both spotted-deer and antelope brought in alive, having been caught in this manner.

Our leave was now nearly expired, so we were obliged to commence a retrograde movement, and, having packed up our trophies, we returned to Bowani, where Mother Garrow, a very Paphian queen, was awaiting our arrival with a formidable array of dusky nymphs. For three days we kept up a continuous nautch, and even after that time we were not tired of gazing upon the graceful pirouettes of the fair votaries of Terpsichore, or listening to the warbling of the dark-eyed songstresses as they sang on the old subjects, "Love and War;" and when the time came for us to take our departure, more than one shed tears as the farewell words were spoken; indeed, if "Rumour with her many tongues" spake true, it was discovered, soon after our departure, that there were vacancies to be filled up in the Pagoda of the dark mysterious goddess.

O D——, "I could a tale unfold" that would raise up a spirit on thy fireside, that all the soft sawder of thy oily tongue would never calm! But I'll spare your feelings for the sake of "auld lang syne," and the jolly days we spent together in the merry green woods.

We got into Trichy just in time, for two days afterwards the monsoon broke, and there was a continuous downfall of rain, which inundated the whole country.

SECTION III.—THE MOUNTAIN RANGES.

CHAPTER XIV.

THE NEILGHERRIES.

> "Primæval woods, and forests vast and rude,
> Where reigns a deep unbroken solitude:
> Eternal teaks, who 've wider stretch'd their arms
> And deeper struck their roots amid the storms."

Index.—Pleasing recollections.—The deep forest described.—The pleasures and excitement of a hunter's life.—The requisite qualifications.—The Neilgherries and their productions.—Variety of game.—Ootacamund.—Englishmen and their love of Sport.—Dawson's Hotel.—Burnside Cottage.—Malamund.—The Todas: their women, habitations, and strange customs.—News of elk.—The start: preliminaries.—The drive.—Game afoot.—A capital shot.—Three deer bite the dust, and Bruin yields up his spoils.—A stag at bay.—The return.—Convivial gathering.—The Major's story.

The Neilgherries. How many pleasing recollections of heart-stirring events are associated with that name; how many glorious days' sport does it recall to mind; how many a dear friend does it bring before me, with whom I have bearded the tiger in his lair, tracked the mighty elephant to his haunt in the pathless forest, and there despoiled him of his trophies, or pursued the watchful ibex from crag to crag, over precipices, chasms, and ledges of rock which men dared not look down in their cooler moments! Many a hand I then clasped has become cold, many a voice I loved to listen to is hushed for ever; he with whom I have often scoured the plain and struggled for the spear after the mighty gray boar, fell a shattered wreck before my eyes in the van of the fight that murky morn when "the Six Hundred" charged. There are times when the past comes before me with sadly painful distinctness, and my heart yearns to return once more to that land where I have passed the happiest years of my life, and to revisit those scenes which are engraven in my memory in strong and ineffaceable colours, although I know that my merry companions are gone, and that their places are occupied by strangers. Who among us have not some sunny spots in their existence, some remembrance of happier days gone by which they love to look back upon with pleasure, however bright future prospects may appear? Almost all of us have some fondly-cherished souvenir or trophy upon which we love to gaze and think of the past, until the soul-stirring scenes of "auld lang syne" again come vividly to mind; and although we feel that they may never come again, we look back with pleasure upon the time when sunshine illumined our path. With some the golden age appears to have been passed at school—with others, later in life. Here a stately old general tells of the glorious time he passed as a jolly sub in the days of powder and pigtails; and there a sturdy old squire of the last generation recounts with glee the doings of his time, "when hounds could run and huntsmen went the pace;" yon phlegmatic-looking old divine, with blanched locks and rubicund nose, which bespeaks his love of the pleasures of the table, relates, with intense satisfaction, the roistering days he spent as a young man in a fast regiment of Light Dragoons, when it was considered a "crying sin" for any one to quit the social board until he had disposed of a couple of magnums under his belt; and that shrivelled-up old relic of mortality, who seems to stand before us as a specimen of what the hand of time can effect on our mortal frame, will prate by the hour of the jolly dogs of his day, and the fascinations of town when he was a gay Lothario. Each and every one has some period of his life on which he loves to look back and think upon, although, perhaps, he may talk much more about the future. The soldier loves to recall to mind the scenes of many a hard-fought day; the sailor, his adventures on the heaving main; the wanderer delights in the reminiscences of travel in many lands; and the fox-hunter in the stiff bursts and glorious runs of bygone times; but the sportsman who has visited the Neilgherri mountains and stricken the mightiest denizens of the jungle, muses by day and dreams by night of the dark deep Wynaad forest.

Those who have never explored a primeval forest can have but a very faint conception of the mysterious effect that absence of light and intense depth of gloom have upon the human mind. The unbroken silence and utter stillness that everywhere pervades its leafy arches, creates a strange feeling of awe and loneliness that depresses the spirits and appals the heart of those who are unaccustomed to wander in its solitudes; and even the stoutest heart feels overpowered with a strange sensation he can neither account for nor explain the first time he enters, for the voice of man resounds with a strange and startling echo, and even the very hound whines with fear, and couches close to his master's side, afraid of being left alone. Solitude is too insufficient a term to convey an idea of the intensely overpowering sensation of desolation and loneliness that pervades these regions; yet to the hunter, who is accustomed to sojourn in their deepest recesses, the wilderness is a home which he would not exchange for any other; and as he roams through its boundless expanse of verdure, with no other companions but the silent trackers and his dogs, and no guide but a pocket-compass and certain jungle signs not to be understood by the dwellers of cities, he imbibes certain feelings that cannot be entered into save by those who have themselves experienced the charms and fascinations of "forest life," and enjoyed its pure and heartfelt pleasures. To him it possesses a peculiar spell, not to be found elsewhere; and, far away from the haunts of man, he gives no care to the turmoil and bustle of the busy world, but loves to study Nature in her grandest forms, and silent unsullied beauty, whilst his heart glows with thoughts that bear him untiring company. There is a peculiarly exhilarating delight passing all description in the wild excitement of this life, which dispels all anxiety, and strengthens the mental and physical energies for the ever-changing scene, delights the eye, and gives pleasure to the intellect; whilst, at the same time, the constant excitement arising from the varied incidents of such a state of existence invigorates the mind and stimulates the powers of thought and observation. The body sustained in continued exertion by constant exercise, enables the hunter to maintain his course for days together through the pathless woods, with that dogged stubbornness and inflexibility which is necessary to insure success in the pursuit of the game he seeks. He moves noiselessly along, without a care as to what he may encounter, for he has implicit confidence in the power of his trusty rifle; and his vigilant eye, piercing the shadowy depths of the jungle, leaves no hollow unsearched, for he and his followers are dependent for their subsistence on their exertions in the chase. Nothing is so conducive to the keen development of the senses as the constant exertion of the different faculties during a sojourn in the jungle; quickness of eye (an indispensable quality in a hunter) and unceasing watchfulness are there attained; habits of observation are engendered, for anything out of the common immediately attracts attention, and the ear is habituated to catch the slightest sound. The hunter should have a thorough knowledge of the habits of the wild animals he seeks, bearing in mind how suspicious they are, and how quickly their attention is attracted by unusual noises, strange traces in the jungle, or even the taint in the air which the presence of man always leaves behind it. The ranger of the forest experiences a thorough feeling of independence and a freedom from restraint in these wilds, that contrasts most favourably with the *désagréments* of artificial existence, and few of those who are fitted to enjoy it ever quit these scenes to return to civilised life without deep feelings of regret that their unalloyed pleasures are at an end; and in after life the murmuring of waters and the sighings of the wind through the trees will recall to mind moments of intense interest, and they will ever feel at heart that there is no music so sweet as the wild voices of the woods.

All forests are gloomy, but they have their comparative degrees of shade, and none present a greater diversity of appearance than that round the Neilgherries. The tall feathery bamboo contrasts most delightfully with the stately teak, ebony, blackwood, and other gigantic trees of the primeval forest, where the air, being confined, is generally close and suffocating. The surface of the ground is everywhere thickly strewn with decayed leaves or dead branches, and underneath the trees may be seen the green of young seedlings which spring up by thousands during the rains, but for the most part pine and die, being deprived of light and heat.

The climate on the tableland is about the finest in the known world—exempt alike from the extremes of heat and cold, it realises as near as any land "eternal spring," for its great elevation (8000 feet above the level of the sea) tempers the heat generally felt in these latitudes, and gives the air a pureness and bracing elasticity peculiarly grateful to Europeans after a lengthened sojourn in the scorching plains; indeed, if cloudless skies, continual sunshine, and pleasant weather were the only essentials to human happiness, the Neilgherries would be the most likely place to seek it of any that I have yet met with in my wanderings over land and sea.

In its peculiar style of beauty nothing can exceed the scenery of the hills. Stupendous peaks, groups of gigantic forest-trees, hanging woods and foaming cascades, alternate with clumps of rhododendrons, covered with crimson bloom, wild camellias, jessamines, and high waving ferns, whilst vines and other climbing-plants hang in festoons from branch to branch; and here and there the landscape is diversified with verdant lawns of velvet turf, natural parterres of scarlet geranium, or orchids of luxuriant growth. Where a view of the low country can be caught through an opening in the thick woods, it is equally grand and impressive, for a blue haze spreads over the scene, softening and blending its beauties, and giving it a dreamy appearance peculiarly enchanting. Wild raspberries and strawberries, noted for their excellent flavour, are to be found everywhere in the woods; and the ferns, buttercups, and daisies that grow on the banks of the numerous rills and burns that flow rippling on every side, present a similarity of appearance that recalls visions of dear old England. Birds of gaudy plumage dart amid the branches, gay butterflies hover about, insects of metallic hue glitter on the leaves, and all nature seems glad in this highly-favoured spot.

I have never yet met with any hunting-grounds to be compared with the great Wynaad Jungle for diversity of game, which includes elephants, bison, elk, spotted-deer, jungle-sheep, hog-deer, tigers, panthers, leopards, cheetahs, bears, hyenas, tiger-cats, boars, wolves, jackals, wild dogs, porcupines, hares, pea-fowl, jungle-fowl, spur-fowl, partridges, quail, and snipe, whilst on the hills are found ibex and woodcock, which are never seen in the low country.

Ootacamund, the principal station, is the most

delightful place of residence in Hindostan. It possesses a handsome church, well-established club, two first-rate hotels, several handsome shops, which are chiefly kept by Parsees, a well-stocked bazaar, and many hundred excellent houses and bungalows, some of which are perfect mansions. The cantonment occupies a great extent of ground, as, the country being extremely undulating, most of the houses are picturesquely situated on slight eminences, and surrounded with large gardens, which are generally extremely well kept up. Apples, pears, quinces, peaches, apricots, plums, cherries, currants, and most European vegetables, thrive well; whilst fuchsias, honeysuckles, woodbine, jessamine, clematis, passion-flowers, and geraniums grow in the wildest luxuriance, and require little care. In the centre of the cantonment is a beautiful artificial lake, round which is the drive or promenade, the "Rotten Row" of Ooty, where in the afternoon may be seen several hundred Anglo-Indians, either on horseback or in vehicles of every description, from the stylish barouche to the humble "bullock-garree," listening to the band or driving about to gain an appetite for dinner.

The Neilgherries being considered among the healthiest spots in Southern India, have been constituted a *sanitarium;* and here may be seen invalid officers from all parts of the Madras and Bombay Presidencies, who have obtained leave of absence from their regiments, for periods varying from six months to two years, in order to recruit their health, during which time they draw their full pay and allowances, which, from some stupid fancy of the East India Board, is not the case when they are obliged to return to Europe. The consequence is, that Ooty somewhat resembles a fast watering-place, and is extremely gay; balls, parties, and picnics being of common occurrence.

Surrounded by splendid hunting-grounds, it is the head-quarters of sportsmen; for wherever there is anything to hunt that promises sport, Englishmen are sure to set out in pursuit. As a nation we are essentially sportsmen, for the chase in all its branches seems indigenous to the country. Taking, for example, the officers of our army and navy, who are scattered all over the face of the globe, thousands of miles from their native land, we find that neither a burning sun and the enervating influence of a tropical climate, nor an icy temperature, can damp their ardour for field-sports, which, notwithstanding every disadvantage, they endeavour to keep up. Such being the case, it is not therefore surprising that in Ooty there is a well-established subscription pack of hounds for hunting the fox and jackal, besides several private ones of beagles, spaniels, and cockers for driving the covers. In no part of Great Britain are woodcock more eagerly followed than on the hills, and every year large sums of money change hands in wagers as to what sportsman will kill the first cock. The season begins in October and ends in March, although solitary birds may be found a month earlier or later.

On my first arrival, Ooty was very full; and as vacant bungalows were scarce, I put up for some time at Dawson's Hotel, where I had every reason to be highly satisfied with the accommodation, for my quarters were extremely comfortable, and the living first-rate; indeed, I have seldom come across such a *cuisine.* There was certainly only another like it on the Madras side, that of the Club of Secunderabad, where the mighty Tatiah ruled the roast.

Having all my establishment with me, including my celebrated hunting-gang, which comprised some of the best trackers in the country, my old chum B—— and I took a snug compact little box called Burnside Cottage, with good stabling, outhouses for servants, and a well-stocked garden; which was most delightfully situated just below the crest of a hill, and overlooking the glen of the Mala-mund, a village inhabited by the Todas, a strange race of people, who are supposed by some to be a remnant of "the lost tribes." The men are generally above the common height, well made, athletic, and with open prepossessing countenances. They have a decidedly Jewish type of nose, large oriental eyes, fine teeth, and oval faces, the lower part of which is generally covered with a fine jet-black beard. They wear no head-dress, but the hair, which grows in great profusion, is parted in the centre, and flows in curls all round the head. Their dress consists of a waist-cloth and a kind of cotton sheet, which they wear like a Roman *toga*, thrown over the body, leaving the arms and legs bare. The men are decidedly the finest-looking race in Hindostan, having a noble independent bearing, and none of that cringing and fawning obsequiousness which is observable in every other caste of native. The women are tall and commanding, with figures for the most part faultless; erect but remarkably graceful, somewhat slight perhaps, but exquisitely rounded; every line full of softness and beauty, every limb in fine symmetry, supple, and delicate. The head is peculiarly small and elegant, the face oval, and generally of the Israelitish type. The features are small and finely chiselled; the mouth beautifully formed, and graced with pearl-like teeth; the eyes large, lustrous, wild, soft and gazelle-like; the eyebrows are much arched and finely pencilled; the lashes very long and full; the hair of the head abundant, full of natural waves, and flowing in ringlets over the neck and shoulders. Their skins, of a softness beyond that of other women, are of a rich, clear, olive colour, several shades lighter than the men, in consequence of less exposure to the weather; and their hands and feet are comparatively small and beautifully formed. They arrive at maturity at a very early age, and it is no uncommon thing to see outside the huts a pretty little girl, under twelve years of age, with an infant on her hip; but as they arrive speedily to womanhood, so their beauty decays; at sixteen they are in the prime of life, and at thirty aged, when they retain no trace of their former beauty. The women have a plurality of husbands, the brothers of a family generally marrying one wife, which practice is also common among the Nairs and other castes on the western coast. Their huts are built in the shape of the tilt of a waggon, of bamboos thatched with turf. They are about ten feet long, seven broad, and six high, and the door (the only aperture in the building) is only about two feet square, so that the inhabitants have to crawl in and out on all fours. Half a dozen huts constitute a "mund" or village, which is generally situated on the side of a hill, in the most picturesque spots on the hills. They are a pastoral people, possessing large herds of the finest buffaloes in India; having a strange language of their own, but no character to express it. The men sometimes wear small gold earrings, and the women silver or brass armlets, and a rude kind of zone, which is worn loosely round the hips. The Toda men call themselves the lords of the soil, and look down with supreme contempt upon the Burghers, another hill race, who are of inferior stature, and cultivate the ground, for which they have to pay the former a certain tribute.

One morning as B—— and I were engaged in superintending the laying out of a piece of ground as an addition to our kitchen-garden, a Toda, to whom I had one day paid some slight attention, came to inform us that he had seen a large herd of elk in a wooded ravine about three miles distant. I immediately wrote off to Major S——, who had a pack of dogs, and W——, K——, C——, and B——, then staying at Dawson's, informing them of the news; and in half an hour they all assembled in their hunting-togs at my crib, with two or three other fellows whom they had picked up *en route*. In the meantime Chineah, my head "shekarry," had mustered the gang, with a dozen extra beaters; and after having partaken of some refreshment, we mounted our nags, and, accompanied by horsekeepers and gunbearers, set off for the cover under the guidance of the Toda. An hour's ride brought us to the spot, and, dismounting, we reconnoitred the ground, so as to make sure the game had not stolen away. No slots were seen to lead us to suppose this had been the case, so we took post along the edges of the cover, whilst the gang-beaters and dogs descended the ravine by a circuitous route, so as to drive the game up the hill, and force it to break towards that side where we were lying concealed. I also ordered the Gooroo and Ali to remain with my polygar dogs on the high ground, so as to be ready in case any of the deer should get away wounded, which afterwards turned out a lucky hit. After nearly half an hour's suspense, certain sounds issued from below which informed us that the beaters and dogs had entered the lower end of the cover, and presently a low yelp told us that one of the pack had taken up the scent. ' Hark to old Ponto!" cried the major, who was ensconced behind a rhododendron-bush a few paces distant from me; and a smile of contentment gleamed over the time-worn and weather-beaten physiognomy of the old sportsman as he recognised the voice of his favourite hound. "Hush! hark! there he goes again. The game 's afoot, take my word for it. He never gives tongue without a cause, so pass the word along the line to keep a bright look-out. There goes Rupert and Gelert chiming in." Shortly after this prelude, hound after hound opened on scent and took up the cry, until at last the harmonious chorus burst forth from the ravine, and awoke the echoes of the surrounding woods. I need not describe to sportsmen the intense excitement and pleasurable sensations this melody raised in our hearts; for we knew that the deer were afoot, and each internally wished that they might break sufficiently near to give him a shot. From time to time the crashing of branches informed us that the herd were close at hand, and each prepared to raise his deadly weapon, but again and again they broke back. At last an enormous buck-elk, with widely-spreading antlers, summoned resolution to leave the cover, and came tearing through the bushes with mighty elastic bounds some distance to my right, and within easy range of W—— and K——, who let drive double shots with apparently little effect, for he continued his course without relaxing his speed for a moment. I tried to get a shot as he was bounding away, but could not catch sight of him on account of intervening bushes, when the old major, who was quietly seated on his right heel, with his left knee thrown well forward, and his left elbow resting upon it, (the best position for steady shooting,) let fly right and left; and although I could not see the stag, I knew from the double "thuds" I heard that both shots had taken effect. "Hurrah! he's down, boys!" vociferated the gallant old soldier, as he sprang to his feet, and picked up his second rifle; but before he could raise it the stag had regained his legs, and a slight undulation in the ground prevented his getting another shot. "Bravo, major!" I exclaimed; "you 'wiped the youngster's eyes' beautifully, and made a couple of excellent shots, for both were over two hundred yards distant. We will now loose Hassan and Ali, and I'll warrant you they will soon give a good account of the quarry." I accordingly gave the necessary orders to lay in the dogs, when just at the moment I heard a crash in the jungle, and two young bucks with velvety horns, and seven does, broke cover, followed by an old she-bear. I brought down one of the bucks, and three of the does fell before a combined volley, whilst the bear received two or three gentle reminders of our presence that did anything but increase her stock of good-humour, for she growled most savagely, and made a serious charge at W——

and K——, who could only give leg-bail, as their rifles were empty. Luckily the dogs caught sight of her, and Hassan seized her by the hind-leg, which brought her up, and gave Ali the opportunity of pinning her by the ear on the opposite side. Both were immensely powerful dogs, (a cross between the bloodhound and polygar,) and poor Bruin stood no chance of doing mischief, although she seemed most maliciously inclined. As soon as I came up I called off the dogs, and B—— gave her a *coup de grace* behind the ear. The beaters and the major's pack now made their appearance; and after the dogs had been collected, I laid Ali and Hassan on the trail of the stag that had been wounded by the major. Large drops of blood marked his course; and as we were following it up a loud deep bellow in a patch of high fern close at hand told us that the stag was at bay. When we came up we found him covered with blood and foam, struggling desperately with the dogs, who had seized him by the throat and held him fast. His bloodshot eyes rolled savagely as we approached, and he lowered his head as if to make a stroke at us with his horns; but he was weak from loss of blood, and stumbled, which gave Chineah the opportunity of drawing his knife across his throat, when he made a feeble attempt to regain his knees, but staggered, reeled, and fell, uttering a deep groan. A convulsive tremour passed over his limbs, and all was still.

As soon as the venison was broken up and slung upon poles, we mounted our nags and returned to Ooty, where we all met round Major S——'s social board in the evening; when, after the cloth was removed, songs went round, and many animated recitals of hairbreadth escapes and perilous encounters with the grim monsters of the forest were related by the old hands, which caused our sitting to last until a late hour. Just as we were about to separate, W—— happened to mention something about a cantonment ball that was to take place shortly; when our worthy host, pricking up his ears, asked if any of us had heard of the direful effects matrimony had upon Geordie S——, a connexion of his. "He was before your time, but no one who knew could ever forget him, for a better or keener sportsman never breathed. It was a pleasure to see him dashing across country after the gray boar, or hear his merry laugh, pithy saying, and jolly song in the evening, round the camp-fire when the sports of the day were over. 'A change came o'er the spirit of my dream,' Geordie got 'touched,' was led to the altar, 'tied up;' and I met him again after a lapse of years—but oh! how changed! The jovial sunburnt face had become long; his laughing eyes, that once beamed with mirth, shot out melancholy glances; the formerly strong arm had become flabby; and the legs no better than broom-sticks! He received me kindly as ever, but looked, I must own, rather sheepish and glum. After some conversation, in which I brought 'old times' to his recollection, he brightened up a little, his old smile returned, and for a moment he looked somewhat like himself again. It was but a temporary glimmer, for a shrill harsh voice in an adjoining chamber, followed by a smart slap and a lengthened squall, reminded him of his wretched situation; and as I rose to avoid meeting his (can I say) *better* half, who was evidently getting herself up for the occasion, he pressed my hand in his old affectionate manner, muttering with a deeply-drawn sigh, 'S——, my dear fellow, you see the unfortunate mistake I made, and what it has brought me to; take warning, steer clear of wedlock, and you'll be a happy man.' 'I'll be —— if I don't,' I replied, feeling at the same time a choking sensation, as I mounted my nag, and rode off just as the temptress was sailing into the room." After a hearty laugh at the major's anecdote we bade him good night, and each made his way home.

CHAPTER XV.

THE NEILGHERRIES CONTINUED.—A NIGHT AFFAIR.

News of a tiger.—His last depredation.—The ambuscade.—Lying in wait.—A night attack.—Exciting moments.—The spoiler vanquished.—The return.—News of ibex, and an expedition to the Koondah range.—Ibex-stalking.—B——'s wonderful shooting.—The game nearly lost.—The ibex described.—Return to Ooty.

TIME passed most pleasantly on the hills, for the days were spent in exploring parties and field sports of every description; the evenings in social gatherings, enlivened by the presence of female society; and the nights in deliciously sound repose, which in itself is one of the greatest luxuries an Anglo-Indian can enjoy, for in the low country during the hot season the unsupportably close and oppressive period between sunset and early dawn is more distressing and enervating than the intense heat of the day; for during this time not a breath of air agitates the branches of the highest trees, candles burn in the open air without flickering, the atmosphere is suffocatingly close, and unless the punkah is kept continually going the European can obtain no sleep, but tosses about restlessly on his couch, and gets up in the morning feeling as weary, tired, and overcome with lassitude as when he laid down. This want of rest is more trying to our soldiers than any privation or fatigue they may experience during their sojourn in tropical climates ; and of late years officers commanding regiments have been empowered by the Indian Government to employ coolies to keep the punkahs going day and night during the hot months, which has been found to have an extremely salutary effect. One day I was superintending the manufacture of a batch of "goorakoo"* for my hookah, according to a recipe I obtained from one of the retainers of Mah-rajah Chundalal, the late Dewan of the Deccan, when Chineah came with the intelligence that a tiger had struck down a bullock belonging to some Mulchers about five miles distant,

* Goorakoo, from the Sanscrit word "goor," sugar, and the Telegoo "akoo," a leaf, is the compound used in the hookah. The following is the best recipe I ever met with :—"Take of tobacco four seers, (16 lbs.,) common treacle four seers, wood-apple (feronia clephantum) half a seer, preserved apples, plantains or pineapple, half a seer, raisins half a seer, and 'goolgund' (conserve of roses) half a seer. Pound these ingredients well together in a large wooden mortar, adding cardamums, sandal-wood, otto of roses, and spikenard, according as you want it more or less scented. When it is well mixed, and has assumed the consistency of a thick paste, add a seer of dried rose-leaves, then put it in an earthen pot, the mouth of which must be made perfectly airtight by being waxed over, and bury it for three months, after which it is ready for use."

and after having sucked the blood had left the carcass, which Naga and Googooloo had gone to watch, to prevent its being carried away by the Chucklars (shoemakers) or Pariahs, (low caste people.)

B—— had gone out to reconnoitre some ibex ground on the Koondah range, and as I did not expect him to return until late in the evening I made preparations to start alone. Tiffin eaten, I set out for the spot accompanied by Chincah, the Gooroo, and a horse-keeper who carried my rifles, and after an hour's ride arrived at a little patch of cultivation surrounded on three sides by dense wood, where we found a fine white bullock lying dead in a pool of blood, with his throat torn and shoulder dislocated. I saw at a glance that the marauder was a large tiger, for besides the holes made in the throat by his fangs, and the marks of his claws in the back of the neck, which had torn up the flesh in ridges, there were several immense "pugs" deeply imprinted in the soft ground, near which the struggle had taken place.

Googooloo and Naga had built an ambuscade in a tree, about ten feet from the ground, which commanded an excellent view of all approaches from the cover; but as I did not imagine that the tiger would return to his prey in the earlier part of the evening, and I should not have the advantage of the light of the moon until late, I determined to await his approach at close quarters, and made the gang dig a hole about four feet deep under a low overhanging bush, much overgrown with creepers and parasitical plants, which was about half a dozen paces to leeward of the carcass. By making my place of concealment in the ground, I knew I should have a better chance of getting a sight of the tiger, and taking more certain aim in the dark, than if I was perched in a tree above him, besides which it seemed something more like *fair play.* Having lined my place of ambuscade with a carpet, so as to make it more comfortable, I carefully loaded my weapons, which were two double ten-bore rifles, a double two-ounce gun, and a brace of large double holster-pistols; arranged my comforts for the inner man, consisting of a stone bottle of strong green tea, a flask of brandy, and a huge pile of sandwiches; and ordered all my followers to return to Ooty, with the horse, excepting Chineah and Googooloo, who were to keep watch in the tree so as to be at hand in case they might be wanted.

All being prepared, as soon as the shadows of evening began to lengthen we took post, and during the few remaining hours of daylight I carefully noted every bush and undulation in the ground, so as to be better able to perceive anything in the dark. As the day declined, the last rays of an unclouded sunset threw a rich purple haze over the whole scene, and the many-tinted foliage of the surrounding woods glistened with golden tints in the light of departing day.

The tuneful songsters ceased their warbling, and

the woods no longer resounded with the sharp strokes of the woodpecker; but the night-hawk was on the wing, and darted swiftly to and fro after the moths, which at that hour were flitting about in great numbers. The air became redolent with the fragrance of numberless flowering shrubs, which seemed to emit a double perfume towards the close of day. The evening deepened into twilight, the twilight darkened into night, and the stars with their mild radiance seemed as if they strove to eclipse the lingering rays of sunset. At length the mighty forest became silent, and no sound reached our ears save the occasional chirping of a cricket, the dismal hooting of the horned owl, the howling of troops of jackals, or the melancholy booming of the great hill-monkey. As the night wore on, the tall trees could hardly be distinguished one behind another, as they loomed darker and darker against an indefinable background.

Time passed slowly, the night air became chilly, and at last I began to fancy the tiger, having satiated his thirst with blood, had no intention of returning for the flesh, (a frequent occurrence;) so I wrapped myself up more closely in my "combley," (a blanket made of goats' hair, impermeable to wet,) and set to work at my pile of sandwiches and cold tea, with occasional nips of brandy, when suddenly I thought I caught the sound of a rustling of leaves, followed by the snapping of a dry twig. I set down the bottle of tea I was in the act of raising to my mouth, noiselessly grasped my rifle, which I raised with the muzzle directed towards the spot from whence I thought the noise proceeded, and listened attentively; but I heard nothing save the palpitations of my own heart, that seemed to be thumping violently against my side; and as to seeing anything, it was out of the question, for the night was so dark and gloomy, that I could scarcely even recognise the outline of the dead bullock. A long anxious hour passed, and I repeatedly heard the tearing of flesh and crunching of bones close in front of me, but the sky was so overcast that I could not distinguish anything, although now and then I caught sight of a pair of greenish-looking eyes, and heard a low purring. At last, finding there was no prospect of getting a fair shot, I resolved to risk a chance one, and having waited until I again caught sight of his eyes, I gave a whistle, which immediately attracted his attention, for he raised up his head, uttering a low savage snarl, and I saw his eyeballs glare as if he was peering through the gloom in my direction. This was the opportunity I wanted. I took deliberate aim between the glittering orbs that shone like burning coals, and pulled both triggers almost simultaneously. A hoarse roar followed the double report, which was re-echoed by the distant hills—something dark passed overhead, and I heard a crashing and rending of wood in the bush immediately behind me, with a loud whine and peculiar grunt which told me that the tiger was hard hit.

I grasped my second gun, stuck my pistols in my belt, so as to be ready for immediate use, and turned towards the spot where the tiger appeared to be, at the same time calling to Chincah and Googooloo, to prevent them leaving their post on any account, for I well knew how dangerous a wounded tiger is at any time, more especially in the dark, when he can see, and man cannot. On receiving the contents of my rifle, he must have sprung clear over the ambuscade, for I heard him struggling in the bush just behind it, grinding his teeth, and emitting strange moaning noises. Every now and then he seemed to be moving restlessly about, and at times I thought, from his hard breathing, (which somewhat resembled a loud snore,) that he was close to me; indeed I fancied once or twice that I felt the bushes shake, as if he was trying to get at me. Although prepared for all emergencies, I remained perfectly quiet, listening intently to his movements, for the darkness was so profound that I could not see my hand before me. Chincah gave a signal to me once or twice, but I dared not answer it, lest I should attract the enraged animal's notice towards the place of my concealment. After a lengthened period of anxious and exciting suspense, I heard the wounded tiger heave a long deep-drawn sigh, which was followed by a succession of smothered groans and gaspings for breath; then came a heavy fall, another violent struggle, a gurgling bubbling sound in the throat as of suffocation, a hollow rattle, and all was still.

I knew my antagonist was dead, but to make sure, I waited a few minutes before leaving my ambuscade, when, hearing nothing, I lighted a bull's-eye lantern I always carried about with me, which fastened by a spring to the front of my belt, and, rifle in hand, I took a cursory view of the bullock, the hinder part of which was half eaten, and then examined the bush, where I found the tiger stretched lifeless on the ground, in some low cover about fifteen paces behind the place where I had been lying in wait. I called down Chineah and Googooloo, who lighted a torch, and we found that both of my shots had taken effect; the first had struck him in the centre of the forehead, ploughed up the skin, and glanced off the bone; the second entered the chest, and apparently traversed the lungs, for the ground about was covered with blood and froth that had issued from the mouth. He proved to be magnificently marked, although not so large as I expected, from the large imprints of his paws.

We now lighted a large fire, wrapped ourselves carefully up in our blankets, and indulged in a brew of hot punch and the "fragrant weed," which never appeared more grateful than on that bitterly cold morning. After some time the summits of the opposite hills began to appear more distinctly against a clearer sky, and presently the moon slowly emerged above the horizon, and her silver rays lighted up the whole scene. After having cut off the centre claw of the tiger's right foot, by way of marking the game, we collected the carpets, blankets, &c., and leaving Googooloo on the platform to watch the body, Chincah and I shouldered our rifles, and made the best of our way to the bungalow, where we arrived just as the first faint streaks of gray in the east proclaimed that day was about to break. After having given orders to the "gooroo" to go with some of the people and bring the skin, I turned in and enjoyed several hours' refreshing sleep, tiffin being on the table before I made my appearance, when I was warmly congratulated on my success by several friends who dropped in to admire the spoils. B—— gave a very good account of the ibex on the Koondahs, having seen two herds on the summit of an isolated ridge overlooking the low country, which he forbore to follow, on account of the weather threatening fog in those altitudes. We determined, however, to make an attempt, and ordered the people to be ready to start with a tent before daybreak the next morning, we intending to follow soon after.

The following morning B—— and I mounted our nags soon after breakfast and sallied forth from the glen of the Mala-mund, equipped in suits of drab moleskin, which colour is the best adapted for ibex-stalking, as at a short distance it is scarcely distinguishable from the bleak crags among which they dwell.

The pursuit of the ibex, although an intensely exciting sport, is the most difficult of all deer-stalking, and proves the severest test of the qualifications of a hunter; for not only are these animals exceedingly shy and watchful, but they are also gifted with remarkably keen sight, and their senses of smelling and hearing are developed to an extraordinary degree. From the almost inaccessible nature of the ground on which they are found, he who would take their spoils should be endued with great strength, perseverance, and endurance, besides which he must have the agility of a mountaineer and a steady head, or he can never follow up his game to their haunts along narrow ledges of scarped rocks and beetling heights, where a false step or a moment's giddiness would entail certain destruction. There can be no doubt but that intense excitement takes away all dread of danger, for I have seen it exemplified many times, not only on the hunting-ground but also on the field of battle. The same spirit which animates a "dare devil" in the front rank of the hunting-field at home accompanies him in the van of the fight abroad, and in both cases, if his career is not stopped by "a fall," he will be found "well in at the death." An ardent hunter, like a daring soldier, possesses a mental energy superior to all thought of peril; for, seeking only the attainment of his purpose, he pursues his course with that dogged stubbornness, inflexibility of purpose, and recklessness of self-preservation that make him invincible and ensure success in the end. In my opinion, the greatest compliment the British army ever received was when the great Napoleon said that "*the men never knew when they were beaten.*" The saying marked the discrimination of the man, as it was that feeling that gained us Waterloo, Inkermann, and numberless other glorious days; for our soldiers, in the words of our greatest bard,—

> "Could for itself woo the approaching fight,
> And turn what some deem danger to delight."

But, gentle reader, I crave your pardon for digressing, having wandered from my subject by musing upon bygone days and the many hard-fought fields that I have seen won. So now to describe the Neilgherry ibex, which is, I believe, of a species peculiar to the range, differing in many respects from those found on the Himalayas or the Caucasus. In shape they somewhat resemble the common Indian goat, but the body is much shorter in comparison with the height. The largest I ever saw—which was killed by B—— on the precipitous heights of the Koondahs, overlooking the low country—measured 6 feet 8 inches in length from the point of the nose to the end of the tail, 50 inches in height at the shoulder, and weighed, I should think, over 200 pounds, as it was in first-rate condition, the rutting season not having commenced. The horns are dark olive with black points, about 10 inches in length, ringed, and 4½ inches in circumference at the base, gradually diverging until the points become nearly 6 inches apart. These ibex are uniformly of a light ash, deepening to dark brown on the hind-quarters and forepart of the legs, with an almost black stripe running along the ridge of the back. The head is fawn-colour, part of the face being of a rich brown, and the muzzle nearly black. The back is furnished with a shaggy, stiff, upright mane, running along the neck and shoulders, which gradually grows shorter on the hind-quarters. The smell of this animal is particularly rank and offensive, and the flesh is scarcely eatable at any time, being so strong-tasted and coarse. Ibex are found in troops, rarely exceeding a dozen in number, amongst the rugged crags of the highest and most inaccessible mountains, their food consisting chiefly of the different mosses and short, crisp, delicate herbage indigenous to great altitudes. A wary old buck who has often quite a patriarchal appearance, is generally chosen as the leader of the herd ; and if he sees anything suspicious, or catches a taint in the air, a peculiar whistle alarms the rest, causing them to collect together and remain on the alert, and on a repetition of the signal away they scamper, always ascending or descending a slope in an oblique direction. Sometimes I have seen an old female lead the herd, and on such occasions I have always found it extremely difficult to get within range, as they are doubly cunning.

Six hours' ride over most picturesque-looking country brought us to our encampment, which

Chincah had chosen close to a small mountain-stream that took its source in a cavern on the side of a lofty peak, which stood out in bold relief, and towered high above the rest. Its rugged summit, round which wreaths of white fleecy-looking clouds were floating in a deep blue azure sky, had the reputation of being the most likely ground to meet with ibex, as from its extreme inaccessibility it had rarely been trodden by man, and the game had been but little disturbed. Having taken a cursory survey of the mountain, in order to endeavour to form some judgment as to the best side to commence the ascent on the morrow, we adjourned to the tent, where we found a dinner waiting to which we did ample justice; and, after making a few preparations, turned in soon after sunset, so as to have a good night's rest previous to the morrow's fag, which we well knew would prove a trying one.

Rising at dawn we found the cold severe and piercing; and, on looking out of the tent door, we saw that the whole range of hills was enveloped in mist, a dense white cloud entirely obscuring the summit of the peak we intended to explore. This was not encouraging, to say the least of it; but towards sunrise the vapours began to open and disunite, and in the course of an hour portions of clouds separated themselves from the main body and moved slowly and majestically down the mountain, some remaining stationary on its side, whilst others hung suspended over the neighbouring densely-wooded ravines and valleys. Seeing that there was every prospect of a fine day we set out, having each selected our favourite rifles, Chineah only being entrusted with a spare gun, whilst Googooloo, Naga, and Hassan carried long ropes and short spears, which were to serve us in the ascent as "Alpenstocks." For some short distance the route was not very difficult, but it soon changed its character and became full of obstructions; for we had often to crawl along the smooth slabs of rocks on our hands and knees, and sometimes were obliged to take off our sambur-skin shoes (which were made purposely with very light soles) in order to get a better footing. The scenery was extremely wild, and a solemn silence reigned around, which was only broken at times by the deep grunt of some one of the gang when he came to a scarped rock or gully more difficult than the rest. On slopes here and there the mountain's vegetation was spangled with dew-drops, which sparkled like diamonds in the reflected rays of the morning sun.

After a severe fag we rested on a ledge of rock to take breath, and, being from constant exercise in rather better training than the rest, I pushed on a short distance in order to reconnoitre the ground, which seemed to be getting more and more difficult as we ascended. Whilst so engaged I heard a slight rustle, followed by a sound like the rolling of a pebble, and to my surprise saw a fine buck-sambur rise from his lair, just below the boulder of rock against which I was leaning, and gaze majestically round with erected head. I noiselessly took up my rifle, and, as he was leisurely trotting along the side of the mountain, brought the sight to bear just behind his massive shoulder and fired. When the smoke cleared away I saw him stretched lifeless on the ground, shot through the heart. The report soon brought up the gang, and having little time to lose, we merely hoisted our quarry—which proved to be a full stag with fine branching antlers—on to a huge boulder of rock, where, having fastened a pocket-handkerchief to one of the tines of his horns to scare away the vultures, we left him until our return. After several hours' clambering over broken ground, scarped rocks, and deep gullies, without seeing any indication of animal life, except a few butterflies, Naga called our attention to something moving along the scarped edge of a high ridge of cliff which frowned like a wall high above our heads, and with the aid of my field-glass I discerned a fine buck-ibex, evidently the sentinel of a herd, poised on a pinnacle of rock nearly half a mile distant. As his head was turned toward us, and he seemed to be watching our movements, I took it for granted that our presence was discovered, so I told Googooloo, Naga, and Hassan to remain quiet where they were, whilst B——, Chineah, and myself made a detour so as to circumvent him.

After intense labour we clambered up the face of the cliff, having frequently to crawl along ledges of rock overhanging precipices down which we dare not look, and with a good deal of manœuvring managed to get above our wary quarry, who was still apparently intently observing the movement of our party below, whilst seven others, confident in his watchfulness, were carelessly browsing on the short crisp herbage close by. By dodging from crag to crag, after some intensely-exciting stalking, we crept behind an isolated boulder of rock about a hundred and twenty paces to leeward of the herd, who were still grazing unconscious of danger; and, as the nature of the ground was such that we could not hope to steal any nearer without great fear of discovery, we prepared for immediate offensive action. Having taken the precaution of putting fresh caps on our rifles, B—— aimed at a fine buck that was carelessly receiving the caresses of a couple of does, whilst I took the sentinel, and firing almost simultaneously, both fell to our shots. I wounded a doe with my second barrel, but it got away with a broken leg; B——, however, was more fortunate, for he stopped a second doe with a ball through the spine, and killed a young buck with the second gun, as it was bounding along a ledge of rocks at least four hundred paces distant. "Well done, indeed, Ned!" I exclaimed, rather taken aback with this splendid display of marksmanship; "that was a shot I envy you for having made, as I have rarely seen a bounding deer bagged at such a distance, notwithstanding I have hunted with the crack sportsman of the day. It would have gladdened old Walter's heart to see one of his pupils do such credit to his 'bringings up.'"

"Yes, Hal, it was indeed a long shot, and I could hardly believe my eyes when I saw him drop, but the credit of it, if any there be, must be given to old Purdey, the maker of your rifle; for never do I think that grooved bore threw lead so true, and I now do not wonder at your luck in bringing down the hatties (elephants) right and left. It's the gun, man; it's the gun! Look after the game, whilst I pace the distance for my own satisfaction."

This was done, and it proved to be five hundred and forty-six paces, or allowing for inequalities in the ground, about four hundred yards. Whilst Chineah was despatching with his knife the still struggling doe that B—— had wounded, and B—— had gone to gather up his game, I went to look after the sentinel, which, to my surprise, was nowhere to be found, although I saw him drop the moment I fired, apparently lifeless. Whilst looking about, I crept on my hands and knees towards the edge of the precipice, and, lying my full length, looked over, when, to my astonishment, I saw the carcass on a narrow ledge of rock jutting out of the scarped cleft about thirty feet from the top. With the aid of my glass I could see that it was a fine specimen with splendid horns, which I determined, *coûte qui coûte,* should not be lost. I scrambled carefully back, and explained the case to B——, who advised me to give it up as "lost game," it not being worth while risking life for the sake of a pair of horns; but I did not like to return empty-handed, and my determination was soon taken, for I despatched Chineah for the rest of the gang. As soon as they arrived, I took the strong silken ropes they carried, on which I made a few knots, so as to enable me to get a better hold, and prevent myself from slipping, then fastening one end securely round the base of an immense boulder of rock, I threw the other down the abyss, taking the precaution of placing my coat and the turban-cloths of some of the people over the rough edge of the cliff, so as to prevent chafing. All being prepared, in spite of the remonstrance of my people, who feared some accident from the snapping of a rope which I knew would sustain a ton in addition to my weight, I commenced the descent, even B—— turning away, as the thought made him feel giddy. To me it was easy work enough, although I must own that I felt rather nervous as I first swang myself off, and hung suspended over a precipice, six hundred feet in depth, by a cord not three-quarters of an inch in diameter, which, not being steadied at the bottom, kept turning round and round, now and then knocking me against projections in the face of the rock. However, my "suspense" was of very short duration, for I soon found firm footing upon the ledge of rock where the dead ibex lay, which luckily turned out to be much wider than I had at first imagined from its appearance from the top. I soon fastened the rope round the buck's head, and on giving the preconcerted signal of a whistle, he was hauled up by the gang, who again threw down the cord for me. I climbed up the rope easily enough, but had great difficulty in scrambling over the crest, as my eyes were nearly filled with sand, which fell from the sides. At last I managed it, and we commenced the operation of skinning, that occupied us nearly an hour, after which we commenced our descent, and taking the head and skin of the sambur *en route* arrived at the tent just before sunset. During the next five days we hunted over these grounds, bagging thirteen ibex and a couple of bison, a herd of which animals came early one morning close to our tent, after which we returned to Ooty.

CHAPTER XVI.

ELEPHANT-HUNTING IN THE FOREST AROUND THE BASE OF THE NEILGHERRIES.

"Trampling his path through wood and brake,
And canes which, crackling, fall before his way,
And tassel-grass, whose silvery feathers play,
O'erlapping the young trees,
On comes the elephant to slake
His thirst at noon in yon pellucid spring."

The elephant-hunter's qualifications, "Mighty Hunters."—The start.—The Coonoor Pass.—The trail.—Signs of a tusker.—The herd.—A bull-elephant dies.—A cow and calf fall.—The bivouac.

ANY sportsman who is a fair shot, cool, steady, persevering, and active, may count upon killing heavy bags of most kinds of game with tolerable certainty; but he who would slay the elephant in his trackless jungle-home must have other qualities combined, or he will fail in his attempt.

The elephant-hunter must have a thorough knowledge of the nature and habits of that sagacious animal, whose keenly-developed senses far exceed that of any other denizen of the forest; he must be well acquainted with its peculiar structure and anatomy, or his bullet, however true, will never reach the vital part with any certainty; he must be an adept at "tracking," or following spoor, and in the understanding of *jungle signs*, which, although a natural gift to the red men of the Far West and Indian jungle-tribes, is only acquired by intense study and long practice; he must be patient and enduring, satisfied with hard fare and short commons, as he will often have to subsist wholly upon his gun, with the ground for his bed, and a forest-tree for his canopy. He should feel with the great poet, that "there is a pleasure in the pathless woods," and "society where none intrudes:" for he must often be content with nature and his own thoughts as companions, and he must not let his spirits be depressed by the solitude and intense stillness of the deep jungle.

The hunter must sleep like a hare, always on the alert, ever prepared and watchful; for he never knows what he may meet, or the danger a moment may bring forth. Inured to peril, he must never be cast down or faint of heart; or he had better not attempt to follow up the spoor of the elephant to his haunts in the dense, deep jungle, where the rays of the sun seldom penetrate, and the woodman's axe was never heard—where the deadliest of fevers lurk in places the most beautiful to the eye; and where, with the exception of certain times in the year, the air and the water are poisoned by malaria, and impregnated by the exhalations of decayed leaves and decomposed vegetable matter, entailing certain death to the hunter, were he tempted to follow up his perilous calling out of season.

Notwithstanding the danger of elephant-hunting, it has ever been a favourite sport amongst the covenanted servants and officers of the Indian army; and the names of Oswall, Rogers, Godfrey, Garrow, Michael, and one or two others, are "as familiar as household words" throughout India, on account of their numerous daring feats and perilous escapades.

Sometimes herds of elephants are tempted to roam, and leave their homes in the deep jungle to devastate the sugar-cane plantations and rice-fields of the ryots, where they commit great damage; and on such occasions the Anglo-Indian sportsman is enabled to get amongst them without being obliged to penetrate the dense forests so pernicious to health.

One evening, on my return to my domicile at Ooty from a very jovial picnic given by P——, a sporting collector of Coimbatore, at the celebrated Dodabetta Peak, (which rises to the height of 8700 feet above the plains,) Chineah, my head shekarry, informed me that a party of Mulchers whom I had sent out to look for game had come up from the low country with the news that a herd of elephants had been seen near the Colunda nullah, a small mountain-stream a few miles to the north-east of the hills.

My gang did not need any orders to prepare; for as I entered the garden, I found them all assembled in front of the gate in full shekar costume, ready to start, and many a knowing look and broad grin they gave me as I passed to don my leather hunting-gear and prepare my battery and ammunition. The cylindro-conical bullets of my rifle, as well as the round ones I used in the smooth-bores, were made of a mixture of lead and zinc, which amalgamation I prefer to any other for elephant-shooting, as leaden balls are too soft, and flatten on striking a bone, and brass balls, which are generally used, are too light to carry truly. My preparations did not take long to make, and in the course of a few minutes I mounted my favourite nag, "Gooty," accompanied by Chineah, Googooloo, Mootoo, and the Gooroo, carrying my guns, axes, spears, telescope, &c., a couple of Mulchers to show the road, and a horse-keeper, who led a baggage-tattoo, loaded with a large "combley" blanket, which served either as a covering or a tent, as occasion required, a change of clothing, some prog and tobacco.

The moon was favourable, being at its zenith as we passed the village of Coonoor, making the night clear as day, and allowing us to enjoy the magnificent scenery of the celebrated Coonoor Pass, where "fern flowers and grasses creep, fantastically tangled," amid gigantic forest trees, and the graceful bamboo contrasts with the darker foliage of the wild fig, and the thickets of rhododendron and wild camellias. The wave-like looking sea of deep forest was diversified with white lichen-covered precipices, and darkly-frowning crags of every imaginable form and shape, some thousands of feet in height, which seemed to shake their fern-fringed foreheads at the passing traveller as he followed the winding road leading down the ravine, every bend of which, like a turn of the kaleidoscope, revealed something new and pleasing to the eye.

Upon the summit of a rugged and almost inaccessible peak, which cast its dark shadow on our path, is the small hill-fort, Hulli kul Droog, built by Hyder Ali, which long since has been abandoned to the birds and beasts of the forest.

As I rode along I frequently heard the sharp bark of the elk above the murmur of the mountain-stream, which glistened like silver in the rays of the moon as it glided over rounded masses of granite and smooth angular pieces of green stone, or, leaping in little cascades, dashed foaming down the steep ravine; and at times I distinguished the distant hoarse roar of the tiger reverberating through the woods, which was immediately followed by a dismal howling chorus from a troop of jackals.

It was past midnight when we arrived at the bungalow at Metrapolliam, a village on the right bank of the river Bowani, and after a few hours' repose, started for the place where the elephants were said to be, just as the first streaks of gray in the east proclaimed the dawn of day; and after a tramp of about twelve miles, some part of the way through very dense jungle, we arrived at the huts of a Mulcher tribe, where I left my horse and baggage-pony under the care of the horse-keeper. They could hardly make their way through the bush.

The Mulchers gave us to understand that the herd could not be at any great distance, as some of their tribe had seen them the evening before, in a valley close to the foot of the hills, and they had been heard trumpeting during the night.

We rested for an hour, and broke our fast by the side of a beautiful little stream, which we followed for some distance, when the Mulcher who served as our guide pointed out to us the spoor of an elephant about three days old, and shortly afterwards we came upon the trail of a herd of eight, which I made out to be about twenty-four hours old.

It was now noon, and the rays of the sun were intensely hot, so we sat down for an hour under a tree, whilst the Gooroo and the Mulcher went to consult with some of the tribe, whom he had left watching the movements of the herd. They returned shortly, accompanied by two other Mulchers, who informed us that they had seen a herd, consisting of a tusker, eight females, and some young ones, passing over one of the lower spurs branching off the Neilgherries the evening before; and under their guidance we soon came upon their trail, which consisted of several footprints of all dimensions, from six to twelve or fourteen inches in diameter.

I held a brief consultation with the gang, and it determined *nem. con.* to follow up the spoor as expeditiously as possible; so we continued on trail through dense jungle, over hills, and almost impenetrable ravines, until the sun had almost sunk below the western horizon, when we collected some dry logs, made a fire to keep off the tigers, &c., distributed some provisions and tobacco, and turned in, two keeping watch by turns whilst the others slept, until the moon had risen high enough to enable us to see the spoor, and continue the pursuit.

A sloth bear (*Prochilus labiatus*) and a half-grown cub were descried by the Gooroo as we went along, and a bull-bison was heard bellowing in a thicket close by; but we left them unmolested, continuing our course by the track made by the herd bursting through the jungle and treading down the brushwood otherwise impenetrable. Huge boughs and branches had been broken off, and trees uprooted or torn up in their passage; in places they had remained for some time browsing on the young wood, tender branches, and succulent plants, and as we passed a watercourse, it was evident from the marks that some of their number had been rolling in the sand.

Here it was I made sure that there was a bull in the herd with large ivories; for I perceived marks in the bank where he had thrust his tusks under the root of a large jungle-tree, covered with creeping oleaster, full of rich bunches of sour scarlet plums, which had resisted all his efforts to tear up.

I saw, from the freshness of the spoor and other traces which remained, that we had gained very considerably upon the herd, and as we all felt rather fatigued, we lay down to repose for a couple of hours, continuing our course when the day broke.

Towards noon, after crossing several densely-wooded ravines and rocky hills, where the elephant, in spite of his great weight, scarcely leaves any trace, the spoor being only indicated by a broken leaf, bruised twig, or a lately-upturned stone, we entered some thick bamboo jungle, and here we found a "jheel," or swamp, where they had remained during the night, and which bore traces of having been very recently occupied. The trail was warm.

Being inspired with fresh vigour, fatigue was forgotten, and after having made our way through a wide ravine, and crossed a stony watercourse, where the spoor was certainly not an hour old, at about three o'clock in the afternoon, we began to ascend a long ridge of low rocky hills—a difficult route, one would think, for such unwieldy-looking animals, but the spoor was plain, so on we went; and after an hour's clambering up a steep and rather difficult ledge of rocks, we arrived at the summit, where I had the indescribable pleasure of beholding the broad backs of the objects of our search, who were quietly browsing, unconscious of danger, under the shade of some tall forest trees. I sent Mootoo, the Gooroo, and the Mulchers, to a high peak, by a circuitous route, from whence they would be enabled to watch the movements of the herd, should they take alarm. After resting for a few moments to reconnoitre the ground and take breath, and having tried the wind, which was favourable, a light air blowing from them to us, I carefully examined my guns, ascertained that the powder was well up in the nipples, and then stole gently forward, taking advantage of any cover or undulation I could find, until I got behind a thick tree, with a patch of low bush at the foot, from whence I could distinctly see the herd about sixty yards distant. The tusker was standing on three legs, swinging his huge carcass to and fro, and fanning himself with the branch of a tree, which he held in his trunk, and near him two females were reposing, whilst several others were standing a short distance off.

I remained a few minutes to make sure that I was well to leeward, and not in any immediate danger of being discovered by their remarkably keen scent, and then making signs to Googooloo to remain concealed, I crept forward with my rifle, followed by Chineah, carrying my other two big guns.

After some very careful and exciting stalking I reached a tree about thirty paces from the group, which, unconscious of our approach, were still in the same position, and taking a moment to draw breath, and wipe my eyes from the perspiration which streamed down my forehead, I crept under the cover of some low bush to a clump of bamboos, within pistol shot of the tusker; which I had hardly reached when I saw that I was discovered, for one of the females sprang up suddenly with a strange wild cry, and rushed a few paces forward, tail on end. The bull also made a simultaneous movement, stretching out his trunk with a grunt to catch the wind, and giving me a fair shot—not a second was to be lost. I threw up my rifle, took a deliberate and steady aim at the hollow above the trunk, (which is about the size of a saucer,) in the centre of his forehead, and pulled the trigger. A heavy fall immediately followed, but before the smoke had cleared away, and I could see the result of my shot, the female rushed frantically forward, nearly capsizing me in her course, and tore up a wild date within three yards of the spot where I was standing.

As she did not appear, however, to notice me, but went off trumpeting in an opposite direction to that taken by the rest of the herd, I did not molest her at the time, for I felt too anxious to secure the tusker, whom I found stone-dead, with his fore-legs doubled under him, his hind ones stretched out, and his tusks deeply embedded in the ground with the fall.

I had hardly made sure of his being dead when

Googooloo called my attention by a signal, and turning round I saw my quondam friend, the female who gave the alarm, helping a young one over some rough ground about a couple of hundred yards distant. As she was going off at a shuffling trot that forbade any hope I might have of overtaking her, I took a steady aim at the young one, hitting it severely and rolling it over. The smoke had hardly cleared away, and I had just snatched a loaded gun from Chineah, (who ran like a cat up a tree,) when down she came on me with a hoarse roar of vengeance. I let her charge to within twenty paces from me, when I gave her a *right and left* full in the forehead, which stopped her career and brought her to her knees, and Googooloo, who stood steadily by my side, handed me my second gun, with which I gave her a "*finisher*" as she was attempting to regain her legs. A convulsive tremor passed over her body, and all was still.

I reloaded the guns, and despatched the young one, which could hardly drag itself along, and as there was no other tusker in the herd, I did not care to follow it up further, so I gave directions to Chineah and the rest of the gang, who came up, to build a hut, whilst I and Googooloo went out to try and kill a deer for food; but after a hard fag our only bag was a large porcupine, a peafowl, a wild cat, and three black monkeys, which latter proved very acceptable to the Mulchers.

On my return to the gang, I found a very com-

The Old Shekarry and his Gang.

fortable hut constructed, a soft bed of leaves prepared, and a tolerably savoury dish ready for me, consisting of an elephant's foot baked in a paste of clay amongst the embers; after having partaken of which, a large fire was made, and we all sat round enjoying "the fragrant narcotic weed," whilst the Gooroo and Chineah by turns chanted an extemporary song in a very monotonous tone, commemorating the exploits of the day, and all the rest took up the chorus.

Being very tired, and perhaps not musically inclined at the time, I fell asleep, and did not awake until broad daylight the next morning, when I found the gang busily employed with their axes in cutting out the tusks, which weighed ninety-four pounds the pair. This job took them about six hours, so that it was nearly noon before we commenced our homeward route, and late at night when we arrived at the Mulcher huts, where we had left the horses. There we slept, returning to Ooty the night afterwards.

CHAPTER XVII.

ELEPHANT-HUNTING IN THE ANNAMULLAY FOREST.

Coimbatore.—News of elephants.—A Poojah to propitiate the Hindoo deities meets with no satisfactory results.—A court-martial held on the recusant Sawmy.—Sentence and execution.—The ghost of the injured Sawmy appears to the Gooroo. —His threat.—The laying of the spirit.—Result obtained.— The start.—M——'s hut at Tunnacuddoo.—His hospitality. —A bison wounded.—Taketty.—News of a herd of elephants. —Our bivouac.—A night alarm.—Elephants astir.—A bull-elephant yields up his spoils.—An immense snake caught.— We follow up the spoor of the herd.—Beautiful forest scenery. —Tracking by torchlight.—Difficulties surmounted.—We swim a nullah.—The trail.—The herd in view.—A bull elephant anchored.—A second tusker wounded.—A charge.— A predicament.—A lucky shot decides the day.—The result of a pat from an elephant.

COIMBATORE has ever been considered one of the most desirable of our military cantonments in Southern India, not only on account of its proximity to the Neilgherry and Annamullay Mountains, and its comparatively cool and salubrious climate, but because it is a single station, where one regiment only is quartered, consequently the duty is extremely light, and "*leave*" easily attainable. The town itself stands about 1400 feet above the level of the sea, in dry, well-cultivated country; is neatly built, and consists of twelve wide and well-ventilated streets. Tippoo Sultan, the Rajah of Mysore, occasionally resided in the old palace, the ruins of which are still standing, and built a handsome mosque.

The officers' quarters are substantially built and delightfully situated outside the native town, by a lake three miles in length, which in the season is covered with waterfowl of every description, and in the reeds and paddy-fields adjoining snipe are to be found in thousands. To the lover of large game this station offers peculiar advantages, as the virgin forest jungle surrounding the Neilgherry and Annamullay ranges are celebrated as being the haunts of all kinds of large game, besides containing abundance of teak, (*Sectona grandis,*) blackwood, (*Dalbergia satifolia,* boxwood,) sandal-wood, (*Santalum album,*) and other valuable timber, which is, however, unfortunately too remote from water-carriage to permit of easy exportation.

The end of December (when the north-east monsoon rains are over, and the sun has gained his most southern declination) may be considered the coldest season of the year in all those countries north of the equator, for at this period the range of the thermometer in the shade is from sixty-two to eighty degrees, and the climate is there delightful, the north-east wind proving enlivening and bracing, and at this time the jungle is considered free from fever, the greatest danger to which the Indian sportsman is exposed.

I had left my eyrie, "Burnside Cottage," near Ooty, having received information that a herd of elephants were said to have been seen near one of the collector's spice-gardens in the Bolanputty Valley, and was staying with M——, who was in the regiment then quartered at Coimbatore, whilst my gang went out to gather intelligence. After an absence of five days they returned, their search having proved a blank, no fresh trails having been discovered.

As was my general custom before the departure of my gang on an expedition, I had distributed some few rupees to purchase sheep, fowls, &c., for sacrificial offerings to their "Sawmies," so as to propitiate the deities, and bring good luck on the enterprise, and on this occasion it appears that the non-success of the reconnaissance had excited the indignation of the whole gang against a certain stone image of Haniman (the monkey-god) in the neighbourhood of the lake, as sheep had been sacrificed, cocks immolated, cocoa-nuts broken, and incense burnt before him, and yet the search for game had proved a failure.

I was enjoying a weed after dinner with M—— and B——, when loud discordant vociferations were heard in the servants' outhouses, and going out to see what was the matter, we found the whole gang holding a court-martial on the recusant Sawmy; to which we listened, keeping out of sight. The Gooroo was gesticulating in an extraordinary manner, and holding out somewhat in this style:— "Soono, Bhai, (listen, brothers,) here we are all very tired, with our feet broken, and our legs and arms full of thorns with tramping for five days through the jungle, and all to no purpose, for the elephants—may their fathers be burnt!—were not to be found, and we had to come back, 'with blackened faces,' before the gentleman and 'eat dirt,' (literally, get abused.) Is not this vile conduct on the part of that monkey-faced Sawmy, to whom we went to the expense of offering sacrifices of sheep and cocks? Are we to suffer him to laugh at us in our trouble, and throw dirt on our beards in this manner? No, brothers, we will pay him out. Heigh! Ali Beg, you are a Mussulman, and do not fear the evil eye of a Hindoo Sawmy, so take the cursed son of burnt fathers and defiled mothers who has dared to bring all this evil upon us, cast dirt upon our beards, and make the master turn his face away from us, break off his nose and ears, put out his eyes so that he can never find his way back, and fling him into the lake." The whole gang highly approved of this sentence, and amidst the hootings, groans, and expletive execrations of the party, the image was dug up from the spot where it had perhaps rested for centuries, and after having been mutilated by Ali Beg, and subjected to the vilest abuse and ridicule, was thrown in the lake; none of the Hindoos, however, venturing to lay a finger upon it.

We slipped quietly away without any of the gang discovering our presence, and after turning over the affair in my mind, knowing the character of my people, I resolved to work upon their superstitious fears to my own advantage; and some few days afterwards, whilst out deer-stalking, I watched an opportunity, when the Gooroo was separated from the rest of the gang, and approaching tolerably near unperceived, hid myself under a large mass of parasitical plants, and called out in a disguised low sepulchral voice, "O Perriatumbie, Perriatumbie!" (his real name, "the Gooroo," being a cognomen given to him by the gang, on account of his having some pretensions to priestcraft and sorcery,) am I not the god Haniman, whom you and your wretched associates caused to be defiled and thrown to the bottom of the tank? I am not dead, as you will find, although I have been eight days in the water; I can see you, although Ali Beg tried to put out my eyes; I can hear, although my ears are disfigured; I can smell your vile carcass, although the end of my nose is off; and I can hardly keep my hands away from your throat, although they are maimed." At the first sound of my voice the Gooroo tried to make a bolt, but in his mad terror he stumbled over the root of a tree, falling heavily his whole length on the ground, when he began writhing about in a convulsive manner, as if wrestling with some imaginary enemy, groaning and keeping his face covered with a cloth. Taking advantage of his terror, I continued in the same tone of voice, "O Perriatumbie! are you not ashamed of having so ill-used your good Sawmy Haniman? Did you not tie seven tails of male elephants shot by your master as a lignum (the sacred thread worn round the body only by the Brahmins) round the image of that pert god, Gánesca? O Perriatumbie! my evil eye will always be upon you, and the rest of those who ill-treated me, to work you evil, until I have also a lignum of elephant tails on me, and my wounds are anointed with the fat and blood of many tigers. I want no sacrifices of sheep and cocks, for the price of them comes out of the pocket of your master, on whom be blessings and good luck, for he never did me any harm, and must not suffer for your ill-doings. Go and show him the fresh trails of elephants and tigers, that he may kill them, and bring me their spoils as offerings, that I may not destroy you all, as your crimes deserve." I then stole quietly away and joined the rest of the gang, but in the course of half an hour I saw the spell had begun to work, for the people collected in groups, and whispered mysteriously to each other; and every now and then the names of Haniman and the Gooroo caught my ears, which proved that a great sensation had been caused by this *supernatural* visitation, which I increased to an awfully exciting pitch by telling them that as I was passing an aspen-leaved peepul (a sacred tree among the Hindoos) I heard a sweet voice, like that of a young girl, exclaim, "Why, O master! do you hunt in these jungles, when the elephants, bound by fate, are waiting for you on the Annamullay Mountains, where you can now follow them well, as there is no fever?" And that, although I looked everywhere to find whence the voice proceeded, I saw no one except an old, queer-looking black monkey, which hobbled away out of my sight in a moment. I told this tale with the greatest gravity and command of countenance, and the effect was prodigious —the whole gang instantaneously exclaiming, shaking their heads, and nodding significantly at each other, that the voice had only spoken truth, and that we had better immediately prepare for an expedition to that part of the country. This was all I wanted; for although at this season of the year the jungle is said to be free from fever, such was the dread of the deadly effect of the malaria of those trackless and unknown forests, that up to this I could never bribe or induce any gang to undertake any very lengthened expedition in those parts, notwithstanding it was known that elephants swarmed, and large game of all kinds was abundant. Having, therefore, attained my object by working upon their credulity and superstitious fears, "I struck whilst the iron was hot," and having consulted with B——, who proposed to accompany me, the morrow was destined for preparation, and the day after for departure.

During the night I heard the shrill notes of the cholera horn and other discordant Hindoo music, and my head servant, Yacoob Khan, a Mussulman, informed me that the gang had that evening fed twenty Brahmins, and that they were then performing Poojah (religious ceremonies) in honour of the god Haniman. The next morning, on my way to the racket-court, as I passed by the lake, I saw the image of the god in its original position, decked out with wreaths of jessamine, and other fragrant flowers, and gaudily painted with yellow ochre and tinsel. Some of the gang must have had a cool dip during the night, for the water was deep where the idol was thrown in.

We were very busy all the next day in getting supplies, casting hardened bullets, and arranging our baggage, all of which was carried on ponies or coolies' shoulders, and in the evening, as soon as the moon rose, the traps started, escorted by the gang, for Annamullay, a considerable village about five miles from the ghaut or pass leading up the mountain. B—— and I rode on at daybreak, and passed the greater part of the day in hunting up villagers who knew something of the hills, in which search, through the agency of the curnum, or head police authority, we were tolerably successful, as we secured the services of three men, whose employment was hunting in the deepest jungle for cardamums. Under their guidance, we ascended the mountains by a steep pass, extremely difficult for our baggage-animals, and after a hard day's fag, arrived at the hut of M——, the celebrated elephant shot, who had established his head-quarters on a little clearing he had made in the heart of the jungle close to the Tunnacooddoo waterfall.

He is the Government agent appointed to collect the revenue of this wild district, and also superintendent of the teak-forests, no tree being allowed to be cut without the payment of a certain tax. The timber when felled is allowed to remain on the ground a certain time to season, after which it is dragged by elephants, who are trained for the purpose, down slopes and slides of the mountain to the low country, were it is collected, and floated down the Ponani River to the town of Ponani, on the coast, from whence it is embarked for Bombay, where much is exported for the purposes of ship-building. M—— received us with great hospitality, and gave me a map of his explorings in the surrounding forest. He also deputed six Carders (some people of a wild jungle tribe he has domesticated) to accompany us in our trip. We lighted a huge box-fire outside his hut, and had a good warm, for the night was very chilly; after which we dined, had a "jaw" as to our future proceedings; and turned in.

The next morning went out after bison, soon found a fresh trail, and M—— got a shot, wounding a bull, which was found dead some days after by the Carders. He recommended us to go to Taketty, and there build a hut as head-quarters, as it was a famous place for elephants, he having killed five tuskers near there at different times. As the jungle was impenetrable for our baggage-animals on the top of the mountains, a part of the gang had to go down into the low country, and ascend the mountains again by a different ghaut. They, however, managed to do this in one day, arriving at Taketty, which consists of three or four wood-cutters' huts, just before sunset.

The next day the gang constructed two huts, one for ourselves, and the other for our servants and the ponies, which would have been taken away by tigers in the night had we left them picketed outside. M—— having some magisterial duty to perform in the low country, could not accompany us, so we bade him adieu, and, under guidance of some of his Carder tribe, joined the gang, whom we found very comfortably established. The next day, sent down into the low country for six bullock-loads of rice and curry stuff, a dozen sheep, a couple of milch goats, and a gross of fowls, for whose reception we prepared places; after which we made a reconnaissance of the jungle round about our hut, near which several old elephant spoors were distinctly visible, and one of the wood-cutters, who accompanied us, told us that some of his people had seen a herd a short distance from their huts at Cawderpuddy, where they were engaged in cutting timber two days previously.

I therefore arranged with B——, who was suffering from dysentery, and hardly fit for hard work, that I should start with Chincah, Googooloo, and two others of the gang, early on the morrow, to reconnoitre, leaving him, with the rest of the people, to get everything ship-shape in the huts. Accordingly, at daybreak we started, under the guidance of the wood-cutter, and a couple of Carders carrying axes, provisions for three days, and large comblies, or goats'-hair blankets, to serve as coverings.

We soon arrived at Cawderpuddy, where we found about twenty men engaged in cutting timber. Here we learned that a herd of fifteen elephants, amongst which were two tuskers, had been seen quietly browsing in a valley some three miles off, the morning previous, by some women, who had gone there to pick "barjee," a kind of wild spinach, and for the inducement of some tobacco one of the men offered to show us the spot. After a couple of hours' fag through thickish jungle, we came upon an open glade, at one end of which was a swamp, where a sounder of hog were wallowing, and here we found the trail of a large herd, not many hours old, which we followed until the sun began to get low in the horizon, when, arriving at a watercourse, I gave the order to halt and prepare the supper, whilst I looked out for a suitable place to pass the night.

Being an old forest-ranger, and used to camping out, I was not very particular, my great object being to secure a flank defence, so as to avoid the possibility of being taken unawares by wild beasts; and a dry bed of sand, under a high shelving bank, from which projected two high boulders of rock, about ten feet apart, seemed to offer a natural fortress, as by making a huge fire in front we were unassailable from without. Chineah and Googooloo spread one of the comblies over two bamboos, so as to form a kind of awning to shelter us from the dew, whilst the Carders collected heaps of dry leaves for our beds, and a sufficient stock of logs to keep a large fire burning throughout the night. Our supper, consisting of curry and rice, was soon ready, and discussed; a cheroot followed, after which the watch was set, arms carefully examined, and we turned in for the night, every one rolled up in a combley blanket.

I had slept for some hours, when suddenly I was awakened by Chineah laying his hand on my shoulder, with a significant low whistle, which signal with the gang denoted that "*something is stirring.*" I immediately sprang to my feet on the alert, and, after listening attentively for a moment, heard a loud crackling of bamboos, as if some large animals were forcing their way through the jungle, accompanied by a curious blowing noise, which at first I thought was the grunting of a bull-bison, but shortly afterwards I distinctly recognised the "trumpeting" of elephants, and the continual crashing of trees at no great distance left no doubt on my mind but that a herd was near at hand. I put fresh caps on my guns, for fear the old ones might have been injured with the dampness of the night air, and taking Chineah (on whose pluck I knew I could fully depend) with me to carry my spare guns, I cautioned the rest to lie quiet until my return, and sallied forth to reconnoitre.

A full moon was nearly at its zenith, so that, except where the foliage was very dense, or under the deep shade of the mighty forest, we had no difficulty in discerning our way, guided by the strange noises and frequent crashing and rending of trees, which sounded at times almost as loud as the report of musketry, as these huge denizens of the forest rushed through the thickets, snapping and tearing up everything before them.

As we were going along, I heard a rustling and a low hissing, and I felt rather startled by seeing a huge snake, which appeared to be of the boa species, coiled round a date-tree, close to which I had passed; as, however, it did not appear to move, I left it undisturbed, and, after a tramp of about half an hour, arrived at a jheel or swamp, at one end of which was a large pool, where three elephants were amusing themselves by sucking up the water in their trunks and spouting it into the air or over their bodies. After a careful reconnaissance I made sure there was no tusker among them, so I left them unmolested, and crept gently round the shady edge of the cover, taking care to keep well to leeward, so as to prevent their getting wind. Passing the swamp,

I entered a rather open bamboo-jungle, when, from the peculiar noises on all sides, I knew I was in the middle of a large herd.

I saw several groups of females browsing about, and threaded my way amongst them, with Chineah close at my side, keeping a sharp look-out for a tusker. We were several times very nearly discovered, although we kept in the shade as much as possible, and always strove to get to leeward. I had counted sixteen elephants without having distinguished any with tusks, when my attention was arrested by hearing a low grunt, and on turning a cover of dense thicket, I perceived a stately bull, with a fine pair of "ivories," swinging himself to and fro, whilst a female was caressing his neck with her trunk.

I stole gently forward, closely followed by Chineah, and, after a little careful and exciting stalking, managed to conceal myself behind a clump of bamboos near which he was standing, which fortunately was to leeward. I remained without stirring for a few moments, the bull not giving me the chance of a fair shot, although I could have doubled up the female half a dozen times over, as I got a full view of her forehead within fifteen paces. At last he swerved round, fronting me, but his head turned towards the female, who just at this moment seemed to have caught scent of us, for she raised her trunk in a very inquisitive manner, and tore down one of the bamboos in front of us. No time was to be lost;

I gave a shrill whistle, which caused the bull to extend his ears, and turn his head in my direction, presenting me with a full view of his forehead. Now was my time; I took a steady aim between the eyes, and gave him both barrels, right and left, at a second's interval. A hoarse scream followed the report, awakening the echoes of the forest, the huge beast staggered back a couple of paces, and reeled like a drunken man, then his sturdy legs gave way under him, and he sunk to the ground in a kneeling position. I snatched a second gun from Chineah, and fearing he might only be stunned, stepped up to him, and sent a ball crashing into his eye, but it was not required, he never stirred, he was dead. The female who was with him rushed frantically through the jungle, trumpeting, and the rest of the herd, taking alarm, dashed down a densely crowded valley at a pace which defied pursuit.

Chineah cut off the tail as a trophy, and after we had examined our prize, whose tusks appeared to weigh heavily, we rejoined the rest of the gang, who were anxiously awaiting our arrival, and once more rolling ourselves in our blankets were soon in the arms of Morpheus.

He who sleeps with a forest tree for his canopy, a stone for his pillow, and the ground for his bed, is not likely to play the sluggard, and I was up and astir as soon as the soft blue light of morning became perceptible along the eastern horizon. A few hours of repose had had the desired effect—restoring both strength of body and vigour of mind—I awoke full of health, and fit for another day's hard fag.

After a hurried ablution in the nullah, I lighted a cheroot, and, guided by my own footprints, proceeded with the gang towards the scene of last night's operations. *En route*, I perceived the snake which had so startled me in the dark, still in the same place, coiled round the date-tree, evidently fast asleep, in a state of repletion. I saw at a glance that it was a beautifully marked "damian" or rock-snake, (a kind of boa,) which is not venomous, and I determined, if possible, to capture it alive, it appearing an excellent specimen. This was soon effected. Chincah fastened a slip-knot to a stout bamboo, and, passing it over its head, pulled, whilst some of the rest of the gang struck the tail with sticks until it unloosened its coil from the tree, and wound round the bamboo, to which it was tied with the stalks of creepers. It proved about eleven feet in length, and over a foot in circumference. A wicker-basket was soon constructed, and in a few days it became quite tame, not attempting to escape when handled.*

Our captive secured, we soon made our way to the spot where the dead elephant was lying, and

* The author subsequently gave it to A. Bain, Esq., of Madras, who transferred it to the Liverpool Zoological Gardens, where it is now, much increased in size.

whilst some of the gang worked by turns with the axe to cut out the tusks, (a tedious and lengthy operation requiring much care,) and others prepared our morning repast, I strolled about with Googooloo, and examined the trail of the herd, in order to ascertain whether there were any other large tuskers in it worth following up.

Our search proved successful, for the troop was evidently much larger than I had at first imagined; and we found the spoor of a very large elephant, which, from the size, I concluded must be a bull with weighty ivories. From the trail, which I followed up for some distance, I perceived that the panic occasioned by my shots, had not been general among the herd, for some of them could hardly have been alarmed, as they had broken off branches and browsed on the young wood, within half a mile from the spot where I had killed one of their number. I therefore made up my mind to pursue, and returned to the gang to hasten them in their work, so as to be sooner on their heels. The tusks, which weighed about 70 lbs. were cut out, and, with the snake, given in charge of Mootoo, Verapah, and three of the Carder tribe, for conveyance to the hut, to which I intended to return on the close of the present expedition.

After a couple of hours' tracking, we came to a purling mountain stream, meandering through dense forest jungle, where we filled our "mushucks," (large leathern bottles,) in case of not meeting with water further on, and continued our course, the spoor leading along the bank.

As we advanced, the woods became more and more open, here and there alternating with beautiful green glades, which much reminded me of the park scenery of "merrie England." On every side were clusters of magnificent teak-trees, interspersed with peepul, jack, and acacia, their branches twined with wild vines, and covered with bunches of deliciously-sweet purple, or rather nearly black, grapes, many coloured convolvuli, or other beautiful flowering parasites. It was a wild garden of Nature's own planting, and, struck with the strange and almost supernatural beauty of the scene, I sat down to contemplate her handiwork. Every sense was gratified. The eye wandered with delight through numerous vistas amid the foliage, and on verdant glades, diversified with parterres of orchids, in full bloom, of every hue and shade, whose presence filled the forest round with fragrant aroma, and loaded the breeze, which was delightfully cool as it played round our heated temples, with pleasant perfume. The bulbul (the Indian nightingale) vied with the other feathered songsters in melody, soft, clear, and harmonious; and for some moments I felt so struck with the transcendent beauty of the scene before me, (so like what I imagine the garden of Eden must have been,) that I became absorbed in thought—imagination, for the time, led me away, and even the elephants were forgotten: short-lived sensations, almost instantaneously passing away, for my eyes soon returned to earth, and my reverie was broken by Chineah laying before me several bunches of delicious grapes that grew temptingly on every side.

After having rested some little time, Googooloo and Naga took up the trail, and we continued the pursuit. As they pressed forward, with bodies half-bent and eyes gliding along the ground, they reminded one of hounds running by scent; but, unlike these, the trackers made no noise, seldom or never speaking when on trail, and then only in a subdued whisper. Tireless, used to constant warfare with the elements, and struggles with the wild denizens of the forest, as the bloodhound loves the trail so did they, and hunger, thirst, weariness, all must be felt to an extreme degree before they would give it up.

We continued the pursuit for many long and weary hours, until at last night set in and arrested our progress, as the spoor was no longer to be discerned. Halting simultaneously, we held a brief consultation as to what was best to be done, and, after some deliberation, my gang, who were all men of jungle experience, and well versed in forest signs, were unanimous in their desire to follow up the trail *by torch-light*, for it was yet early in the night, and many hours must intervene before we should have the light of the moon, as it would not rise until nearly midnight, and during this time the herd, which, from the freshness of the spoor, were evidently not very far ahead, might travel a long way.

I therefore determined to be at once on their heels, and lighting a large bull's-eye lanthorn (which one of the gang always carried) and branches of dry resinous wood, we continued the pursuit, following the trail almost as fast as before. I counted that we should get over many miles before morning, and perhaps even come up with the herd; at any rate, we might expect to fall in with them before the next night.

Notwithstanding we were tired and hungry, we did not linger, but followed up the spoor with every precaution, keenly scrutinising the ground in advance of us, in the hope of perceiving the objects of our search.

After some time we descended into a deep valley, and there encountered an obstacle that proved not only a serious barrier to our progress, but almost brought our tracking to a termination. This was a tract of *dense* bamboo-jungle, with thick underwood, which we could hardly penetrate without the constant use of our axes. Our lights also proved very insufficient, and for several long weary hours we followed the trail, the greater part of the time crawling on our hands and knees. At last the long-wished-for moon shone forth, lighting up the forest with her cheering rays. Darkness passed away, and the night became clear as day.

Extinguishing our torches, on we pressed with

renewed vigour. The roar of water sounded in our ears from the direction towards which the trail was leading us, and after a short time we came to a formidable torrent, which, freshened by recent rains on the mountains, came tumbling down its rocky bed in a succession of foaming cataracts.

To my surprise, I found from the spoor that the herd had crossed, although by what means was not evident either to myself or any of the gang, as the stream was extremely rapid and appeared too deep to be forded. Here and there, among the boiling frothing eddies, broken rocks of greenish hue were seen above the surface, but they were only the crests of large boulders, and between them the stream ran dark and rapidly. How the young elephants, of which there were several in the herd, had managed to get over I could not imagine, as no swimmer, however strong, could have stemmed the torrent for a moment; he must have been swept down and dashed to pieces against the rocks.

At last I bethought me that perhaps the "fresh" had come down only lately, and that the herd had crossed before the torrent became so swollen, and by placing sticks by the edge of the stream I found my opinion was correct, and that the volume of water was still increasing. This was certainly not satisfactory, to say the least of it, but "Never say die" was ever my motto, and we knew the elephants were on the other side, and that if we intended to be amongst them, we must go too. How? was the question. To cross where we were was impossible, but after some reconnoitring we found that below the falls the current ran much less rapidly, forming a kind of pool about a hundred yards across or more. This was not the first time that either I or my followers had crossed a river without a ford, and many a stronger current had I stemmed in my time than that then before me; the only difficulty was to get the guns and ammunition over dry.

After a moment's consideration, I made the gang collect a number of dry logs and bamboos, and with the aid of the stalks of creepers, which served as ropes, I tied them together and made a small raft, on which I securely tied the guns, tools, &c. I then stripped, and throwing my clothes on the top, cautiously entered the stream, and by laying hold of the raft, with the assistance of Chineah and Googooloo, pushed it before me. Plunge, plunge, plunge, I heard behind me, until the last of my gang had taken to the water, and was swimming silently to a smooth ledge of rocks on the opposite side, where, one after another, we landed, donned our toggery, and made sure that our arms had not got wet; after which we clambered up the bank, and by keeping along the stream soon recovered the trail.

Feeling considerably refreshed with our bath, we made short work with what little cold provision we had left in our wallet, and forgetting our fatigue, once more pushed on at a rapid rate.

Hours rolled by, and daylight found us still on

trail; hunger, fatigue, and weariness were all forgotten in the excitement attendant on the pursuit, for from the freshness of the spoor, and other unmistakable signs, we knew the herd could not be far distant.

The utmost care was now necessary in following up the trail, as the slightest noise might have given the alarm: indeed, I felt apprehensive lest the elephants should get wind of us, as their senses are more acute in the early part of the morning than at any other time.

We had crossed a broad belt of open teak-forest, and were once more in dense bamboo-jungle, when suddenly I saw Googooloo, who was half a dozen paces ahead, make a stand and turn his head as if to catch a sound; a low grunt (a sign of satisfaction) was followed by an expressive hiss, (his ordinary mode of attracting attention,) and then I felt as sure that game was afoot as any English sportsman could be on seeing his favourite dog point. I laid my ear to the ground but heard nothing, and the jungle was too thick to allow me to see any distance round; I therefore carefully followed up the spoor, creeping along as cautiously as possible, when again one of Googooloo's peculiar sounds attracted my notice, and after listening attentively a few moments, I heard a distant, low, rumbling noise, which I immediately recognised as being that made by elephants from the water rattling in their stomach.

I ordered Chineah and the rest of the gang to halt, and having looked to the powder in my nipples, and made sure of the direction from which the sounds proceeded, stole noiselessly forward, accompanied by Googooloo only, who carried a couple of spare guns. We soon came up with the rearmost of the herd, a group of five females, who were browsing upon the young and tender shoots of the bamboo and other succulent plants which abounded in that part of the jungle. As they were beneath my notice, I gave them a wide berth, and Googooloo and I separated, in order that we might have a better chance of finding the trail of a bull.

I soon came across a spoor larger than any of the rest, and Googooloo not being in sight, I followed it up alone. After half-an-hour's tracking, in which I passed a young male and three other females, I saw a huge tusker standing alone by several large boulders of rock, against one of which he was rubbing his hind-quarters.

Immediately I caught sight of him I dived into the deeper jungle, and, by making a circuitous route, got well to windward of him. I then regretted that Googooloo was not with me, as I had no spare gun, and I felt nervous lest my prey might escape. However, there was no help for it, so, after carefully reconnoitring the ground, in order to avail myself of any cover it afforded, I crept forward on my hands and knees, and, after a few minutes' intensely exciting stalking, managed to ensconce myself behind a low ledge of rock, from whence I could observe every motion he made.

He was standing on three legs, the 'off' hind-foot being raised from the ground, and leaning carelessly against the other, whilst the fore-part of his body was swinging to and fro. Although he was not more than twenty paces distant, I could not get a fair shot, as his head was turned directly away from me. I waited nearly ten minutes for a chance of his altering his position, during which I had ample time to admire his stately proportions and magnificent tusks, but he never moved an inch. I could not get round in front of him on account of the wind, and as I did not like to risk the chance of losing so fine a fellow by an uncertain shot that might not prove mortal, after a few seconds' deliberation, I determined to try another plan, which, as I had not a spare gun, was attended with considerable danger.

I examined the ground carefully, so as to be prepared in case I had to make a run for it, and then taking off my leathern gaiters and extraneous clothing, so as to have my limbs as free as possible, noiselessly crept on my hands and knees behind him, and placing the muzzle of my gun almost close to the centre of the hind-foot which was raised, I pulled both triggers almost simultaneously, and sprang out of the way. A shrill shriek of agony followed the double report, and I just escaped a ferocious blow aimed at me with his trunk, being fortunately out of reach. I ran round to the back of the rock before I ventured to look over my shoulder, when, finding he was not on me, I re-loaded as quickly as possible; this done, I felt secure, and again approached the scene of action.

I found my plan had proved completely successful, for my antagonist was entirely disabled. My gun (which was a double two-ounce smooth-bore, by Westley Richards) had been heavily loaded, having about six drachms of powder in each barrel; and the bones of the foot were so completely shattered by the double shot, he could not put it to the ground, and every time he attempted to make a step forward he fell heavily. He must have suffered intense agony, for he uttered most piteous cries between his bursts of rage. As I approached, he strove to charge with a shriek of despair, but he fell heavily to the ground, and, as he was rising to his knees, I stepped up and discharged both barrels into the hollow over the trunk, the contents of which penetrating the brain, he fell "never to rise again."

After having taken a cursory survey of "the spoils of the fallen," and made an estimate in my own mind as to the probable weight of the ivory, I hastily reloaded, and retraced my steps towards the spot where I had left Googooloo. A shrill whistle twice repeated soon brought him to my side, and I learnt that my shots, being so far distant, had hardly disturbed the herd, for most of them were still browsing in the same place. He showed me the spoor of another bull, which we followed for nearly a mile up a narrow ravine, or rather gorge, in the mountain, where we found him drinking in a rocky nullah, and accompanied by two females. After having watched his movements for a few moments, I saw that it was advisable to gain the opposite bank, as it was much higher, and afforded good cover. This I accomplished, after some trouble, for the underwood was very thick, by making a circuitous route, crossing the stream some distance to leeward, and creeping along the banks of the nullah until I got behind a tree, about thirty paces from the group.

Although I kept well under cover, I could see, from the elephants' movements, that their suspicions had been aroused, for they kept sniffing about with their trunks, as if they were aware that "there was something strange in the wind."

At last the bull moved forward a couple of paces, and stretched out his trunk, as if to discover from whence the taint in the air proceeded, at the same time fully presenting his broad forehead to my view. This was the opportunity I sought. I took a steady aim at the vulnerable spot, just over the root of the trunk, and dropped him with a single ball, like a rabbit riddled with buck-shot.

The females, taken aback at the fall of their companion, rushed trumpeting down the stream, when just at this moment a cry from Googooloo attracted my attention to a crashing of underwood in the jungle close at hand, and I had hardly time to snatch up my second gun as a mighty bull and seven females dashed hurriedly past at a distance of about fifty paces. I threw up my rifle, and, aiming behind the ear, let drive a couple of snap-shots for the chance of stopping him, the last of which took effect, for it brought him to his knees; but he immediately regained his legs, and, separating from the females, tore frantically through the forest, which he made resound with his angry roar.

I snatched my second spare gun from Googooloo, (a heavy two-ounce double rifle,) and, jumping down the bank, ran with all speed to cut him off at the gorge, which was extremely narrow, as the torrent made its way between a huge cleft in the rock, through which I knew he must pass in order to join the rest of the herd. I was running down the bed of the stream, on either side of which rose high banks, when I heard a rattling noise among the stones behind me, and on turning my head I saw the wounded bull tearing after me, with his eyes flashing fire and his tail straight on end, about forty paces distant.

Speed I knew would not avail me; he would have been down upon me before I could have clambered up the bank, so I swung round and dropped on my knee, to take a more steady aim.

On he charged with a fiendish shriek of revenge; I let him come to within fifteen paces, when I let drive, aiming between his eyes (my favourite shot); but whether it was that I was unsteady, being breathless from my run, or that my rifle, which weighed sixteen pounds, was too heavy, I know not; but my left arm dropped the moment I pulled the trigger, (not from nervousness, for I was perfectly cool, and never lost my presence of mind for a moment,) and my shot took effect four inches too low, entering the fleshy part of the root of the trunk instead of penetrating the brain. It failed to stop him, and before I could get out of the way the huge brute was on me; I saw something dark pass over me, felt a severe blow, and found myself whizzing through the air; then all was oblivion.

When I came to, I found myself lying on my face in a pool of blood, which came from my nose, mouth, and ears. Although nearly choked with clotted gore, a sense of my perilous situation flashed across my mind, and I strove to rise and look after my antagonist, but he was nowhere to be seen.

I picked myself up, and although fearfully bruised and shaken, found that no bones were broken. I was lying on the top of the bank, although quite unable to account to myself how I got there.* In the dry bed of the nullah I saw my rifle, and after much painful exertion managed to crawl down and get it. The muzzle was filled with sand, which I cleared out as well as I could; and then, sitting by the edge of the stream, began to wash away the blood and bathe my face and head. Whilst so em-

* The elephant must have flung me a considerable distance with his trunk, as the bank was upwards of six feet high.

A Close Shave.

ployed I heard a piercing shriek, and saw Googooloo rushing towards me, closely followed by the infuriated elephant, who was almost mad from the pain of his wounds. Luckily a hanging branch was in his way, and with the agility of a monkey he caught hold of it, and swung himself up the steep bank, where he was safe.

The elephant, balked of his victim, rushed wildly backwards and forwards two or three times, as if searching for him, and then, with a hoarse scream of disappointment, came tearing down the bed of the nullah. I was directly in his path, and powerless to get out of the way. A moment more and I saw that I was perceived, for down he charged on me with a fiendish roar of vengeance. With difficulty I raised my rifle, and taking a steady aim between his eyes, pulled the trigger—it was my only chance. When the smoke cleared away I perceived a mighty mass lying close to me. At last I had conquered. Soon after this I must have sunk into a swoon, for I hardly remember anything until I found myself lying in my hut, and B—— leaning over me.

It appears that Chineah and the gang had carried me in on a litter, and, finding my body very much swollen from the severe blow I had received, my back being black from the waist upwards, had applied a native remedy, and covered the bruised part with leeches, which had the effect of counteracting the inflammation, although I shall carry their marks to the grave. As it was, I was entirely laid up, and had to return to Ooty to recruit.

B—— sent a part of the gang to fetch in the ivory, which altogether weighed nearly three hundred pounds—not a bad bag for three days' "shekar."

CHAPTER XVIII.

THE GREAT ANNAMULLAY FOREST.—TIGER-HUNTING.

Our plan of operations.—The hunting-grounds.—Preparations. —The journey.—Jungle travelling.—Our bivouac.—A lonely glen.—Signs of game.—The ambuscade.—Foreign signs and jungle melody.—Googooloo gives tongue.—The spoiler spoiled.—An unexpected rencontre.—A wounded tigress.—Her retreat stormed.—Fatal accident.—Retribution.—The Shekarry's grave.

TOWARDS the latter end of May, having become somewhat weary of the commonplace routine of ordinary cantonment-life in Ootacamund, I determined, before the monsoon broke, to have a fortnight's hunting with my old chum B——, in that immense tract of virgin forest which lies to the south of the Neilgherry mountains, and extends over the Annamullay range, and along the Western Ghauts. This region, which in the most recent maps is still left blank as an "unexplored district," is one continuous wilderness of mountains and dense waving forest, veined with broad rivers and streams, extending over an area of several hundreds of square miles, inhabited only by a few wild, uncivilised tribes, said to be the aborigines of the country, who for ages have shrunk from intercourse with the rest of the world, living in hollow trees or caves, and subsisting upon wild fruits, jungle-roots, and such small animals as they can bring down with their arrows.

These woods, in which the sound of an axe is seldom heard, are the haunts of the largest denizens of the forest. Here vast herds of elephants and bison (*Bos gaurus*) wander through the leafy solitudes unmolested; and tigers, panthers, and bears are so numerous, that after nightfall they may be heard in different parts of the jungle howling and calling to each other, with those peculiarly wild and deeply melancholy intonations which appal and strike awe into the hearts of those who are not accustomed to such serenades.

The natives in this part of the country have a strange superstition about these hunting-grounds. They say that in the inmost recesses of the forest, where the eye of man has never yet penetrated, there is a lake, to the banks of which elephants, when they feel the approach of dissolution, go *to die.* Perhaps this popular belief may in some measure be accounted for by the fact, that the body of an elephant that has died a natural death has rarely, if ever, been found in the woods. Some say that the remains of the dead are buried by their companions in the herd.

Hunting trips being every-day occurrences, but little time was required for preparation either by myself or my companion. I examined my battery (which consisted of a pair of double rifles of ten-gauge by Purdey, a pair of double smooth-bores by Westley Richards, carrying two-ounce round balls, and a couple of fowling-pieces), and saw that all were in perfect order, and fitted with ammunition.

I then paraded my "Skekarries," or hunting-gang, which comprised Chineah, Googooloo, Naga, Veerapah, Hassan, the Gooroo, Ali, and Ramasawney, eight stalwart fellows, all well tried and true, and inspected their hunting-gear, clothing, and equipments, so as to make sure that all were in perfect marching trim, and fit to commence a jungle campaign. My baggage ponies having been re-shod, then passed muster with their burdens, consisting of a small hill-tent, carpet, blankets, cooking-apparatus, rice-bags, &c., and finally my dogs, four huge creatures, any two of which would bring a bear to bay, or a hog to a standstill.

In the meantime B—— paid a visit to Framjee's celebrated emporium for what the French term "*comestibles*," and filled out two pairs of large "cowry"* baskets, with everything necessary for the support of the "inner man," at the same time engaging a couple of stout coolies to carry them.

All being in readiness, I gave orders to Chineah,

* Round wicker-baskets, which are slung at each end of a bamboo, and carried over the shoulder.

my head shekarry, to proceed at once, with the gang, guns, and baggage, to a hut I had built on a previous hunting expedition at the top of the Taketty Pass, which was four marches from Ooty, and there await our arrival.

Although this was the hottest season of the year, the temperature on the table-land of the Neilgherry Hills was rarely much over 80°, but knowing from experience that it would be at least 40° higher in the plains, we determined to get over that part of the journey by night, in palanquins, with posted bearers, so as to avoid any unnecessary exposure to the sun, and get fresh to our ground.

Having made arrangements with the police Ameen to this effect, on the next day but one after the departure of our people, we left my snug little domicile, Burnside Cottage, at about three in the afternoon, arriving at the travellers' bungalow, in Metrapollium, at the foot of the Coonoor Pass, by sunset, dined, and afterwards proceeded to Coimbatore, where we remained only a few minutes, and again started for the Annamullay Hills, the base of which we reached by 10 A.M.

Here, to my surprise, I found Chineah, the Gooroo, and one of B——'s followers with our rifles, who informed us that they had come across a couple of Mulchers, (a jungle tribe,) who had taken them to a ravine alive with game of all kinds, which they begged we would try before ascending the Ghauts. At first I did not care to alter my former plan of exploring the table-lands of the Annamullay range, but after a consultation with B——, it was resolved to follow Chineah's advice; so, having donned our hunting-gear, we dismissed our bearers, who returned with the palanquins, to Ooty, shouldered our rifles, and struck off by a jungle-track leading along the base of the hills.

The heat was intense in the extreme, and we perhaps felt it the more, having so lately left the vernal freshness of the hills; but signs of game were to be seen on every side, which encouraged us to proceed, and after what B—— called "a moist tramp" of nearly four hours, we arrived at the dry bed of a mountain torrent, which we followed for nearly three miles through a narrow gorge between two densely-wooded hills. During this part of our route we were entirely sheltered from the oppressive beams of the sun by overarching trees, which were so densely covered with convolvuli, and similar delicate climbers of every colour, as to form an impervious shade overhead; indeed it seemed as if we were traversing a vast leafy bower.

At last, after a good hour's clambering over huge boulders of granite, ledges of rock, and loose shingle, we came to a bed of sand, where we recognised the pugs of two full-grown tigers, and innumerable slots of deer, hog, and jungle-sheep. Here, from a small open glade in the forest, I got a glimpse of our route, and found that we were approaching an apparently insurmountable barrier of mountains by a ravine so deep that nothing but the cloudless blue sky was to be seen overhead; whilst on each side frowned perpendicular cliffs and stupendous peaks, so high that it strained the eye to look upwards to their summits. Whilst we were admiring the impressive grandeur of the scenery, a dull roaring, like distant thunder, caught my ear, and on inquiry Chineah informed me that the sound proceeded from a cascade near which we were to bivouac.

Having rested for a few minutes, we again pushed on, and shortly afterwards fell in with the rest of the gang and a party of Mulchers, who were busily engaged in the construction of a bamboo hut under an overhanging rock, which formed an impervious shelter against the piercing beams of the sun.

Feeling exhausted with our fag, after having paid a visit to B——'s investment in the cowry-boxes, and partaken of sundry refreshing drinks, we resolved to look out for a suitable place for a bathe, and strolled along the tortuous and winding bed of the watercourse for a short distance, until we came to a huge plateau of granite overlooking a wild, rocky glen, or cleft in the mountain, which looked as if it had been torn asunder by some convulsion of nature, for on three sides rose perpendicular cliffs, so high that the gigantic forest-trees which fringed the scarped edge of their summits looked diminutive as ferns. From the rugged side of one of these giddy heights, a mountain stream came gushing down, roaring like distant thunder, as it fell foaming and boiling upon massive boulders of rocks below, and causing a misty vapour to arise, in which numberless mimic rainbows appeared and vanished with magical rapidity. At the base of the fall was a clear pellucid pool, about two hundred yards in diameter, surrounded by live rocks of gray granite, rising high above the water's edge, except upon the side near which we were standing, where there was a shelving bank of sand.

"What a glorious place that is for a dip, in the shade of those overhanging rocks!" cried B——, after we had gazed for some moments upon the romantic beauty of the scene.

"Yes," I replied, "if we are sure that it is not infested with 'muggers,' (alligators,) but I must confess I should not like to venture the first plunge until I have made a careful examination of the bank, for I never saw a more likely-looking spot for such kind of vermin."

"You do not say so," replied he. "By Jove! how lucky it is that you are with me, for, had I been alone, I should most assuredly have taken a header into that clear part without ever dreaming that such horrid brutes could be concealed in so lovely a spot."

"I have often met with them in such places," said I. "However, we can soon find out if there are any trails or prints of their claws upon the sand, where they are most likely to bask when the sun enters the ravine at mid-day, and if we do not find any, we will send in the dogs to make sure; but until this has been done I should advise you to confine your ablutions to 'chatties' (earthen pots) of water on shore." So, sending Chineah for the dogs, we clambered down the rock, and strolled by the sand along the edge of the water.

Here we saw the fresh pugs of two tigers, a cheetah, and several bears, besides the old spoors of elephant and bison, with innumerable slots of different kinds of deer, including the "Sambur" or black Rusa deer, commonly called the Indian elk, (*Rusa Aristoteles;*) the "Chetel" or spotted deer, (*Cervus Axis;*) and the "Muntjac" or jungle-sheep, (*Cervus Muntjac;*) besides the marks of a sounder of hog, a pack of jackals, peacocks, and jungle-fowl; but I could not distinguish any trail of alligators.

It was evident that this was the place where most of the wild animals of the surrounding jungle came to slake their thirst, so I determined to build a moat, or place of ambuscade, on a huge isolated boulder of black rock, which commanded all approach to the water within easy range of our rifles. As the sides were scarped we had some trouble to get to the top, which was covered with bush, thorny brambles, and creepers, but with the aid of our axes we soon cleared a space sufficiently large for three or four of us to lie down at full length, on which we constructed a kind of hut, by stretching a "combley" blanket over poles, and covering the outside with creepers, so as to make it resemble a bush from below, leaving loopholes all round to fire through; we then manufactured a rest for our rifles, and a bamboo ladder to go up and down more easily, after which we carpeted the interior, and furnished it with a couple of mattresses, pillows, and sundry refreshments.

Whilst we were busy preparing our ambuscade, a young buck spotted-deer came out of one of the "runs" leading towards the water, within pistol-shot distance, and was leisurely proceeding to drink, when he caught sight of some of our people down below, which startled him. He stopped, threw back his head, pawed the ground, and coolly retraced his steps, apparently but little alarmed at the sight of man. Had our rifles been near at hand, he might not have got back so easily, for venison is always desirable, especially when there are many mouths to feed.

I forbade any of our people to go near the pool on the side frequented by the jungle animals, but made them draw what water they required in leathern buckets from the rocks, fearing lest their footsteps might betray our presence.

Our work being completed, we had a refreshing bath, and adjourned to the hut, where we saw the stores distributed, so that each man received his allowance of meat, rice, curry-stuff, "ghee," (clarified butter,) and tobacco.

Having dined, we inspected the arrangements that had been made for the comfortable housing of our people and baggage-animals, and then returned to the ambuscade; Chineah, Naga, and Googooloo accompanying us, to keep a look-out for game, as we ourselves felt too fatigued with our day's fag to depend much on our watchfulness.

As a light air was blowing from us across the water, and we were perfectly concealed from view, some ten feet above the level of the ground, there was no danger of the scent of tobacco being "winded" from the jungle, so we lighted our cheroots, (a most unorthodox proceeding when lying in ambuscade for large game,) and amused ourselves with observing the different species of animal-life that frequented that lonely spot.

The margin of the lake was visited from time to time by different kinds of aquatic birds and water-fowl; amongst which I noticed a flock of flamingoes with their magnificent rose-coloured plumage, stately pelicans, besides ibises, storks, herons, egrets, plovers, sand-larks, and crows, which latter birds assembled in noisy groups, and seemed to revel in the luxury of a bath. A toucan, with its awkward flight, was seen wending its way from tree to tree in search of the reptiles and small birds on which it feeds, and a jungle-cock, whose plumage gleamed like gold in the rays of the declining sun, came with his consorts, and scratched on the ground for food within a dozen yards of our hiding-place.

Each period of the day has its accustomed visitants, every hour has its "certain signs," that can be read and understood by those only to whom jungle voices are familiar, and who, from long habit and experience, have been enabled to observe and mark the systematic order of Nature's handiwork.

During the intense heat of the day, whilst the sun is still high above the meridian, all animated nature seems to yield to his overpowering influence. A strange stillness, a profound silence, reigns throughout the jungle, which in early morning seemed to teem with life and motion. Every living creature disappears into the deepest shade of the woods, in order to escape from the exhausting heat and oppressive glare; except, perhaps, the eagle, hawk, and falcon, who are seen hovering overhead in circles, like specks in the cloudless sky, or skimming, with strange, wild cries, over the tops of the jungle in search of their prey, and the green enamelled dragon-flies that still flit over the water from leaf to leaf. Then the sturdy hunter, overcome with lassitude, suspends his toil, and seeks the grateful shade of some gigantic forest tree or overhanging rock, where he reposes until the mid-day heat is passed, whilst his dog, also sharing in the universal languor which seems at that hour to oppress the whole face of nature, lies panting upon the ground, with his legs extended to the utmost, and his tongue hanging far out of his mouth.

The weary hours roll on, and nature revives; the woods again resound with the melody of the voice of birds; butterflies of varied hue flutter across the open glades; bees flit from flower to flower; and lustrous beetles, exhibiting metallic hues of green and blue, that rival the deepest shades of the emerald and the sapphire, hover round in circles, making a peculiar booming noise from the flutter of their wings. Myriads of insects keep up a perpetual hum in the solitudes of the jungle, and other gentle sounds murmur softly from every side, like spirits in the air, and produce an effect singularly strange, soothing, and dreamy. At times, above this jungle melody, may be distinguished the distant cry of the peacock, the shrill wild note of jungle-fowl, the call of the coppersmith, the tapping of the woodpecker against some hollow tree, the chattering of a troop of monkeys as they pass in the distance, bounding from bough to bough; the peculiarly soft and melancholy note of the turtle-doves, as they flutter in pairs from tree to tree; or the shrill screams of flights of paroquets, whose brilliant plumage shines with exquisite lustre in the light of the sun, as they dash close past, unconscious of danger in their forest home.

As the day declines, birds of all kinds are seen returning homeward from their distant feeding-grounds; pelicans rise heavily on their unwieldy wings from the marshes, and wend their way to their nests on the highest trees in some secluded spot. Flying-foxes leave the shady grove where they have hung suspended during the heat of the day, and are seen in numbers darkening the sky as they roam through the twilight; whilst multitudes of bats flit about in all directions in search of the insects on which they feed.

As the sun sets, moths of all kinds issue from their retreats, and mosquitoes are constantly heard buzzing about, increasing in the audacity of their attacks as the night wears on. The shrill voices of innumerable crickets, the croaking of frogs, and the continual hum of other insects, keep up a perpetual serenade long after darkness has covered the earth. Then is heard the whooping of the great rock-monkeys, the bark of the elk, the mournful howling of the hyena, the unearthly shrieking of jackals, the trumpeting of elephants as they crash through the underwood; at intervals the distant roar of a prowling tiger is re-echoed among the hollow arches of the forest, as he leaves his lair, in its inmost recesses, to search in the plains for prey; and great horned-owls flit past on muffled wings with strange sepulchral cries, like evil spirits of darkness.

All these nocturnal animals return to their haunts in the deep jungle on the first appearance of dawn, when the jungle-cock sounds the "réveille," and pea-fowl are heard in all directions calling to their mates. Herds of bison and deer retire slowly from the open glades where they have pastured during the night, and again seek the shade of the thick cover. As light increases, the notes of the earliest of the feathered songsters are heard; and herons, cranes, and waders, may be seen on high, soaring away in the direction of their feeding-grounds.

At this early hour there is generally a cool breeze, and the morning air is fresh and bracing; but very shortly the whole of the eastern horizon glows with ruddy lustre, and the sun bursts forth in a blaze of living light, and seems to travel on his way in the heavens with much more rapidity than in northern climes. This is the moment for the lover of the beautiful to see the forest, for the dew-drops on the leaves and ground sparkle like brilliants, and at no other time are the varied colours of the verdure so vivid. The lights and shade show to the best advantage, and a peculiarly harmonious charm reigns over the whole face of nature, which must strike upon the heart even of the most apathetic spirit, and make him feel, with the great poet, that

> "There is a pleasure in the pathless woods."

But I am digressing, and must return to our ambuscade, where we were lying at our ease, whilst Chineah and Googooloo kept watch. Numbers of pea-fowl, jungle-fowl, and spur-fowl came to drink from time to time, and their wild cries were heard on every side of the deeply-wooded valley. Presently we heard the low bark of a buck-elk calling to his hinds, and as the sun was sinking below the horizon the roar of a tiger awoke the echoes of the surrounding hills, and was immediately answered by another, at no great distance from the lake. Peafowl took up the cry on every side, and the wood resounded with the voices of wild animals. Chineah and Googooloo smiled grimly at each other as they caught up each cry, and named the animal that it came from, and each gave me a significant look as I proceeded to put fresh caps on my pet rifle, which I had previously carefully loaded.

"You forest music goes cheerily, Hal, and does one more good than all the *sol-fa-ing* we have lately heard at Ooty," whispered B——.

"Yes, Ned, it strikes upon the heart of a ranger of the woods like an old well-loved strain upon a wanderer's ears; but I imagine that we shall have a view of the performers before morning, as the Mulchers say there is no other water about here nearer than the Bowani, and it is evident from the pugs we saw on the sand that they frequent this place."

Just at this moment we heard a movement in the bushes, and an old gray monkey, evidently a scout, came creeping cautiously into the plain. After peering about a few moments in a very inquisitive manner, seeing all appeared clear, he turned towards the woods, uttering a sharp cry, and immediately a whole troop of his followers came leaping and swinging themselves from the trees, screaming, chattering, fighting, and making grimaces at each other, as they rushed frantically to the water's edge to quench their thirst. Then, after gambolling about for a little time, and picking up a few berries, they again disappeared in the woods. Towards dusk two jungle-sheep followed, and remained for some time, but we allowed them to retreat unmolested. Shortly afterwards my attention was attracted by a low grunt from Googooloo, whom I saw cautiously putting his head forward and raising his body, so as to get a better view of something, whilst he motioned to Naga to hand me my rifle.

"Kya hy?" (what is it?) whispered I. Googooloo made no answer, but still continued to strain his eyes in the direction of a large low bush about thirty yards from the place of our concealment, at the same time making a sign with his hand for me to wait. We remained for some minutes in the utmost silence, all of us keeping a look-out through the loopholes, but nothing was to be seen.

"Kuch na hy," (there is nothing,) at length whispered Chineah, who was rather jealous of Googooloo's having drawn attention to a sound which his quick ear had not caught up, and B—— again laid down, fancying it was a false alarm. I, however, remained on the alert, having the same confidence in the Yanadi's warning as a huntsman would have when his best hound gave tongue or a sportsman when his favourite dog made a dead point. I had often previously trusted to his natural instinct and quickness of hearing, and scarcely ever found him wrong, so I kept my eye upon him, prepared to act. Although he maintained a dignified silence, I could see by the contemptuous curl of his lip that he was evidently disgusted with Chineah's remark and vexed at B——'s mistrust; but when he saw, as his eye caught mine, that I believed in him, he gave his accustomed grunt of satisfaction, and continued to peer into the dark-tangled forest before us.

A few minutes passed, when he again turned his head on one side, as if to drink in some fancied sound, and I noticed a grim smile of satisfaction illumine his expressive face as he raised both hands over his eyes as if to get a better view of something. At this moment I caught sound of the light crackling of a twig, and a rustling as if some animal was moving amongst dry leaves, and again was heard Googooloo's low grunt as he pointed to the bush which had before attracted his attention, whispering beneath his breath, "Bagh hy!" (there is a tiger!) I cocked both barrels of my rifle, moved noiselessly forward, and kept it pointed in the direction indicated, but nothing was to be seen, although we waited for many moments in anxious suspense.

Chineah, who twigged the noise this time, now took the Yanadi's right hand and pressed it to his own forehead, a silent acknowledgment that he had been in the wrong, and from the satisfactory smile that passed over Googooloo's face, I could see that peace was made between the two friends and rivals in "forest lore."

"Do you think it was a tiger, Hal?" whispered B——. "I rather suspect it must have been a jungle-fowl scratching up the ground, or a snake gliding amongst the leaves."

"It might have been the latter," I replied, "but jungle-fowl are all gone to roost by this time, and I have often heard a tiger or a panther steal along with as little noise."

For a time an intense quiet reigned, not a leaf stirred, and no sound was heard but the dull monotonous roar of falling waters, or the plaintive cry of a stray plover in search of his companions. The sun had been gone down some time, and the moon, which was then at the full, had not risen sufficiently high for her silvery light to penetrate the deep ravine in which we were.

Both B——'s patience and his cheroot were well-nigh exhausted, and as I saw he could hardly keep himself awake, I bade both him and Chineah sleep whilst Googooloo and myself kept the first watch. We remained for nearly a couple of hours listening anxiously to every sound that issued from the jungle, and although during this time we distinctly heard the growling of a bear just below us, and could distinguish in the gloom the dark forms of a sounder of hog wallowing in the pool, still there was not sufficient light to take aim, and I did not pull trigger. At last the moon appeared over the scarped crest of the mountain, sailing in a cloudless sky—a flood of light glistened like silver on the lake, and caused every object to be seen as distinctly as at noon-day.

Struck with the fairy-like beauty of the scene before me, I became absorbed in thought, from which I was roused by Googooloo laying his hand on my shoulder and pointing to something standing in the shade of a lofty forest tree. At the same moment I heard the low short bark of a spotted deer, and a fine buck with broad-spreading antlers came forcing his way through the tangled brushwood, and stood before us in bold relief. I threw up my rifle, brought the sight to bear upon his shoulder, and was just about to pull trigger when a huge monster of a tiger sprang from the very bush that Googooloo had been so attentively watching, and fastened upon his shoulder with a low growl. Like a flash of lightning my trusty rifle belched forth its deadly contents right and left: a roar, a smothered whine, followed the double report, and the stricken brute rolling over and over was gasping in its last agonies. A convulsive movement was succeeded by a stifled groan, a moaning cry, a bubbling sound, and all was still.

"What have you killed, Hal?" cried B——, awakened by the shots, and cocking his rifle. "Ha! ha! I see—a fine pair of horns too—but he is not dead," he continued, raising his piece and putting an end to the poor buck, who was still struggling on the spot where he had been struck down.

"Look a little to the right, Ned, under the shade of the bush," replied I, "and you will see the result of my shots—he felled the deer."

"A *yaller hair,* by the powers!" exclaimed B——. "Well, you are in luck; but it serves me right for not believing in the Yanadi's warning."

"Yes, Googooloo was not mistaken, for the tiger must have been lying in wait in that bush for some hours before," I replied, as I finished reloading. We then descended from our place of concealment, and were examining the dead tiger, when Naga, whom I had sent to the hut to call up some of the people to help to carry away the carcass, came rushing back with fear depicted on his countenance, exclaiming that he had seen another tiger.

Beckoning Chineah and Googooloo to follow with spare guns, we both rushed down the pathway that the people had cut through the bush, as a short way to the hut, in which Naga said he had come face to face with the tiger, and sure enough there were the pugs close to the prints of Naga's toes. The tiger must have been as much astonished at the rencontre as the man, for he had evidently turned back, as we could tell by the trail.

Whilst we were examining the pugs, in order to note which direction he had taken, my attention was attracted by a low whimper, followed by a yawn, which appeared to proceed from the bed of the watercourse, and after some little trouble we forced our way through the thick underwood to the bank, from whence we saw a tigress coolly picking her way among the stones, in the bed of the "nullah," (watercourse.) We put up our rifles and both fired at the same moment; uttering a deep angry growl, she fell forward, evidently hard hit, although the distance was nearly two hundred yards, and the light none of the best. When she rose, I thought her foreleg seemed to dangle from the shoulder as if broken, but she still went on, notwithstanding we let fly again and evidently hit her, for she gave a terrific roar and turned short round as if to charge, but her heart seemed to fail, and she slunk into some cover close at hand in the centre of the nullah.

"The light is not good enough for accurate shooting at this range, Hal," said B——, as we were reloading our rifles, "but I do not think she can travel far. I am sure she carries lead in her."

"Of that there can be no doubt," I replied, "as I heard the soft 'thud' of the bullet distinctly; however, we will follow her up, for I saw her enter that isolated patch of bush in the nullah, from which it would be an easy matter to drive her out with a few rockets. I was only considering whether we had not better wait until daylight, when we could almost make sure of her, for the moon will only favour us a short time longer, as the gorge will be in darkness as soon as she sinks below yon wall of rock."

"No time like the present, Hal," cried B——, climbing down the steep bank into the bed of the nullah; "so send Naga to the hut for rockets and some of the people, whilst you, I, and Googooloo watch the cover in case she may attempt to steal away."

Knowing from experience the difficulty of making accurate shooting by the light of the moon, which is very deceitful, it was with some reluctance that I ordered Chineah to take a rifle and go with Naga to the hut for the rest of the gang, and I regretted it almost as soon as I had done so, for I felt a strange presentiment of some accident occurring, being aware of the extreme danger of beating out a wounded tiger from thick cover in such an uncertain light; however, I determined to take every precaution, and clambering down into the nullah, followed by Googooloo, we watched each side of the cover in which the tigress had been seen to enter, until Chineah and the rest of the gang, accompanied by our coolies, joined us. We then formed up in line, B—— taking the right and I the left flank, with Chineah well provided with rockets in the centre, and all the rest armed with the short spears they generally carried when beating the jungle.

Having distinctly warned them not on any account to straggle or separate, and seen that our spare guns were at hand, we moved into the cover, which, although not more than fifty yards long by twenty broad, was very dense, being covered with low tangled bushes and coarse grass about four feet high. We could easily have driven the tigress out by firing the grass, but I did not do so as the blaze would have scared all the game away from the surrounding jungles. We had beaten our way steadily through almost half the patch, when we heard a low grumbling, which appeared to proceed from a large bush much overgrown with creepers and high spear-grass.

"Dekho! sahib, dekho!" (look, sir, look!) cried Chineah, throwing a couple of lighted rockets into the retreat, which evidently annoyed her, although they had not the effect of causing her to break—for she set up a low angry growl which lasted some time. Two or three times I thought I saw the bush shake as if she was about to spring, and once I caught a hurried glimpse of her outline, and threw up my rifle, but I put it down again as I did not like to fire a chance shot with uncertain aim.

Again Chineah's rockets flew hissing about her, and one of them caused her to move, for B—— caught sight of her, and let drive right and left when out she sprang with an appalling roar, and struck down poor Ali, who, notwithstanding my orders, had separated himself from the rest in order to pick up a stone to throw into the bush. His piercing death-shriek rang through the night air, striking terror on every heart; and, although I felt that I was too late to save him, I determined he should be amply revenged, and dashed forward towards the spot where the infuriated tigress was savagely growling, as she still shook the senseless but quivering body of her victim. No sooner did I get a glimpse of her than I knew that I was perceived, for with a short angry roar she left the corpse and crouched low to the ground, with her head down, her back arched, and her tail lashing her heaving flanks. At this moment, before she could make a spring that might have proved fatal, carefully aiming between her eyes, which glared upon me like balls of fire, I let drive—she reared up full length on her hind-legs, pawed the air, and fell back dead.

Vengeance satiated, I went up to poor Ali, whom I found shockingly mutilated; his death must have been instantaneous, as the tigress, with the first blow of her paw, had crushed in the skull (for the brains lay scattered about the place) and then made her teeth meet in his throat and shoulder, breaking the arm in two places, and lacerating the fleshy part of the thigh.

B—— and the gang came up shortly afterwards, and long and loud were their lamentations, for Ali was much liked by them all, and a great favourite with his master, to whom he had ever proved a willing and devoted follower.

We bound up his head, covered his face with a cloth, and by the aid of our axes constructed a litter of bamboos, on which we carried him towards the hut, where Yacoob Khan, Hassan, and Cassim, B——'s "kidmudjar," (butler,) who were also Mussulmans, performed the last rites of "the Faithful;" and we buried him in a deep grave, under an overhanging rock near the lake, in which the nose, whis-

Retribution.

kers, and claws of the tigress had been previously thrown.

To show our respect to the memory of the shekarry who had come to such an unfortunate end, we all attended, and, at the request of the gang, three volleys were fired over his grave. Strange to say, that hardly had the echoes of the last report died away, rumbling amongst the hills, than the roaring of another tiger was distinctly heard several times.

Whilst the grave was being filled in, many of the gang were much affected, but not a word was uttered by any except Chineah, who, with his eyes still streaming with tears for the loss of his companion, pronounced the following oration:—"*Boht utcha Shekarry tha, lakin murgia, kya kurna? Nusseeb hy.*" (He was a very good Shekarry, but he is dead —what can we do? It is his fate.) Then each man fetching a large stone, placed it reverentially over the grave, so as to form a kind of cairn, and making salaam to both of us, returned to the hut, we following with heavy hearts. As it still wanted some hours to dawn, we turned into bed; but that fearful death-shriek still rang in my ears, and, although tired and weary, I could not sleep.

CHAPTER XIX.

THE GREAT ANNAMULLAY FOREST—*continued.*
BISON-HUNTING.

Our hut.—A gigantic carp.—Fish-shooting.—His dimensions.—Discovery of a cave; an exploring party.—The tiger's spoils.—His dimensions.—"Away with melancholy."—Chineah's *reconnaissance* and bag.—Our open council.—Jungle harmony.—Our proceedings and plan for the morrow.—The turn-out.—The start.—A hard fag.—A fresh trail of bison struck.—Googooloo has the ear of a hare.—Two buck-elk and a hind bite the dust.—We follow up the bison's trail.—Heavy work.—Land-leeches.—The find.—A heavy bag and a good day's work.—The gigantic dimensions of the patriarch of the herd.—The game bushed.—Again *en route*.—A teak forest.—The head of the fall.—Magnificent views.—Our bivouac.

BEING fatigued with our night adventure and the previous day's fag, it was late in the afternoon before either B—— or myself made our appearance outside the tent, which, notwithstanding the intense heat of the weather, was comparatively cool and comfortable, being completely shaded from the scorching rays of the sun by the overhanging rocks above.

Chineah, Googooloo, and a couple of Mulchers had gone into the forest to reconnoitre and look out for trails, and the Gooroo and the rest of the gang were busily engaged in denuding the dead tigers of their spoils.

After breakfast we strolled towards the lake, where we found Hassan, who attracted our attention to an enormous fish which lay basking as if asleep on the surface of the water, whilst several others of the same species, but smaller, kept rising from time to time in different parts of the pool. He informed us that he had been trying for several hours to catch one of these monsters with a rod, but that they were too cunning to take any bait. Knowing from experience that Hassan was a first-rate fisherman, I felt sure that I (who at the best of times am but a bungler with the rod) should have a poor chance of succeeding if he could not, so I left B—— to amuse himself with bait and fly, whilst I returned to the hut to make preparations more in my line.

I took a common musket which Chineah used for wild-fowl shooting, and to the centre of the iron ramrod I firmly attached a piece of double wire, about two yards in length, to the end of which I fastened a strong log-line. This done, I loaded the piece with powder and a thick felt-wadding, and then inserted the ramrod, with the flat head downwards, keeping it in its place in the centre of the bore with a second wad which fitted tightly in the muzzle.

My preparations completed, I returned to the

pool, and creeping up as cautiously as possible, I got to within twenty paces of the huge fellow who was so coolly enjoying his "siesta," took steady aim and fired. The ramrod flew like an arrow true to the mark, passing through the fish and dragging the wire and part of the line with it. Immediately the creature found itself wounded it sprang high out of the water, and then dived, pulling so hard that our hands were badly cut with the cord running so fast through them as we gave him play.

For some time it raced round and round the pool, but at length seemed to grow exhausted, and allowed us to pull it to the surface of the water, when, as if endued with fresh vigour, it gave another great spurt, and again spun round and round, until at times I felt afraid that the cord would break. After a good hour's play it turned on its belly and gave in, and we managed to land it with some trouble, on account of the great weight.

It was evidently of the carp species, having large round scales, one dorsal fin, forked tail with rounded lobes, and yellow olive sides, deepening to black on the back. Not having any scales at hand, we could not determine its weight exactly, but I constructed a rude pair with some ropes and a bamboo accurately suspended in the centre, and by that we made out the weight to be about sixty-three pounds, as it weighed down two bags and a quarter of shot, which were supposed to hold twenty-eight pounds when full. The flesh proved to be coarse, rank, and tough, but some of the gang, who made part of it into a curry, said it was not bad eating.

As we were strolling about the ravine with our rifles whilst the gang were engaged in skinning the dead tigress, B—— discovered the entrance of a cave in the scarped overhanging cliff near our hut, and having nothing better to do we determined to explore it. Naga and Ramasawmy were accordingly despatched for torches, blue-lights, matches, &c., and after carefully examining our rifles so as to be ready in case we found it tenanted by bears or hyenas, (not an unlikely occurrence,) we crept in, Naga leading with a torch, I following with B——, and Ramasawmy with another torch bringing up the rear.

The entrance was about four feet high and three broad, but it shortly became much more lofty, and from the light of our torches we saw numbers of pointed stalactites hanging from the roof in every direction, which threw perplexing shadows as we advanced, and every now and then made us think that some animal was moving towards us.

After proceeding for about forty yards, we came to a vast chamber, where we were very much annoyed by myriads of small bats that, alarmed at our intrusion, came dashing up against our faces, and almost put out the torches.

Having peered about carefully to make sure there were no beasts of any kind likely to molest us, I lighted a couple of blue-lights, which enabled us to see every part of the grotto distinctly. The cavern appeared to be about seventy yards long by forty wide, and varying from ten to sixty feet in height; it was vaulted with live rock covered all over with elegantly-formed stalactites which glittered like brilliants from the reflection of the blue-lights. The ground was very uneven, and covered with fine sand, except on one side, where there were enormous boulders of black granite. We saw several fissures and crevices, which appeared to be passages stretching out further in different directions into the bowels of the earth, but did not care to explore them on account of the close heat and insupportable stench, as well as for fear of snakes and scorpions, several of which reptiles we discerned moving about the place.

We therefore wrote our names and the date on a huge slab of smooth rock with charcoal, for the benefit of any one who might come after us, and retraced our steps into daylight, glad to breathe the fresh air once more.

We found that the Gooroo and Veerapah had finished skinning the tigress, and were busily engaged in searching for our bullets; she had received five wounds, besides the last, which entered between the eyes and penetrated the brain, causing instantaneous death. The tiger had been skinned in the morning, having been previously carried some distance away from the lake for fear the scent of blood might taint the air, and prevent other animals from approaching the spot to drink. He proved to be a fine specimen, his dimensions being as follows:—Length from tip of nose to point of tail, 10 feet 2 inches; length of tail, 3 feet 1 inch; girth of body, 6 feet 1 inch; girth round fore-arm, 2 feet 10 inches; height at shoulder, 3 feet 9 inches; circumference of head, 3 feet 5 inches. The tigress was much less, not measuring more than 9 feet 5 inches from the tip of the nose to the point of the tail, and her limbs smaller in proportion.

The melancholy fate of poor Ali had spread a gloom upon us all, and the camp, which usually resounded with mirth, seemed strangely still and silent; so, to give the people something else to think about, I ordered a couple of sheep to be killed and distributed with an extra allowance of tobacco, which had the desired effect, for in the course of a short time cooking-pots and brass curry-dishes were boiling and bubbling on every side, and the busy hum of voices was heard throughout the bivouac as usual.

Towards evening, Chineah and his party returned from their *reconnaisance* with three young "squeakers," (hog,) which the dogs had captured alive, and they reported that they had come across a large herd of bison, browsing in some bamboo-jungle half-way up the hill, and had left them undisturbed, so that we should most likely find them near the place on the morrow.

After having dined substantially upon a prime haunch of roast venison, and grilled sucking-pig, we adjourned to our camp-fire, which was lighted in a deep cleft of the rock, where it could not be well seen at any distance from the surrounding jungle; and here we found the gang and all our people assembled, according to their usual custom when out in the jungle on a "Shekar" expedition. The Gooroo and Veerapah were enlivening the party with some extemporary chanting, and at the same time accompanying themselves on the "sitarr" and "sarinda," * whilst Chineah and the coolies performed on tomtoms, and Ramasawmy gave occasional discordant flourishes on the cholera horn, which we were obliged to decline, as B—— declared it would make his dinner disagree with him.

As we took our seats on a carpet spread over a heap of dry leaves which had been prepared for us, the concert ceased, and each man produced his pannikin or cocoa-nut shell, for it was my custom to give every one in camp a glass of rakee, and tobacco or cheroot, when we assembled in council round the camp-fire in the evening to consult as to the morrow's proceedings. As soon as the grog had been served out, and all were enjoying the fragrant weed, I opened the proceedings by expressing my regret that such an untoward event should have befallen the gang as to lose one of their number; but I explained to them that poor Ali had lost his life by disobeying my positive orders in foolishly straggling from the rest, and I hoped his sad fate would be a warning to the gang to be more careful in future.

* Rude instruments somewhat resembling the violin and guitar.

I also suggested that the gang should each subscribe some small sum towards making up a purse for his father, (an old pensioned Havildar,) to which B—— and I would contribute a hundred rupees; and I was glad to see that when Chineah went round with his cocoa-nut shell, every one present, even to the coolies, put in his rupee or whatever he could afford.

We then proceeded to deliberate on the plan for the morrow, and to detail each man his duty. Veerapah and Naga, with two Mulchers, were to ascend the Ghaut on the left, to find out if the Carders (a jungle tribe who inhabited that side of the mountain) had seen any elephants lately, and afterwards to join us at the head of the fall. Hassan was to go into Coimbatore with notes from B—— to K—— and C——, informing them of our whereabouts, in case they could manage to join our party. Ramasawmy was to continue the preparation of the skins, and Chineah, Googooloo, and two Mulchers were to accompany us in a trip up the side of the ravine, where the herd of bison had been seen. These matters being settled, we sat smoking and chatting for a couple of hours, and then turned in.

Next morning the moon had only just set, and there was but a slight tinge of gray in the eastern sky, when my factotum "Five Minutes" entered the hut with hot coffee flavoured with eau-de-vie, which is the best morning-cup for a sportsman when in the jungle, as it prevents any ill effects arising from inhaling the vapour which still hangs upon the ground at that early hour. Our toilet was soon completed, and on stepping outside the hut we found the gang all wrapped up in their combleys and couched over a wood-fire, for the early morning was damp and chilly; so I ordered a glass of grog to be served out, and Chineah distributed the spare guns, blankets, stores, &c., that each had to carry in case of our being benighted in the jungle, which was a common occurrence.

In tropical climates the interval between the first faint glimmering of dawn and daylight is very short, and as soon as we could distinguish objects pretty clearly we entered the forest, where we heard jungle-cocks already crowing merrily.

The first living creatures we encountered were two great hooded-owls, who, like drowsy revellers after their nightly carouse, sailed hooting past, leisurely flapping their wings as they returned to their haunts in some hollow tree. Shortly afterwards we surprised a troop of monkeys who were evidently making their way towards the pool for a morning draught, but who fled, skipping from branch to branch, chattering and showing their teeth as soon as they detected our presence. Every now and again the dun sides of deer flashed for an instant before us, as they bounded across the open vistas of the forest and disappeared in the dense cover. The fresh morning air was loaded with the perfume of different flowering jungle-plants, and the forest resounded with the melody of feathered songsters.

We followed the trail that Chineah's party had made in their *reconnaisance* the day before, and after an hour's painful climbing up the dry bed of a mountain-torrent, filled with loose round stones which rolled from under the feet at every step, and somewhat tried our powers as mountaineers, we arrived at a natural clearing in the midst of the dense forest, where the gang had seen the bison browsing the day before. We examined the ground carefully, and found numbers of old marks, but no fresh ones, so we continued our route up the side of the mountain, and after a couple of hours' severe toil found ourselves in a patch of bamboo-jungle, where Chineah detected the fresh trail of a herd of bison.

Being thoroughly exhausted and done up with our exertions, we sat down upon a ledge of rock to regain our breath and rest ourselves before following up the trail, and were indulging in the indescribable luxury of weak brandy-panee and cheroots, never more enjoyed than in the jungle, when an exclamation from Googooloo caused us both to jump on our feet and seize our rifles that were leaning at our heads against a tree. I made a motion to our people to lie flat on the ground, and listened for a couple of minutes without hearing anything; but a glance at Googooloo's speaking features told me that he had caught sound of something, and I remained on the alert.

Just at that moment we heard a sharp bark,

which I knew came from an elk, and, stealing as gently as possible to a ledge of rock which commanded a view of the slope, I had the satisfaction of beholding a herd of sambur feeding in a glade about eighty yards below us. A fine stag with sweeping antlers was grazing, unconscious of danger, within easy range, and a second was lying down in the shade chewing the cud, surrounded by hinds.

"Now, Ned," whispered I to B——, who had joined me, "take that fellow well behind the shoulder, and he 's your own."

He raised his rifle, took deliberate aim, fired, and the stag, leaping with a convulsive bound high into the air, fell dead. The second hart, startled by the shot, sprang on his feet, and threw up his head with a wild snort, which gave me a fair shot, and I sent a two-ounce ball crashing into his brain, when he tumbled heavily forward in the high grass; and, without removing the rifle, I brought the sight to bear upon a fat doe, and dropped her with a broken shoulder; but she immediately regained her feet, and would have given us a long run, or perhaps have got off altogether, if B—— had not given her the contents of his second barrel, which again rolled her over, and, whilst she was struggling, Chineah sprang forward and buried his long knife in her chest. Her dark, languid eye rolled wildly round for a moment, and distending her wide nostrils, she gasped painfully for breath, heaved a convulsive sigh, stretched out her limbs, and all was still.

We immediately set to work and broke up the deer; and, after reserving a portion for present use, slung the remainder by creepers to the branch of a tree, tying a red pocket-handkerchief like a streamer to keep off the vultures, who otherwise would soon have scented it out and left us nothing but the bones. I also despatched one of the Mulchers with the heads to the hut, as the horns were good, giving him orders to collect some of his tribe to carry down the venison, and leave the skins with my servants.

This little matter arranged, we followed up the spoor of the bison, and in a little time fell in with the trail of a large herd, which, from unmistakable signs, we knew could not be far in advance.

It was very lucky that we came provided with leech-gaiters, made of very fine long stockings, which we wore over our ordinary hose and breeches, and under the gaiters, as we found the land-leeches swarming in the damp grass and rank vegetation. These pests of the jungle are very insignificant in size, not being above an inch in length, or thicker than a knitting-needle, but when distended with blood they attain double that length, and are about as thick as a good-sized quill. They have the power of planting one extremity on the ground, and poising themselves erect to watch for prey, towards which they advance rapidly by doubling up the body and holding on with their head and tail. They are of a yellowish-brown colour, streaked with black, with one greenish line along the whole length of the back, and a yellow one on each side. Their bites scarcely give any pain at the time, the punctures being so small as hardly to be perceptible, but they cause an uncomfortable irritation, and with persons in a bad state of body often occasion nasty ulcers, which are slow to heal. The gang were accustomed to smear their naked legs with some peculiar kind of grease mixed with ashes, the scent of which prevented the leeches from biting, otherwise they would have been seriously inconvenienced by their attacks.

After following the trail for some miles, Chineah and Googooloo, who were creeping along a ragged hollow, which appeared to have been the pathway of an impetuous torrent, some little distance in front, made a sign to us to keep silent, and shortly afterwards they beckoned us to advance. With great caution we crept noiselessly forward, stopping from time to time to listen, and after crawling on our hands and knees for nearly a hundred yards, we gained the crest of the hill, where we had the satisfaction of seeing a large herd of bison quietly browsing on the green herbage in a patch of open teak-forest.

Having satisfied myself that we were well to leeward, and in no danger of being discovered by their remarkably keen scent, I raised myself cautiously behind the trunk of a tree to reconnoitre ; and after pointing out to B—— a fine bull, who, surrounded with cows, was lazily nibbling the young and tender shoots of a clump of bamboos, about a hundred yards distant, I begged him to reserve his fire until he heard my signal, as I intended to try and stalk the patriarch of the herd, a stately fellow with enormous dew-lap and immensely deep shoulders, who was pawing the ground fretfully, and uttering deep cries as if impatient for the herd to retire to the depths of the jungle for shelter from the rays of the sun, which were beginning to feel oppressive.

I descended a short distance down the side of the hill, and crept along the brow until I got under the cover of a clump of bamboos, whence I again caught sight of him. Here I had nearly been discovered, for two cows and a young calf sprang up close to me, and rushed tail on end towards the rest of the herd, who lifting up their heads seemed to gaze anxiously in my direction. I therefore remained a few moments perfectly quiet, keeping my eye upon the mighty bull who was standing about three hundred yards distant; and when I saw that their alarm had in some degree subsided, I crept gently forward, and, taking advantage of any cover I could find, managed to ensconce myself behind a large rhododendron-bush within a hundred and twenty yards of him.

I then blew a shrill blast on a silver call I always wore round my neck, as a signal to B——, and shortly afterwards heard a double shot, followed by three others. The first report attracted the bull's attention, and he trotted forward a few paces to reconnoitre, tearing up the turf with his hoofs, and lashing his tail as if indignant that his sylvan retreat should be intruded upon. Whilst in this position he offered me a fair view of his brawny shoulder, and I planted a heavy cylindro-conical bullet just behind it, which brought him to his knees with a surly roar. Mad with pain he regained his feet, and staggered forward on three legs, when I gave him the contents of my second barrel in nearly the same place, which rolled him over. Chineah now handed me my other rifle, and I quitted the cover; when no sooner did he catch sight of me than again springing up, with a deep tremulous roar, he charged headlong at me, tail on end, his eyes flashing fire, and mouth covered with blood and foam. I let him come to within six paces of where I was standing, when I stopped his mad career with a ball in the centre of his broad massive forehead, which again made him bite the dust: he gave a desperate plunge forward, and rolled heavily over on his side dead. The others, alarmed, were now tearing frantically over the plain, so I slipped behind the cover of a bush to reload, and again stealing forward, managed to bowl over a cow and wound another badly, before the terrified herd sought safety in flight by rallying in a body and crashing through the dense bamboo-jungle which clothed the side of the hill. After reloading, I despatched the second cow with a bullet behind the horns, as she was lying disabled by my first

THE DEATH OF A BULL BISON.

shot, which had passed through the small of her back and paralysed her hind-quarters.

I now looked out for B—— and Googooloo, who were nowhere to be seen, but a dead cow and a young bull-calf showed that they had not been idle. Whilst I was examining the latter, and cogitating upon veal-cutlets and marrow-bones, I heard two double shots in the cover just below the crest of the hill, which were immediately followed by a loud whoop from B——; and on running up I found him standing breathless over the carcass of a huge bull, which was evidently just killed.

"By Jove! Hal," exclaimed he, as I approached, "I'm regularly done up; this brute has led me such a chase. I hit him fairly between the eyes, and doubled him up like a rabbit with buck-shot, for he dropped without a struggle, dead, as I thought, and I paid no more attention to him; but letting drive at the herd as they bolted away, I killed a cow and a calf and wounded a third, when suddenly my friend picked himself up, shook his head savagely, gave an angry grunt, and charged right at me. Every barrel being discharged, I stepped on one side and got out of his way, when he directed his attention to Googooloo, who dodged him amongst the trees easily enough; for, half-blinded with blood from his wound, he reeled and tumbled about as if he was groggy, every now and then falling heavily. As soon as I had reloaded I gave chase, but all at once missed him, and it was only just now that the Yanadi pointed him out to me in this clump of high grass, where he had cunningly lain down to conceal himself. As I came up he again charged, when, stepping aside, I allowed him to pass, and gave him the contents of both barrels well behind the shoulder, which brought him up, and to make sure of him this time I administered a couple of pills in the back of the head as he lay writhing and gasping upon the ground; and here he is safe enough. But what have you done?"

"About the same as yourself," I answered; "I have killed the big bull and a couple of cows, which makes six bison and three elk bagged. Not a bad day's work for two guns."

"No, indeed," replied B——; "would it no make the folks at home stare?"

"*Mulcher log boht kush honga, Sahib!*"—"The Mulcher people will be very happy, sir!" exclaimed Chineah; "there will be meat in their huts for many days to come, and the gentlemen's great shekar will be spoken of for a long time in far off jungles."

"Yes, Chineah," I replied; "I dare say we shall soon have more mouths to fill, but remember you impress upon the minds of the Coorchi moopen * of the Carders, and the head men of the Mulchers, that in return for the game we give them I shall expect to hear of elephants."

* A high priest, or rather "holy-man" of a tribe.

"*Ho ba-shuck, Sahib!*"—"Yes, without doubt, sir; the tribes will build 'jopreys' (huts made of branches) near our camp, and we can send the men into the jungle every day to look out for trails."

"All right," I replied, "that's your affair; in the meantime hand me the tape, and come and help me to measure the other *kulgha*, (bull-bison,) as I think it is the largest I have ever killed."

So saying we retraced our steps to the big bull, and, with the aid of a straight bamboo, I took the exact dimensions and entered them in my note-book as follows:—

"Perpendicular height from the bottom of the hoof to the top of the shoulder, not following the curve of the body, 6 feet 4 inches; height to the top of hump, 6 feet 9 inches; length of body from the tip of nose to insertion of tail, 11 feet 4 inches; length of tail, 3 feet 4 inches; girth of body, 9 feet 3 inches; girth of fore-arm, 2 feet 10 inches; girth of neck, 4 feet 10 inches; breadth of forehead, 2 feet 5 inches; circumference round base of horns, 1 foot 9 inches; length of horns, 1 foot 4 inches; colour, black along the back, light dun under the belly and inside the thighs, the legs below the knees and hocks dirty white; the cows much less in proportion, with hardly any hump or dewlap, the head smaller and more graceful."

"Well, Hal," exclaimed B——, as we finished measuring the gigantic animal; "I think there are few finer fellows than this even in the whole Wynaad

Jungle: he is fully two inches higher than any we have hitherto met with, and both you and I have tumbled over a good few in our time too. What a farce to compare the American buffalo with this stately fellow, nineteen hands at the shoulder, and twenty and an inch extreme height. I wonder what the folks at Smithfield would think of him."

"I wish we had the little stock we have bagged this morning, Ned, in that neighbourhood," I answered; "they would be worth a twelvemonth's pay and allowances to us, and as a contrast we might also exhibit at the same time a 'Yak,'—for the smallest as well as the largest of the genus *Bos* are to be found in Hindostan,—the bison being over twenty hands and the yak not exceeding nine. But, Ned, we have yet a good trudge before we reach the head of the Fall, and I do not think we shall have more than four or five hours' daylight, so we had better set the people to cut thorns and bamboo-stakes at once to cover the animals, so as to scare away the jackals, and then make the best of our way."

"All right," replied he; "we'll blow a cloud whilst they are at work, for it would be a pity to have the skins spoiled, they would cover us such a famous basket-boat to float down to the coast in, by the Bowani and Cauvery;" which latter flows into the sea near Tranquebar, passing through the towns of Trichinopoly, Tanjore, and Combaconum *en route*.

After having cut out the tongues, which we generally salted, and packed up a few marrow-bones, we superintended the "bushing" of the game, and shouldering our rifles again made a start. We followed a course parallel to the crest of the ravine, taking care not to go too close to the edge, as the turf was smooth and slippery, and in some places we might have fallen several thousand feet before reaching the ground.

We now entered a forest of gigantic teak-trees, so dense that the rays of the sun never penetrated, and the light resembled faint and dubious twilight. None but those who have explored an Indian forest could have any conception of the depth of gloom and strange silence that pervades these solitudes. Emerging from the dense forest-jungle that covered the high ridge along which our course had hitherto lain, we descended through a rocky gorge into a beautiful valley clothed with short luxuriant emerald-green grass, through which a softly-murmuring stream of clear pellucid water glided smoothly along until it plunged over a jutting cliff, when, bounding from ledge to ledge, it formed a succession of foaming cataracts, and at last, rushing in its headlong course down the almost perpendicular slope of the mountain, swept over the scarped precipice at the end of the ravine in which we had built our hut.

We made our way to the first fall, and lying flat upon the ground, crawled to the edge of the precipice, and peeping cautiously over, we beheld a scene which amply repaid all our toil. The glowing plain of the low country lay stretched like a map before us some thousands of feet below, and we could trace the winding course of the Bowani river for some scores of miles as it gleamed in the rays of the sun like a silver thread. To our right, rose a grand amphitheatre of frowning heights, every portion of which, save only the scarped face of some perpendicular cliff, was covered with primeval forest, and far off could be discerned the fringed outline of more distant ranges, blue and indistinct in the fading light of departing day. It was a landscape of transcendent beauty, which has left a vivid impression on my mind, for perhaps the gorgeous sunset, which gilds all eastern scenery with a beauty peculiarly its own, may have rendered this more charming, by casting those rich golden tints upon the lofty peaks and rugged cliffs which the painter loves to throw over his picture.

The day was fast drawing to a close, and it was time to think of preparing our bivouac for the night, so we selected a rising ground for our encampment, under the lee of a huge boulder of moss-covered rock, flanked by two strange-looking trees, whose dark dense foliage, gnarled branches, and tortuous roots, reminded us much of those ancient yews that are so often met with in the country churchyards of old England. This arcadian nook was embellished by natural parterres of orchideous plants, wild camellias, rhododendrons, and other flowering shrubs, whilst here and there were scattered clumps of stately forest-trees, from which hung festoons of the *pusivel creeper* (*Entada pursætha*) with its gigantic pods nearly six feet in length, and other blooming parasites.

Chineah and the people were not long in constructing two huts (one for us and the other for themselves) by sticking bamboos into the ground, bending their tops together, which they fastened with creepers so as to form an arch, and wattling the sides with twigs. A trench was then dug, the earth heaped up all round, and the whole covered with a combley which was well pegged down, making an impervious shelter. In our tent a carpet was spread over a bed of dry leaves, a rest for our rifles constructed, and a bull's-eye lanthorn hung up ready for lighting.

I was accustomed to make myself at home and comfortable when in the jungle, being always very careful in the selection of my sleeping-place, for although, after many long years' campaigning, my constitution has become more hardy and less susceptible of injury from cold and damp, still I have seen so many fine fellows succumb to dysentery and fever, the seeds of which diseases were laid by careless exposure to the night air, after extreme heat and exhaustion, that I always take care of myself; besides which it is wretched beyond description to be shivering beneath a scanty covering, and feel the night air cut through one until the life-blood is almost frozen, when a little care and forethought would have prevented it.

The sun had now gone down, and the fast expiring twilight was deepening into night, and barely sufficed to disclose the beauties of the surrounding scenery, so we adjourned to the camp-fire, where all were busily engaged in preparing the evening meal; and the consequent bustle which ensued presented a strange contrast to the dreamy stillness that a few minutes before pervaded this romantic sylvan dell. After a smoke and a chat round the fire, we set the watch and turned in, well satisfied with our day's sport.

CHAPTER XX.

THE GREAT ANNAMULLAY FOREST—*continued.*
A ROGUE ELEPHANT.

Naga's party join us.—News of a *rogue* elephant.—Chineah despatched for the bison's spoils.—B——'s luck.—The start.—We strike a fresh trail.—Fall in with the tusker.—Our proceedings.—B——'s excellent shot.—The *ivories.*—A discussion on "rogues."—The cutting-out of the tusks.—Return to the low country.—Arrival of our guests.—Dinner.—B——'s adventure of a "griffin."—The lion and tiger compared.—My first lion.—We again ascend the Ghaut.—Good cheer.—Consultation.—Elephant-spoors.—The trail followed up.—K——'s rashness.—An escape.—A small tusker falls.—Return to the hut.—B——'s bag.—A storm.—Return to cantonment.

SHORTLY after we had retired to rest, I was awakened by an extraordinary noise and bustle outside our hut; and, on calling for Chineah, found that Naga and Veerapah, with a party of Carders, had come in, having missed their way until attracted by our fire. Naga reported that the Carders had told him of a bull-elephant, with large tusks, that had been seen several times lately in a wooded ravine about two coss (four miles) distant; and that he and Veerapah, under the guidance of the party then in camp, had been to look for him, and whilst they were following up his trail, and talking as they went along, he made his appearance and charged right at them, but that they had made their escape by climbing into trees, where they remained until he moved away. The Carders also knew of the whereabouts of a herd at no very great distance among the hills; and they reported that bison were to be found at any time in the teak-forests. Having made up my mind to go after the solitary tusker, whom I suspected to be a "rogue" that had been driven out of a herd by his companions, from his vicious attack on the people, I turned over and slept until called by Chineah in the morning.

A venison-steak broiled on the embers of our fire, a cup of coffee, and a couple of chapaties (girdle-cakes made of rice-flour) formed our breakfast; during which meal I informed B—— of Naga's news, as he had not heard it, being asleep at the time. I then despatched Chineah, Veerapah, and a party of Carders and Mulchers, for the bisons' skins and horns, which they were to take down to our hut in the low country, and there remain until our return. As there was only one elephant, according to our usual custom in such cases, we tossed up for the "shot," and B—— won, as he generally managed to do; after which we set out and followed the course of the valley for about a mile, when we entered a beautiful open forest of magnificent teak-trees, where we soon came upon the old spoor of an elephant, which we followed into a patch of high waving bamboo-jungle, that had evidently been his place of abode for several days, as we could tell by the number of trails we met with on every side, all of which appeared of the same size, and varying from one to ten days old.

Finding, from the freshness of the spoor, that he could not be very far off, I ordered all the party, except Googooloo and Naga, who carried our spare guns, to mount into trees, so as to be out of the way in case we met with him; and shortly afterwards we came to a sandy watercourse, which he had evidently only just crossed, as the water was still flowing into the imprints of his mighty feet. Whilst examining these marks, Googooloo, whose every muscle quivered with excitement, whilst his expressive countenance was lighted up with intense animation, made a sign for us to listen; and above that strange, indescribable, low buzzing hum caused by the insect-world, from the depths of the forest on every side, I plainly heard a low "*urmph,*" "*urmph,*" which noise I knew was caused by the elephant blowing through his trunk. We now took the spare guns from Naga and Googooloo, which we flung over our shoulders, first taking the precaution of putting on fresh caps, so as to ensure against miss-fires.

Having made signs to our attendants to mount into trees, which was much against their inclinations, as they wanted to see the fun, we crept as noiselessly as possible towards the spot from whence the sound proceeded, and in a little while had the gratification of seeing a very fair-sized tusker rubbing himself most energetically against the trunk of a large teak-tree. We made a circuit through the wood in order to get well to *leeward* of him, and then, cocking our rifles, cautiously approached, taking advantage of whatever cover we could find from clumps of bamboo and natural undulations of the ground, he seeming so much engrossed in his occupation (that of scratching himself) that he did not perceive our approach, and allowed us to get close behind him, where we stood watching his movements for a few moments. Seeing that B—— was perfectly ready, I gave a shrill whistle, which immediately attracted his attention, for his ears distended, and he swang heavily round, with a hoarse grunt, fully exposing his broad forehead to our view. Quick as thought, B—— threw up his rifle, and fired a double shot. A heavy fall, a subdued sigh, followed the report, and when the smoke cleared away I saw he had pitched heavily forward, and buried his tusks nearly a foot deep into the ground. I stepped up to give him a "*coup de grace*," but it was not required, both bullets had struck the vulnerable place immediately above the trunk, within an inch of each other, and, penetrating the brain, death was instantaneous.

"Hurrah!" cried B——, as he threw up his cap,

"those '*ivories*' must weigh heavily, and will help to replenish the shot in my locker, for old Framjee will give me a pagoda * a pound for them. Was it not neatly done?"

"Yes," I replied, "most scientifically, for he dropped to your shot like a stone; however, you had better superintend the cutting-out of the tusks yourself, as he has fallen in an awkward position to get at; and, if you do not take care, the fellows will chip the ivory with their axes, which will spoil the appearance of the tusks."

"All right, Hal, I'll see to it; but do you think this fellow was really a rogue, for he does not look as if he was particularly vicious, judging from the cut of his 'physog,' although he has several old scars, barely healed, over his hind-quarters?"

"I do, for several reasons," I replied. "First because the Carders, who are generally tolerably truthful, say so; secondly, because of his solitary habits; and thirdly, because I fancy these scars are the results of encounters with others of his species, who will not allow him to associate with them. An elephant who has once lost his herd or family is an outcast from the rest of the race, for he is not permitted to join any other troop, although he may frequent the same feeding-places. I fancy that their solitary life causes them to become morose and vicious; for rogues, whether male or female, are always found alone. I think I told you that the old rogue

* A pagoda, three rupees and a half—about seven shillings.

with a broken tusk, that I killed in the Ballyrungum Hills a short time ago, used to attack every animal he came near, and did not fear man in the least, for, whenever he heard the sounds of an axe in the part of the jungle he inhabited, he would rush shrieking, and chase the woodcutters; who went about their work in fear and trembling until I rolled him over with a single ball as he charged me, when I caught him bathing in a small pool of water."

"I remember it well," answered B——; "but here come the men with the axes, so bear a hand, and we will show them how to begin ourselves."

When the people came up, we set to work cutting out the tusks; which task, even with the aid of heavy axes, a saw, and fresh relays of operators, took us nearly three hours before it was accomplished, when, cutting off the end of the tail and the tips of the ears and trunk to send to the "Cutchery"* for the Government reward, we slung the ivory on bamboos, and the Mulchers carried it on their shoulders.

We descended the Ghaut by a shorter route than the one we came by, and arrived at our hut by sunset, where we had the gratification of finding K—— and C—— enjoying a bath in the lake. We joined them, and, after a most refreshing dip, sat down to a famous dinner, in which my *chef de cuisine*, "Five Minutes," outvied all his previous performances by indulging us in a most delicious pie made of the bison's marrow. After due justice had been done to

* Cutchery—the collector's office.

the good cheer, and we had received the hearty congratulations of our guests on our shooting achievements, we adjourned outside the hut, to indulge in the "fragrant weed" and the cup that cheers but does not inebriate, and B—— much amused us by relating an account of Paddy Lynch's first *rencontre* with "wild bastes." Paddy landed as a cadet at Madras, and was very shortly afterwards despatched to join a party of "griffins"* at Poonamallee, who were going up-country to join their respective regiments. Pat sent on his traps the day before, and early the next morning commenced his march, accompanied by his horsekeeper, who had a smattering of English. He had heard of bears and tigers up-country, so he went fully armed and equipped. After he had got a few miles from Madras, he came to a tank, in which he saw two strange black-looking creatures swimming about, that he took to be alligators or hippopotami, (he was not sure which.) He immediately dismounted, drew his shot, and, loading with ball, stole as gingerly as he could towards his game, which, to his surprise, allowed him to approach tolerably near, when they snorted in his face. Pat, taking a fair aim at the head of the first, let drive, and immediately the animal sank; he then blazed away at the other, and wounded it so severely that it began spinning round in the water. He loaded again, and after some more discharges, he

* Griffins—officers who have not completed their first year's service.

"cooked its goose," and was in great glee at having killed his first "*large game.*" He, however, forbore going into the tank to fetch them out, as he said "he felt a bit scared-like for fear there might be any more o' the craturs at the bottom of the wather," so he called upon some villagers to help him. When he had pointed out his game, to his great surprise they began a series of vociferations and lamentations, beating their breasts, and howling in a most frantic manner. "By the Powers!" says Pat, "sure it's one of their sacred alligators I've been shooting!" So, mounting his horse, he set off at full speed to Poonamallee, where he arrived just as they were sitting down to breakfast. He immediately told his adventure. The griffins listened with wonder, but a cloud passed over the face of the officer in charge, who, turning round in a very grave manner to Pat, said, "Mr Lynch, I am afraid you have killed a brace of niggers, and got yourself into a mess." Pat declared he had not, but remained very glum all the rest of the time at breakfast, when suddenly a row was heard outside. Pat recognised his horsekeeper's voice, flew out of the door, and in a moment returned shouting, "Sure, Captain, they arn't niggers at all, but just a fine brace of sea-cows I've bagged, for they're being brought in slung on poles." Need I say that Pat had killed a couple of tame buffaloes as they were swimming in the tank with their noses just above water, and he only got out of his mess by the prompt payment of some forty rupees, and a good "wigging" from the commanding officer of the station.

After B——'s story, which was deservedly much applauded, whilst we were discussing brandy-panee and cheroots, and talking over the events of the day, B—— and K—— had a lively discussion regarding the relative size and strength of the lion and the tiger, and as I had had some experience with both, the question was referred to me. I gave it as my opinion that the tiger was the larger and more powerful of the two, but that the lion, generally speaking, showed the most pluck.

"That is just what I have been contending, Hal," exclaimed B——; "but give us a Cape yarn to pass away the time, and afterwards we will have a song or two, and turn in, so as to be up betimes in the morning."

"All right," I replied, wetting my whistle, "I'll give you an account of my first lion. I was rusticating at Natal, with an old chum who had given up the service to turn settler, a little way up-country, and was about to convert his sword into a pruning-hook, when one day, as we were sitting under a mat awning in front of the house smoking our manillas after breakfast, a Dutch pedlar, of the name of Vanderhalt, (a well-known character in that colony,) came up and informed us that he had seen a herd of spring-buck in the Berere, a large belt of jungle some few miles distant. S——, who was also very fond of sport, gave him some tea and a bundle of cheroots, provided he would accompany us and show us their trail, and mounting our nags we set out with our guns and rifles, and, after a ride of five hours, came upon the slots of the herd. These animals, which take their name from the amazing springs they make over bushes, or any obstruction that lies in their path, are rather less than the common deer, and about the same colour, with a white stripe on each side, and a black stripe or mane along the back, which they have the power of closing or expanding. They are sometimes caught with greyhounds, but it takes a good dog to run them down. Confident in their fleetness, it is very amusing to see the contemptuous way in which they treat their pursuers; as they allow them to come near, and then, giving a bound and a snort, expand the hair on their backs, and change colour, appearing white. They are extremely graceful creatures, jumping beautifully, with the head thrown back, the legs doubled quite under, and the body curved, so that they appear for the moment as if suspended in the air.

"We were all, the Dutchman included, well mounted on beautiful Cape horses belonging to S——, and accompanied by a native servant, who had followed his master's fortunes over the 'Kala Panee,' (Black Waters,) and a Hottentot boy of the name of Hans Kleine, (John the Lesser,) who was quite a *lusus naturæ*, for—

'His back went in, and his belly stuck out,
And his lips resembled a grunter's snout.'

But he rode well, and carried a goat's skin full of water, some grog, and a couple of bottles of cognac. S—— was armed with a double fowling-piece; the Dutchman with a huge antediluvian single rifle, nearly six feet in length, called a 'roah;' and I had my pet double rifle (ten-gauge), loaded with Jacob's cylindro-conical balls, and a smooth-bore of the same calibre, besides pistols in my holsters. We followed the trail for some time, passing through a series of grassy plains, separated from each other by copses of the delicate-leaved mimosa, covered with golden-yellow blossoms, which emitted a delightful perfume, until we came to a river, the banks of which were covered with reeds, twenty yards in breadth; and as the stream was low, there having been a drought for some time, we managed to find a ford, the water coming up to our saddle-girths. When we arrived at the other side, we perceived from the slots that the herd had scattered over the plain, as if they had been suddenly alarmed; and, on closer investigation, we found the pugs of two full-grown lions and a pair of half-grown cubs, which fully accounted for the panic that had taken place. It was evident that these animals had been lurking in a mimosa-grove, by the side of the river, and lying in wait for their prey as they came to drink; and, from the freshness of the pugs, I felt sure they could not be far off, so I followed their spoor for about a mile over the plain, (which was hard, firm, and good riding-ground,) until I came to a low cone-shaped hill, which I ascended, to get a better survey of the surrounding country. I was sweeping the horizon with my field-glass, which was not of much use on account of a mirage that obstructed the view, and made all distant objects look dim, when 'Kleine,' the Hottentot boy, tapping me on the shoulder, pointed out a flock of vultures that were circling in the air at some short distance, saying, 'Dar ist der verdamt tau!' (There is the cursed lion!) I turned my glass to the spot, without distinguishing anything, but on cantering ahead, I soon had the gratification of seeing a full-grown lion and lioness, with two half-grown cubs, feasting on the remains of two spring-bucks. I looked to my nipples, to see the powder was well up, and rode towards them; but my horse did not at all like the sport, and became so extremely violent and restive, from fear, as to be almost unmanageable, and finding that I should have had no chance of firing from the saddle with any precision, I had to return to S——, who, with the Dutchman and servants, had pulled up, on observing the lions, which were game none of them seemed inclined to attack, for although S—— was a fearless hunter, he had been suffering from an inflammation and weakness of the eyes, caused by the excessive glare of the sun reflected from the sand, and his sight was so much affected that he could no longer depend upon his aim as in days of yore. I therefore dismounted, and prepared to open the campaign on my own hook—trusting to a steady hand and good weapons to see me safely through it. On my retreat, on account of the restiveness of my horse, the lion had advanced nearly two hundred yards from the spot where the dead spring-bucks lay, leaving the lioness and cubs still feeding, and he was now coolly surveying our party, stretched out at full length on the grass, with his paws out before him, and yawning listlessly, about four hundred yards distant. On perceiving me advancing towards him, he made a long, low moaning noise, like thunder rumbling among distant hills, by which he thought perhaps to intimidate me; but finding it had not the desired effect, he got up and sat on his haunches like a dog, making curious whining noises, and turning his head every now and again to look at his mate and cubs, who understanding from his growling, which was becoming more and more savage, that something was up, withdrew to some low sand-hills, a short distance away, which I was rather thankful for. When I got to about two hundred and fifty yards distant, I stopped to unsling my second gun from my shoulder, so as to be ready; on which my friend sprung to his feet, and made three or four huge bounds towards me, lashing his tail from side to side, showing his teeth, and giving a tremendous roar, which seemed to shake the earth, and caused the horse I had been riding to break from the grasp of the Hottentot, who was holding it, and scour over the plain. On seeing me advance, he again stopped, and, couching low on his belly, growled in a most savage manner. I felt that 'the die was cast,' and there was no retreating; it was a regular duel between man and beast, and was beginning to be rather serious work, for we were barely sixty yards asunder. The lion still lay with his head couched between his paws, although every now and then he appeared to rise, and tear up the earth with his hind claws. His eyeballs glistened with rage, his mane stood erect, his tail lashed his flanks, and I felt he was watching my every movement, and that further delay was dangerous. I therefore quietly cocked my second gun, laid it by my side on the ground, and then gave a loud shout, at the same time flinging my pith hunting-cup towards him. This had the desired effect; he sprung upon his feet, and at this moment looked grand beyond conception. Now was the moment. I threw up my rifle, took deliberate aim at his broad and massive breast, and let fly. I heard the soft 'thud' of the ball as it entered his chest, saw him spring high into the air, and fall upon his back. I rushed up to give him a *coup de grace*, but it was not needed; a convulsive tremor passed over his sturdy limbs, blood gushed from his nose and mouth, the under-jaw dropped, and my first lion was dead. He was a noble animal, measuring over eleven feet from the tip of his nose to the end of the tail. The lioness and cubs, on hearing the shot, made for a small copse about a mile distant; and as it was too late in the day to pursue them, after S—— had caught my horse, we skinned the lion, cut off his head as a trophy, packed them behind Kleine's saddle, and made the best of our way back home, where we arrived late in the evening."

After my yarn, songs passed round until a late hour, and as my old hunting-chaunts had begun to be very stale from frequent repetition, and new ones were not obtainable, I extemporised the following words, and sang them to old English airs, when my turn came round:—

THE BRITON'S SONG.*

There's a magical charm in the land of our birth,
Which, seek where you will, is not found else on earth;
You may search till you tire, from the pole to the zone,
But where will you find such a land as our own?
Her daughters are fairest, and what nation dare brave
The Isles'-men of Britain, the Queen of the Wave?
I have roam'd through the world, but I cannot compare
Any men with her sons, any maids with her fair.

CHORUS.

Then fill up your bumpers, and drink to my toast!
I pledge ye "The Island" we all love the most:
The gem of the ocean, the pride of the earth,
The bulwark of freedom, the Land of our birth!

The red cross of Britain is the pride of the main,
An emblem of freedom, a flag without stain;
Go search through creation—on the land, o'er the wave—
That standard ne'er floats o'er the head of a slave.

---

* Afterwards set to music by H. W. A. BEALE, Esq.

Like a meteor it shines, for 'tis borne to the field
By those who may die, but who never will yield;
Go search in Fame's volume, you 'll find there its story,
And Britain's fair name, midst a halo of glory.

CHORUS.

Then fill up your bumpers, and drink to my toast!
I pledge ye "The Island" we all love the most:
The gem of the ocean, the pride of the earth,
The bulwark of freedom, the Land of our birth!

THE OLD SONG.*

There 's something in the well-known tone
Of ancient ballad lays,
That calls to mind, though years have flown,
The friends of early days.
I 've seen them cause the tears to start
From sternest soldier's eye;
No modern strains could touch his heart
Like those of days gone by.

CHORUS.

Then sing to me the songs of yore!
For, though they make me sigh,
They bring to mind dear friends once more,
And happy days gone by.

I love to hear the ancient lays
My mother used to sing!
They tell me of my childhood's days,
And fond thoughts backwards bring.
I dream of days of hope and joy,
Whene'er I hear that strain;

---

* Afterwards set to music by H. W. A. BEALE, Esq., and published by Messrs OLLIVIER, Bond Street.

I think that I am still a boy,
  And hear her voice again.

CHORUS.

Then sing to me the songs of yore!
  For, though they make me sigh,
They bring to mind dear friends once more,
  And happy days gone by.

The echoes of the wood were several times awakened by our rattling choruses, which reverberated in a most strange manner against the face of the cliff overhanging our retreat, and the moon was high in the heavens before we turned in for the night.

We slept long and soundly, as hunters generally do after a hard day's fag, but as soon as the gray light of dawn appeared, the stirring strains of K——'s bugle rang through the valley, and, obeying its cheerful summons, we hastily arrayed ourselves in our hunting-gear, assembled round the fire, and partook of a hurried collation previous to ascending the Ghaut. The coolies accompanied us with supplies, as it was our intention to remain for a day or two at my former bivouac at the head of the Fall, in the hope of falling in with the herd of elephants reported to have been seen by the Carders some days previously. We entered the jungle as day was breaking, and, after a tedious ascent, arrived at the head of the Fall about noon, where we immediately commenced building a commodious hut, as our former one was too small. As soon as our arrangements were completed, B—— and I started on a pot-hunting expedition, K—— and C—— being too much done-up to accompany us, and, after half an hour's beating, managed to bag a couple of jungle-fowl and five hares, which latter were very much larger than those found in the low country. On our return to the hut with our game, we found such a feast awaiting us that we hardly knew what to commence with. An immense round of Dawson's celebrated spiced beef was backed up by a Yorkshire ham, a roast squeaker, and a marrow-pie; besides which, cakes smoking hot from the oven, pilau, curry, and piles of wild raspberries and strawberries garnished the board. Having done ample justice to our good cheer, we withdrew to the watch-fire, where all our people were assembled, and, after distributing the usual allowance of tobacco and grog to every man in camp, we held a consultation, in which it was determined that we should divide into two reconnoitring parties on the morrow: B—— and C——, with Chineah and four of the gang, forming one; and K——, myself, with Googooloo and three others, the second. This settled, we retired to the hut, and after a rubber of whist turned in.

We were up long before the sun the next morning, and, after a hearty breakfast, started at a good pace towards the spot where the Carders had fallen in with the elephants. After half an hour's tramp we came across an old trail, which B——'s party followed up, whilst mine continued our route through beautiful open teak-jungle, carpeted with green turf, most deliciously soft and elastic under foot.

There were plenty of bison-tracks everywhere to be seen, some of which were quite fresh; and Googooloo pointed out to K—— a tuft of herbage that had been very recently torn up by one of those animals, as saliva was still remaining on it. We followed up the trail for a short distance, in the hope of obtaining a shot, but could not get a glimpse of them. Towards noon we fell in with the spoor of an elephant, that appeared to be about twenty-four hours old, and we continued to track it up until late in the afternoon, when, my companion giving evident signs of fatigue, we made preparations for passing the night, by building a couple of huts close to a small rivulet, which looked clear and sparkling as a trout-stream in Scotland. It was a beautiful spot for a camp, as on all sides rose hills covered with dense deep-green forest, intersected with innumerable mountain-streams, which emerged from the trees, and glistened like silver threads in the light of the setting sun.

Our day's fag told upon us; for within half an hour after our dinner we were all coiled up in our blankets fast asleep, and did not stir until Googooloo informed us that dawn was breaking, when, giving ourselves a shake, we adjourned to the brook to perform our ablutions whilst breakfast was preparing.

This finished, we again started on trail; and as we were following up the spoor of the day before, I found unmistakable signs that a herd of elephants had passed by within a very short time. We immediately followed up at our best pace, and in a couple of hours fell in with the rear-guard, consisting of three females, which I had some difficulty in preventing my companion from firing at, as they were the first wild elephants he had ever seen. I never cared to pull trigger at the "gentler sex," and, as the herd appeared to number about eleven, I concluded there must be a bull amongst them. I told K—— to wait under cover as quietly as possible, whilst I went forward to reconnoitre; but I had hardly left the spot, when I heard a double shot, followed by a scream of rage, and, turning back, to my horror I saw my companion running for his life through the jungle, with a tusker closely following him tail on end. The elephant, notwithstanding his apparently unwieldy shape, gets over the ground much faster than one would suppose, and poor K—— would have had no chance if he had not been able to dodge him, by running round trees. I could not for the moment get a fair shot at any vulnerable part; but, seeing that the elephant had got so near that he could almost have reached him with his trunk, I let drive a double shot at his ear, and brought him to his knees, which gave K—— time to clamber up into a tree. It was a very near touch. for he was breathless, and another few seconds would have seen him trampled under foot; as it was, I was able to despatch the tusker with my second gun, which Googooloo handed to me just as he began to recover himself, and was getting on his knees. K—— told me that the moment I left him he heard a slight rustling in the cover close to where we were standing, and almost immediately the tusker made his appearance, coming directly towards him, when he fired a couple of hurried shots and took to his heels, seeing that he did not drop. I fancy that he must have lost his presence of mind when he saw the huge brute advancing towards him, as only one of his shots had taken effect, and that high up in the forehead. I congratulated him upon his escape, which was certainly due more to good luck than good management, as, in the position I was in, and the distance, it must have been entirely a chance shot of mine that dropped him. The sound of our guns caused a great panic in the herd; and they rushed about crashing through the jungle at a great pace, which led me to suppose that they would not pull up until they had covered a good deal of ground; and as K—— found he had sprained his ankle in his flight, which prevented him from walking comfortably, we gave up all thoughts of further pursuit. Leaving two of our people to cut out the tusks, which were small, not exceeding thirty pounds in weight, we made the best of our way back to the hut, where we found B——'s party busily occupied in preserving the skins of two bison, which they had killed the day previous.

During the afternoon, heavy banks of dark clouds arose, which I knew prognosticated a storm; so we strengthened our hut, and spread extra combleys on the weather-side, so as to make it impervious to the weather. Hardly were our preparations completed, when the sky became uniformly black and gleamless, except when illuminated at intervals by the flashes of bluish-white lightning, and the thunder, reverberating among the mountains like the rolling of distant artillery, now came nearer and nearer, until it seemed to peal directly overhead, whilst the rain, in a perfect deluge, poured down upon the hot earth with that peculiar hissing sound heard only in the tropical climates. Later in the evening, the storm passed over, and the night became bitterly cold, dense vapours rising from the ground, which could not be otherwise than unhealthy; so it was determined to commence a retrograde movement. We accordingly started early the next morning for our hut in the valley below, packed up our traps, and halted for the night at the public bungalow near the village ot Annamullay. The next day we pushed on to Coimbatore, where we remained a couple of days, as B—— was suffering from diarrhœa, and then returned to my domicile at Ootacamund

PART II.—CIRCASSIA.

CHAPTER XXI.

Omer Pacha.—My followers.—Bashi-Bazouks.—Houssain the Arnout.—Ahmed the Koord.—Ali the Nubian.—Mahomed the Arab.—Sied Cassim the Dervish.—Abdulla the guide.—Captain Dymock's grave.—Godova.—Wild-fowl.—A heavy bag.—The climate of Circassia.—The inhabitants: their manners, customs, and dress.—Circassian women.—The Illori chieftain.—The "Faithful," and the "forbidden indulgence." Omer Pacha a humbug.—His reputation amongst the Turkish officers.—His wound accounted for.—His acquisitiveness and plunder.—A fearful chase by wolves.—The Turkish Colonel's advice.—Sulleiman Pacha.—His purchase.—Revolt of the Hareem.—The catastrophe and finale.

AFTER the fall of Sevastopol, I was attached, with several other British officers, to the general staff of that part of the Ottoman army under the command of Omer Pacha, which was destined to relieve Sir William Williams and the brave garrison of Kars, then closely invested by General Mouravieff; but, disgusted with the dilatory and vacillating conduct of a leader whose cowardice or treachery allowed the sole object of the expedition to fail, I obtained leave to throw up my appointment and return to the Crimea, where I hoped again to partake of more stirring deeds. But it was not to be—"the de'il confound the ministry!" they began to make peace at the time we had just warmed to our work, and when we were best able to carry on the war the armistice was signed, peace concluded, and "Othello's occupation gone." Finding it was uncertain when a steamer was likely to touch at Tchamshira, the nearest point of embarkation to Sugdidi, where the head-quarters of the army were established, I resolved to go to Suchum Kaleh by land, amusing myself with shooting amongst the lower spurs of the Caucasus *en route.*

Besides a guide, I had five well-tried followers, whom I had picked up from amongst the Bashi-Bazouks during the campaign of the Danube: a fearless set of men, ever true to their salt, who cared neither for laws nor Pachas, and who, being used to campaigning and foraging, were just the fellows to have about one in a country where "might is right," and "he may take who has the power, and he may keep who can;" for, although the Russians had vacated those districts some time previously, predatory bands of Abassians, Mingrelians, and Circassians were continually prowling about, not particularly nice as to whom they plundered. We were all well armed and mounted on Arabs, or sturdy little Kurdish horses, besides having three shaggy mountain ponies to carry our baggage, or rather to carry whatever we might pick up, for a Bashi-Bazouk always returns heavier laden than when he set out, if he knows his trade.

The cognomen "Bashi-Bazouk" is a composite Turkish word for a class of individuals who would be allowed to exist in no country in the world save Turkey, or perhaps Central America, where the term "filibuster" appears to be almost synonymous. It is derived from "Bash," *a head;* "ba," *without;* "zouk," *brains*—literally, though not in reality, "*a head without brains:*" certainly not an appropriate name for men who have to live by their wits. Among the horde I commanded on the Danube before our troops landed at Varna, I counted men of twenty-seven different nations and castes.

My troop were a queer set, and merit a slight description. Hoossain, an Arnout, had been a "chaus" or sergeant, in one of the Turkish regiments engaged at Silistria, and having been deputed to wait upon me by Moosa Pacha, (the gallant Arab leader who was afterwards killed on the ramparts by the explosion of a shell during the siege,) found my service preferable to soldiering, at the nominal pay of twenty piastres per mensem, (then twenty-two months in arrears,) and, as he was a plucky, honest, and useful fellow, I kept him always with me. Fortune had dealt kindly with him; and as he had managed, by hook or by crook, to amass a sufficient quantity of gear and sundries to enable him to smoke his pipe in comfort for the remainder of his life, he had given up all intentions of joining his regiment again. In camp before Sevastopol, during the siege, he was a well-known character, glorying in the name of "Ingleese Jonnie," for, by dint of "*wrinkles*" picked up from an old corporal of Zouaves, my *chef de cuisine*, and sundry lessons from poor old Soyer, now, alas! gone to "kingdom come," he was no despicable cook, and formed a great addition to any party "*sub tegmine fagi*," whether out foraging in front of the enemy near Baidar, or picnicking with amateur campaigners at the Monastery of St George.

The second, Ahmed, was a Koord, one of the followers of the Princess Kara Fathama, and a "mulassim," or lieutenant, of Bashi-Bazouks; a fearless, devil-may-care kind of fellow, who, having received some fancied insult and extortion from a Pacha, hated all Turkish authorities like poison, and seemed to glory in setting them at defiance. He was strikingly handsome, a splendid horseman, a famous fellow in a brush, and the *beau-idéal* of a Bashi-Bazouk.

The third, Ali, commonly called "Kutchuc," (the Little One,) was a Nubian of colossal proportions and gigantic strength, who was devoted to me, I having saved him from the Cossacks in an affair on the Danube, after he had been disabled by several severe wounds, and abandoned by his comrades.

which service he amply repaid afterwards, when I, in my turn, was laid on my back, by his constant attention and unwearied care for my wants.

The fourth, Mahomed, was an Arab, or rather a Khabyle by birth, who had fought with the Emir Abdel-Kader against the French, and, having been obliged to fly his country, had entered the corps of Bashi-Bazouks, from whence I took him to look after my horses, he being a first-rate groom.

The fifth, Sied Cassim, was a Hindostanee from Northern India, who, being of a roving disposition, had turned "Fakeer," or dervish; and, after having performed the "Hadj," or pilgrimage to Mecca, had wandered all over Asia Minor and Persia, and at last enrolled himself in the ranks of the Bashi-Bazouks. He was a trustworthy fellow, and, being a good scholar in Persian, Hindostanee, Arabic, and Turkish, used to act as paymaster, or rather as the divider of the spoils, and keep the accounts, from which he usually went by the name of the "Vakeel," or secretary. He claimed also to be a descendant of the prophet, and always wore the significant badge, a green turban.

Our guide, Abdulla, was likewise a Hindostanee by birth, but had left his country when a child with an Arab cloth-merchant, who had sold him to the Circassians, by whom he had been adopted as one of themselves. He was a great chum of Cassim's, and I took him into my service, as he had a good knowledge of the Circassian and Abassian languages, as well as the various dialects of the different mountain tribes, and was well acquainted with the country. Being quite a youth, he generally went by the name of "Chojuck," (the Young One.) His office was that of interpreter, and he was charged with the care of five very handsome greyhounds and a pointer, which fell into my hands by the fortune of war, and furnished me with many a game dinner when nothing else was procurable.

We left Sugdidi early in the morning, crossing the Ingur by the redoubt which was thrown up by the Ottoman troops after they had forced the passage on the morning of the 7th November, when poor Captain Dymock fell, shot through the heart, whilst he was leading the column to the attack. We buried him close to where he fell, under two beautiful trees, covered with festoons of wild vine. I stayed a few moments to take a hurried sketch of a brave comrade's last resting-place, and then rode on to Godova, on the coast, where we arrived about three P.M.

I was most hospitably received by an old colonel of infantry, who, with his regiment, was left in charge of some stores; and in a marsh near the village I killed a couple of pintail ducks, three couple of snipe, and a bittern, and "Guimish," (Silver,) one of my greyhounds, caught a hare.

The country round about Godova is densely wooded; oak, ash, chesnut, walnut, and most kinds of European fruit-trees seeming to grow indigenous and in the wildest luxuriance, whilst the loveliest flowers bloom in perfection; amongst which I noticed the tulip, anemone, hyacinth, ranunculus, rose, pink, jasmine, and violet, besides numberless other species with which I was not previously acquainted. The lower spurs of the Caucasus, the grandest of mountain ranges, rise about seven miles to the eastward of the village, and run parallel to the coast. The lower ranges are clothed with dense and almost impenetrable primeval forest, whilst the higher are covered with perpetual snow, and generally enshrouded by mists.

The heavy falls of rain, and the melting of snow and ice on the mountains, in the summer, when the power of the sun is strong, swell the numerous rivers and watercourses into mighty torrents, causing them to overflow their banks and inundate the surrounding country; forming large marshes or bogs, which, at certain seasons of the year, are almost alive with waterfowl of different kinds, whilst snipe and woodcock are to be found in thousands.

It is my belief that swans, ducks, and geese of all kinds, besides snipe and woodcock, choose these secluded and almost inaccessible spots to breed in, migrating here for that purpose from all the other countries of Europe. I have killed seventeen different species of duck and teal in one jheel, the water in places where the weed abounded on which they feed being black with them. They were evidently unaccustomed to the sound of a gun, for, when the echoes of the report died away in the distant hills, they would settle down in the same place without taking alarm, although each discharge brought down about a dozen of their number. The bag that might be made may be estimated from the fact that I killed in one day in a jheel near the foot of the Abassadagh Mountain, fourteen miles from Tshamshira, thirty-four brace of woodcock, eleven couple of snipe, seven geese, and sixty-one ducks ; and could have continued the slaughter, were it not that the villagers, for whose benefit it was intended, declared that they could not carry more away. I think I must have flushed that day at least a hundred brace of cock, besides snipe innumerable. I hope my reader will not imagine from this account that I at all countenance or am in favour of such wholesale destruction as a general thing ; but it must be remembered that at this time I had many mouths to feed, that food of any kind was at a premium, and I had nothing in store except mouldy Turkish ration biscuit, full of weevils and other such indescribable animalculæ.

The climate, soil, and magnificence of scenery render the east coast of the Black Sea one of the most beautiful and interesting countries in the world. It is abundantly irrigated by numberless rivers flowing from the mountains, and the valleys are extremely fertile, producing cotton, rice, wheat, millet, Indian corn, hemp, flax, and quantities of excellent grasses, with little labour ; yet the inhabitants are generally poor, holding in contempt agriculture and all employments of a peaceful kind. They are divided into several nations, tribes, and castes, which are again subdivided. The principal are the Tcherkesses, the Kabardines, the Abassians, the Mingrelians, and the Georgians. The Tcherkesses, or Circassians, said to be derived from the Tyches, (who settled in the country several centuries ago,) are essentially mountaineers, and have many qualities in common with the Scottish Highlanders of the olden day. Their element is war, and they possess all the characteristics peculiar to the inhabitants of lofty regions, being divided into tribes and clans, each of which is governed by a chief invested with the power of life and death over his followers. They chiefly profess the Mohammedan religion, but, having no written language, their faith differs considerably from that of other Mussulmans ; a traditionary history and code of laws, which has been transmitted from age to age, and become hallowed from its antiquity, being substituted for the Koran. The old men act as judges, and settle all the affairs of the community, subject to the supreme authority of the chief, whose will is law. They are an exceedingly fine and handsome race, the men being tall, well-made, and muscular, though rather of slight build, with pleasing features, flowing beards, and remarkably small hands and feet.

The dress of the common people in some respects resembles that of the Tartars, but is more elegant ; it consists of a sheepskin cap with high peak of gray cloth, white or yellow linen tight-fitting trousers, yellow boots, and shirt-like tunic, bound with gold or silver lace, having on each side of the breast cases made of morocco for holding cartridges. Their arms are a kind of rifled matchlock, pistol, sabre, and broad, heavy, double-edged poniard. Their chiefs or nobles, however, present a much more brilliant spectacle when in full dress, being clad, like our knights of old, in coats of mail composed of rings of steel joined together with the most beautiful workmanship, and armed with damascened sabres, daggers, and richly-ornamented pistols, often inlaid with gold.

Their women have long been celebrated for their extreme beauty, the harems of Constantinople being kept supplied from the descendants of slaves, though not, as is generally supposed, from the families of the free tribes. They are of slender and elegant figures, with regular features, white skin, and dark brown or black hair, with blue eyes. They are in general neither reserved nor confined, but at the age of ten or twelve years they are incased in a broad leathern band tightly sewn round the waist, which they wear until marriage. Over a low-cut chemise they wear a long laced jacket with wide trousers, and they heighten their beauty by painting their eyebrows with a preparation of antimony called "soormah," and stain the nails of the toes and fingers with henna. Their hair is generally plaited and falls down the back, and a small sheepskin cap, with the upper part embroidered, is commonly worn.

Their villages consist only of "konaks" or log-huts, plastered with clay inside, and seldom containing more than one room. A wooden bench or sedan runs all round, and one part, covered with matting, serves as a bed. The only furniture or garniture are the saddles, arms, and a few brass or copper cooking utensils.

The customs of ancient Sparta are in some degree in force amongst them, the youths being brought up in all bodily exercises calculated to increase strength and agility—such as riding, running, wrestling, shooting, and they are accustomed to endure hunger and fatigue. To fall in the field is considered an honour, and to kill an enemy a triumph; stealing is also allowed and encouraged, that is, provided it is not found out, for if the culprit is detected, he is bound to restore the stolen property sevenfold. Murder or crime is generally punished by fine, more or less, according to the rank of the victim.

Some of the Kabardines and Abassians profess a kind of Christianity, but they are a more degenerate and treacherous race than the Circassians, who, though cruel crafty enemies, are extremely hospitable and more to be depended upon.

A petty chieftain, who lived with his tribe in the mountains to the northward of Illori, dined with us; and as he spoke Turkish tolerably well and was exceedingly communicative, I gleaned a good deal of useful information about the country and the kind of game that was likely to be met with. According to his account, bears of an immense size, as well as wolves, hyenas, and jackals were to be found on the mountains, besides red-deer, wild cattle, hog, wild goats, and sheep, (which latter proved to be ibex and chamois.) He invited me to visit his "konak" *en route*, and undertook to show me game of different kinds, which offer I was glad to accept.

When the repast was over, coffee served, and the servants out of the way, I produced a little keg of brandy; and notwithstanding we were all supposed to be good Mussulmans, it went round merrily, and opened the hearts of "the Faithful."

The "cratur" made the eyes of the old Osmanli colonel glisten again, and as the keg passed round pretty often, it soon began to show its effects, rendering him extremely loquacious, and he recounted several very amusing incidents of his early service, besides expatiating, in the strongest of Turkish Billingsgate, against the Sirdar Ekrem Omer Pacha, whom he denounced as an arch-humbug, who has usurped the credit of other men's acts, and gained the position he held by cringing servility, base intrigue, and despicable chicanery — being totally destitute of all those qualities which he ought to possess, not only as a general, but a man. He was said never to have been under fire except on one occasion when he could not help himself, (at Eupatoria ;) and the small scar he has on his wrist, which he often brags about, and shows to strangers as a wound, was thus accounted for :—During one of the outbreaks of the "Ryahs" or Christian subjects of the Porte, in Southern Turkey, he was sent in command of a body of troops against a walled village not very far from Monastir, which was vigorously defended by the inhabitants, armed only with matchlocks and ataghans. A long-continued drought had dried up most of the wells in the enceinte of the place, and the besieged had to obtain their supply from a spring in the ditch outside the walls, which task was generally undertaken by the women and children after nightfall. This fact was communicated to Omer Pacha by some of his sycophants, and he ordered the small brass rifled mountain-piece, which he always keeps in front of his tent, to be pointed so as to command the source on a rising ground far out of range of the small-arms of the garrison. During the night a noise was heard in the ditch by some of the advanced sentries, and the Pacha was informed that the villagers were drawing water: he immediately rushed to his gun and loaded it, not knowing that one of his staff had previously made it all ready for him. When he applied the match, the piece, being doubly charged, recoiled violently, knocking down the Pacha on the broad of his back, with half a dozen of his hangers-on, and injuring his wrist. Thus is the only wound Omer Pacha ever received accounted for, and it is not to be wondered at if he never mentions how and when he got it.

Omer Pacha had appropriated to himself the whole of the plunder of Princess Dadien's palace at Sugdidi, despatching for his own use, at Constantinople, a magnificent collection of furniture, consisting of chairs and couches covered with crimson velvet, beautiful inlaid tables, magnificent chandeliers, and articles of *virtu*, which looked like recent importations from Paris. The tame deer and peafowl were killed for his table, and the exotic plants transported to his garden at Stamboul.

Story-telling is a great amusement amongst the Turks, and each of us in his turn had to contribute some anecdote for the amusement of the rest.

The Abassian chief gave us a very thrilling account of the loss of five of his tribe, with some prisoners, by wolves, during the winter of 1852, when the whole country lay covered with snow for months together. It appears that a force had been collected and sent out in the plains to harass and annoy the Russians, but having met with a reverse, they scattered, and each tribe made the best of their way homeward. The Abassian party, to which the narrator belonged, consisted of eleven men fairly mounted and armed with matchlocks, pistols, and swords, with five prisoners—four Russian soldiers and a woman. As they were traversing a vast steppe or plain they perceived a pack of seven wolves slowly following them, of which number they killed two or three with their matchlocks, for the sake of the fur, and, dispersing the rest, continued their journey. Shortly afterwards a strange howling noise was heard in the rear, which at first sounded like the roaring of the wind, but afterwards increased to such a pitch, that they thought Jehannum (the infernal regions) was turned loose, and that the cry they had heard was the exulting laugh of the "gins" and "afrits," (evil spirits,) whom they believe to inhabit the impenetrable snows of Mount El-bruz. At length their attention was called to a dark mass of black objects spreading over the snow, like a cloud on the horizon, and the full extent of their danger now burst upon them, for they knew they were pursued by a horde of wolves.

Their horses were already fatigued with a long day's journey, but terror seemed to give them wings, for they tore along as if they knew their peril, and for a while seemed to hold their own. The nearest "konak" or hamlet was at least two "saat" or seven miles distant, and the ground was in many places so deep with drifted snow that their horses could hardly get along. The crisis was now evidently fast approaching, for the advanced troop were almost within gun-shot, howling and yelling as wolves only can. A brief consultation was held, and it was determined to sacrifice the prisoners one by one, so as to gain time for the rest to escape. The woman met her fate first. One of their number stepping behind, drew his sabre across the hocks of her horse, hamstringing it, and causing both to fall heavily to the ground. Her shrieks, as well as the cry of the horse in his death agony, rang through their ears for a moment, and then all was still. They anxiously looked back, and found that this desperate expedient had enabled them to gain a considerable distance on their pursuers, but it was not for long; they were soon again on their heels, when a Russian soldier was sacrificed by shooting his horse; a second, third, and fourth followed, and much time was gained and a considerable distance covered: still their insatiable foes pressed on, apparently more ferocious than before, for their appetite was whetted with the taste of blood. They now commenced discharging their firearms amongst them, but it was of no avail, for although many fell, the rest rushed on, and the course of the horde was not stayed. The horses of two of their number now gave up, and fell with shrieks that told they knew the fate that awaited them; and although their riders were swift of foot, they could not keep up their speed for any length of time in the deep snow, and soon became fatigued, so bidding their comrades farewell, they resigned themselves to their "kismet," (destiny,) drew their yatagans, and shouting their battle-cry, died like men, fighting to the last. The survivors were now within a couple of miles from shelter,' but their horses were almost worn out, the leading wolves hardly a pistol-shot behind, and gaining upon them rapidly—another moment, and they expected to feel their fangs, when an old man, whose two sons were also present, seeing the hopelessness of the case, bade his comrades farewell, and shouting out the "imaun" (Mohammedan creed) as a death-song, felled his horse to the ground with the heavy butt of his pistol, as he could not rein up the scared animal, and offered himself a willing sacrifice to save the rest. On tore the survivors, now reduced to eight in number, and on followed their relentless pursuers, now again only half a dozen horses' length behind. In spite of all their efforts, their doom seemed sealed, and their case hopeless, when their chief, giving an expressive look to the narrator, drew his pistol and shot the man nearest to him through the head. He threw up his arms and dropped the reins, but although stone-dead he sat firm in the saddle, the affrighted animal carrying him until a second discharge brought both to the ground. Again the pursuit was checked for a time, and the konak appeared in view; luckily the door was open, for it was deserted, men and horses rushed in, the door was closed, and a ponderous bar drawn across inside, when suddenly a loud heart-rending yell was heard from without, above the howling of the wolves, and they saw through the chinks between the logs, one of their comrades whose horse had broken down and lagged behind, unperceived by the rest, surrounded by the horde and fighting desperately—a moment more and he was pulled from the saddle, and both man and horse devoured before their eyes. Then the wolves surrounded the hut, and, finding themselves balked of their prey, began to fight with each other, at times endeavouring to scratch away the earth under the logs or force their ways through the crevices, but the hut being substantially constructed resisted all their efforts, and a deadly discharge of firearms was kept up from the interior, which thinned their numbers, and revenged their fallen friends, but the dead wolves were speedily devoured by the survivors, who remained howling and shrieking round the hut until the night of the second day, when a violent storm arose, and they took themselves off in the dark, much to the relief of the six survivors, who, seeing the coast clear, made the best of their way to their homes.

"Allah kereem, (God be merciful,) but you had a wonderful escape!" exclaimed the old colonel, when the Illori chieftain had finished his story. "I thank Kismut (fate) that I was not with you on that day, or I should have stood but a poor chance in your desperate race for life, (he weighed at least eighteen stone,) and a shudder comes over me when I think of it; and if I were you, O Ingleese Bey! (so he termed me,) I should give up all idea of rambling about this desolate country, where one sees nothing but mountains, trees, rivers, and mud; may go a moon's journey without falling in with a *café*, and where fighting comes oftener than one's dinner. Be advised, and embark at once for Stamboul, where you may enjoy your 'kieff,' (a dreamy state of listless idleness, peculiar to the Turks,) and smoke your chibouk, surrounded with dark-eyed beauties, whose voices are more melodious than the cries of jackals, whose kisses are more desirable than the bites of wolves, and whose embraces are preferable to the hugs of bears. Heigh Allah! when shall I see the blessed place again?"

"Shabash! (Bravo!) Bey Effendi!" I exclaimed; "you are too greedy, and it is fortunate that every one is not of your opinion, or some would come poorly off; for where are all the women to come from, if every man required a troop? I am more moderate, being content with one at a time; besides which, I do not like having a continual 'karabalik' (disturbance) in the house, which is always the case when women get together; for I am of the same opinion as the sage, who says that it is an easier task to rule a thousand men than to control two women; and to prove that my theory is correct, I will relate to you the sad fate of a man you all knew, who owed all his misfortunes to taking one woman too many in his establishment.

"Sulleiman Pacha, late commandant of the first brigade that landed in the Crimea, was formerly a collector of customs in the Pachalik of Widdin, and subsequently held some lucrative civil appointment at Stamboul. Tax-gathering, for a number of years, had made Sulleiman Aga a rich man; and through the interest of Mehemet Ali Pacha, backed up with a large packet of 'kaima,' (paper-money.) the Aga was made a Lever Pacha, (General of

Brigade,) and things went on swimmingly for a time. One day, however, the horizon of his destiny was darkened with the cloud of misfortune; for as he was enjoying his chibouk at a *café* near the 'Buyuk Chouk,' (Grand Bazaar,) he was accosted by an old friend, and in an evil moment accepted an invitation to accompany him to a slave-merchant's 'khan,' in order to select a Nubian eunuch as a guardian for his harem. This matter settled, the slave-merchant took them to see a magnificent Georgian damsel, who was considered to be the finest importation for many years. Her price was eighty thousand piastres, (about six hundred pounds sterling,) and Sulleiman Pacha became so captivated with her appearance that, notwithstanding he was an elderly man, and had three wives at home, he became the purchaser; and the object of his affections was ordered to be conveyed to his garden-house near Scutari, *on the extreme quiet,* so that his other wives might hear nothing about it. The Pacha thought he observed a diabolical twinkle in the eye of the slave-dealer when, after he had received his money, he wished him 'every felicity;' but at the moment he merely thought he had been cheated out of some piastres, which, being rich, he did not care about, never imagining that he would have such cause to repent his bargain. The cunning old fox then went home, and informed his wives that he was obliged to start on a journey, and after taking an affectionate farewell he set off for his country house. His reception could not have proved very satisfactory, nor did he ever disclose to me what actually passed, for although he has often related his grievances to me, at this point he invariably worked himself up in such a rage, that I could make out little but a long string of curses against a cat-like fiend who must have escaped from 'Jehanum,' (the infernal regions,) so I concluded he got his face clawed. However, he admitted that he spent the night in a neighbouring *café*, and when he went home the next morning he found a mutiny had taken place in his harem; for whether his scratched face and disordered appearance told tales, or some maliciously inclined persons had given his wives an insight into the affair, he knew not, but he was received with torrents of abuse. One knocked his turban off, a second pulled his beard, the third spat in his face, and they all left the marks of their nails on his person, besides belabouring him with the heels of their slippers until he was almost insensible, when the guardians of the fold of the 'third sex' came to the rescue, and enabled him to get out of their clutches. Finding himself driven out of house and home, he grew desperate, and, being weary of his life, went for a soldier, thinking to terrify the household into subordination, for he had no idea of going to fight; and the Seraskier (Minister of War) gave him the command of a brigade of 'redifs,' (militia,) which, unfortunately for our hero, were the first troops ordered out on active service in the Crimea, and he was obliged to go. Although not actually engaged, he saw quite enough at the battle of the Alma to turn his stomach against the profession he had chosen, and satisfy himself that the smell of powder did not agree with his constitution; so, after a solemn consultation with his second in command, Colonel Haleem Bey, as great a poltroon as himself, both parties decamped one fine morning, without beat of drum, and found their way to Stamboul; for which act the Seraskier Riza Pacha brought them up before the Mejlis (Council of War) on a charge 'of having cowardly abandoned their post in the field before the enemy;' and in the presence of all the troops they were degraded from their respective ranks, and are now vegetating in prison.

"This *finale* was, however, against my interests, as one evening before the Pacha left the Crimea, when we were talking about the chances of an engagement at an early period, he said, 'You are an Englishman, and like fighting, and cannot be afraid of a woman; so what do you say to taking my eighty thousand piastres' worth off my hands? She is as good as when I bought her, and I will give you a house and garden with her, and adopt you as a son.' Of course I closed with his offer at once, but our little arrangement was put an end to by his sentence; so you see, my friends, that the old adage is true which says, 'Wherever there is misfortune, a woman is sure to be at the bottom of it.'"

CHAPTER XXII.

Circassian scenery.—A false alarm.—The Bey's konak.—Rifles and revolvers.—Circassian cuisine.—A goose cooked à la Mrs Harris.—Uninvited company.—News of a bear.—A night prowler.—A huntsman's toilet.—The route through the ravines.—The lair.—The Bey's dogs give tongue.—An enor mous bear wounded.—A man mauled.—The Bruin bites the dust.—The bivouac.—Horses stolen.—Mussulman apathy.—The pursuit.—The trail.—The plunderers surprised and taken. —Their punishment.

THE next morning we all set out with the Illori chieftain, and after a four hours' ride through a densely-wooded country, arrived at the gorge of a romantically picturesque valley, which appeared to wind its way for several miles between two lofty mountain ridges, forming a part of the chain of the Caucasus; a tortuous path, so narrow that we were obliged to ride in single file, and keep a sharp look-out that we did not come in contact with overhanging rocks or branches of trees, wound along the edge of a chasm, in which a foaming mountain-torrent dashed impetuously; and at times we passed along the brinks of precipices which made the head giddy to look over. Here and there gigantic forest trees stood out in bold relief, and towering crags of castellated form rose in every direction, whilst patches of gorgeous flowers of various colours were seen among the luxuriant herbage, adding their rich tints, as if to harmonise with the exquisite beauty of the surrounding scenery.

As we were picking our way over the strong bed of a mountain-stream which had cleft a wide opening through the forest, I was rather startled by hearing the sharp crack of a rifle, and the "ping" of a bullet high over our heads, which, from the streak of smoke, evidently came from a high rocky crag commanding the ford on the opposite bank; and, instinctively, both myself and followers, apprehensive of treachery, unslung our rifles, and prepared for action by springing from our saddles and taking advantage of the cover of huge boulders of rock that were scattered about in every direction. But the Illori Bey, who was much amused by our proceedings, informed us that we were approaching his "konak," and that the shot we heard was merely a signal from one of the outlying scouts of his tribe, who, being at feud with their neighbours, were obliged to keep a strict watch on the defile leading to their hamlet. One of his followers answered the signal by discharging his pistol, and in a few moments a number of young men came galloping up on rough mountain-ponies, who gave us a cordial welcome, and saluted us by touching our feet with the tips of their fingers, and then raising them to their foreheads.

On the slope of a hill, surrounded by a small patch of Indian corn, stood the hamlet, which consisted of about half a dozen log-huts, each containing a single apartment; and one of the largest, by the orders of the Bey, was cleared out of its occupants, consisting of an indiscriminate medley of men, women, children, ponies, sheep, goats, cows, buffaloes, geese, fowls, &c., and given up for the accommodation of my people and horses, being sufficiently roomy to contain all comfortably.

I was conducted to the "dewan-khana," or guest-house, and introduced to the elders of the tribe as the "Ingleese Bey," where, after pipes and sherbet had been handed round by boys, I had to undergo a long series of cross-questioning as to the recent events of the war.

At last my revolvers, which I aways wore loaded in my belt, in case of accident, attracted their attention, and they all jumped up thunderstruck when I explained their action; but I was not believed until I had exhibited their powers by lodging ten bullets in a small circle of a walnut-tree about twenty paces distant from the door of the hut. In order more strongly to impress upon their minds the nature of our armament so as to guard against any attempt at treachery, I directed one of the boys to hang a dry gourd, which served as a water-vessel, on a stalk of Indian corn about a hundred yards distant, and sent a couple of bullet shots through it with my double rifle; and, whilst they were examining the weapon, I slipped the extra loaded chambers in my revolvers and again fired them off, much to their consternation and wonder: indeed, they looked upon me as very closely allied to the "the nameless one," for I heard them congratulating themselves in an undertone that none of their enemies had *demon-inspired* pistols that were of fatal aim and never required loading.

When we again adjourned to the hut I found that breakfast had been served, consisting of several dishes, but I was most woefully disappointed in the cookery, which was wretched in the extreme, I may say execrable; for, although hungry, I could hardly manage to swallow half a dozen mouthfuls · the bill of fare consisting of rank goat's-flesh boiled up with millet-seed, black broth, sundry preparations of sour milk, smoked kouskous, and pillaf made of rancid butter, roasted Indian corn, and black-looking maize cakes. At last the repast was over, and, making some excuse about looking after the horses, I bolted to my people, whom I found comfortably established and supplied with all they required.

One of them had managed to get hold of a goose, and, as I felt nearly ravenoüs, I devoted him to "sudden death," converted him into a savoury mess in less than ten minutes, by an old campaigning receipt which, for the benefit of future foragers, I give *à la* Mrs Harris's:—"First catch your goose, cut off the head, pull off the feathers with the skin, cut the meat from off the bones in small square pieces, and chuck them into a frying pan, with butter, pepper, and salt, if you have any, letting them stew until they assume a rich brown colour, when you may begin to eat." Bread or biscuit fried up with the fat is a considerable adjunct.

My hunger satiated, the gang, according to their usual custom, made a huge fire of dry logs on a piece of open ground a short distance in front of the hut; and, spreading my carpet to windward, I prepared to enjoy the "fragrant weed," and cogitate upon the programme for the morrow, whilst our *tents d'abri* (of which each of us carried a part in front of his saddle) were being pitched: it being considered preferable to sleep under canvas to remaining in the hut, on account of vermin; fleas having been found so large and numerous that Kuchuk declared that he was afraid of molesting or annoying any of the race, for, if they made a combined attack, and all pulled one way, he felt sure they would be able to drag him bodily out of the hut.

There is no time more pleasant in the life of an old forest-ranger than the setting in of the night after a good day's sport, when the hunters recline round the log-fire, shaded from the evening dew by the canopy of some gigantic forest tree, and talk over the events of the day or the hopes of the morrow. Then the soothing cheroot and comforting can of grog are indeed luxuries, and old familiar airs and stirring tales go round cheerily, carrying the heart back to happy bygone scenes of home, and dear old friends, far away in "Merrie England." None of my sporting chums caring to accompany me in this trip to regions marked in the best maps as "unknown tracts," I was without companion, and time hung heavily on my hands when not *en route*, or on the look-out for game, so I was very glad when the Bey Effendi came to consult me as to the most suitable arrangement for the morrow's battue. He was accompanied by a very intelligent young fellow of his tribe, who, whilst watching the cattle out at pasture, had discovered the lair of an immense bear, whose depredations had been severely felt during the winter months, when, emboldened by hunger, he had carried off horses picketed close to the "konac."

I decided to beat him out, if possible, and, after a long smoking-match, and some talk with the Bey as to the best plan of proceeding, he went to warn his people to be in readiness to start at the first appearance of dawn on the morrow, and I crept into my tent, rolled myself up in my blankets, and, being tired, was soon in a sound sleep, from which I was awakened by some one, as I thought, unceremoniously shaking me by the shoulder; but the visitor proved to be a half-famished prowling jackal, who was trying to drag away the buffalo-robe which served as an outer covering. I scared him away by shouting, and he vented his indignation by setting up a melancholy howl, which started a most infernal chorus from half a dozen packs in the neighbouring woods; but being well accustomed to such "jungle melody," I turned over, and once more composed myself to sleep.

When I awoke the next morning, I found my followers busily employed in rubbing down the horses, and the whole of the male portion of the tribe, with the exception of a few left to guard the village, preparing for the field. I gave myself a shake like a spaniel, and washed out my mouth, (the ordinary toilet of a hunter of the deep jungle, who generally performs his ablutions in the first stream he comes to,) and after hastily swallowing a cup of coffee and a biscuit, I mounted my horse, and hastened the departure of the party, which consisted of about forty individuals, most of them mounted on rough mountain-ponies, and armed with matchlocks, pistols, attaghans, &c.

The track lay through a gorge in the mountains, and, when day broke, presented a magnificent scene, as the sun dispelled the fog and mists which seemed to cling to the gigantic masses of rock piled on each other in endless variety of shape and extraordinary confusion; but I felt too much absorbed in surmising upon the different kinds of large game that were likely to be met with in such a vast extent of virgin forest, to pay very much attention to the picturesque beauties that lay in my path.

After about three hours' riding we came to a large log cattle-shed, used only in the summer months, when the best pasturage is to be found on the lower spurs of the mountains; and here we had to leave the horses under the charge of a guard, as the track became impracticable for them.

The Illori chief described this bear to be a terrible animal, standing as high as a pony; but, as I had a double-gun and rifle, and a brace of revolvers, I considered myself more than a match for him.

The herdsman now led the way, and under his guidance we climbed, in Indian file, a steep rocky hill, which caused us to puff and blow, and made our knees tremble before we got to the top; where, by dint of scrambling on our hands and knees, creeping along the edges of break-neck precipices, and hanging on to perilous ledges, we managed to work our way along the crest until we came to a deep rocky ravine on the other side, which appeared to have been denuded of the dense bush that generally covered the face of the country, by the violence of numerous mountain-torrents, which, when swollen by the rains, or the melting of the snow, dashed down the steep descent with immense force, and swept away all the underwood in their course. Here our guide assured us the lair was, and, indeed, it looked a likely place to meet with queer customers, for in all my peregrinations I never saw wilder country.

After an hour's careful investigation, during

which I came across several trails of red and roe deer, hogs, wolves, jackals, and foxes, as I was crossing a patch of sand in the dry bed of a stream I perceived the fresh footprints of a bear, which I instantly saw must be a very large one from his long stride and the size of his pugs, my hand hardly covering them.

I followed up the trail for some distance, but lost it on some rocky ground, and was making casts in different directions in order to regain it, when some of the Bey's dogs, which had gone on some short distance ahead, gave tongue, and immediately after I heard a sullen roar, followed by four or five dropping shots. I sprung upon a boulder of rock and discovered an enormous, dirty, white-looking bear in full pursuit of four or five Abassians, who were running shrieking up the hill-side about two hundred yards distant. One of them, in his frantic flight, tripped over a stone, and before he could rise the brute was upon him. Although the hinder-quarters of the animal only were presented to me, I threw up my rifle and let drive; whether it was that my hand was unsteady that morning, or that I feared hitting the man, I know not, but the first bullet fell short; the second, however, struck fair, and the bear, with a sharp hoarse cry of pain, quitted the fallen man, and again made after the rest. I reloaded as quickly as possible and ran up towards the wounded man, when I again saw Bruin for a moment, and got a couple of snap-shots at him as he bolted into some cover, having been turned by a straggling volley from some of my gang and the Bey's people. I found the youth who had fallen into the bear's clutches severely bitten in the shoulder, besides having his side clawed, and being considerably bruised and shaken, though not dangerously hurt; so, after bandaging his wounds as well as I could, I collected the people together, and prepared to make another effort to dislodge Bruin from his shelter.

One of my people had seen him enter some thick underwood between two large rocks, and I tried to coax the dogs to go in and drive him out; but it was of no use, they only ran yelping round the thicket. Two of their number had been killed in the first onset, and some of the others severely mauled, which damped the courage of the rest; so, finding that nothing could be effected with their assistance, I posted all the people in groups as safely as I could at one end of the cover, in case the game might break without showing fight, and followed up the trail, which was very plainly marked with blood, alone.

The brushwood was very thick, and much impeded my movements, so I got on but slowly; but, by dint of creeping on my hands and knees and scrambling, I managed to get some distance into the cover, when I heard a savage growl, followed up by a low grunting noise, evidently not far from me.

Bruin's Charge.

I peered through the bush, but could see nothing; so, resting my rifle against the trunk of a tree, I endeavoured to swarm up in order to have a better look round. I had hardly raised myself a couple of feet from the ground when, with a terrific roar, the brute, which must have got wind of me, charged. Luckily, the bush was so thick in front that he could not get at me very easily, but had to make a turn which gave me time to seize and cock my rifle; and as his monstrous head, with flashing eyes and open jaws, appeared about a couple of paces from me, I gave him the contents of both barrels, which almost stunned him, for he spun round and round, and I had time to follow it up with my smooth-bore, both bullets taking effect in the head; but such was the enormous tenacity of life that he managed to tear out of the cover, rolling over and over as he went.

After reloading carefully, I followed up and found him sprawling about on the ground, moaning piteously. As I got out of the bush he caught sight of me, and made another headlong charge, reeling from side to side as he came; but I stopped him with another bullet in the head, which made him bite the dust. He rose again, and got up on his hind legs as if to look round, and whilst in this position he looked a fearful object, standing, as he did, with his fore-paws raised about seven feet high and the blood pouring in torrents out of his mouth. I now had a fair shot at his chest, and inflicted a mortal wound, for he rolled over and over, making his teeth meet in the root of a tree with his last dying effort.

He proved to be the largest bear I ever met with, standing over four feet high at the shoulder, and, from the number of men it took to lift him, I should think he could not have weighed less than eight hundred pounds. He appeared to be of the same species as the hill-bear of Circassia and the Himalayas, being covered with long whitey-brown hair. He had received eleven wounds, six of which were in the head; but I found that the round leaden balls from my smooth-bore had flattened on the skull without penetrating, whilst the conical projectile from my rifle splintered the bone. By the time the skin was taken off, the carcass cut up, and the flesh divided among the people, the sun had sunk low in the west, and we had to beat a hasty retreat in order to reach our bivouac (the cattle-shed) before nightfall. Here we found a supply of sheep, fowls, and forage had been brought in during our absence; so, after we had pitched our tents and made the "inner man" comfortable, our battle with the bear was fought over again as we reclined round an immense fire, until some of us began to nod, when we rolled ourselves up in our blankets and turned in for the night, well satisfied with our day's sport.

I was awakened some time before dawn by Kuchuk, who informed me that my baggage-pony and three horses belonging to the Bey's people were missing, and it was suspected that a predatory party of Kabardines, known to be lurking in the neighbourhood, were the culprits, and had paid us a visit in the night.

The loss of a good baggage-animal is, at any time, a serious inconvenience when travelling; but in a wild and desolate country, like that of the eastern coast of the Black Sea, it is almost an irremediable misfortune, so I jumped up immediately to consult with the Bey as to the best measures to take for the recovery of the stolen property. I found him still encased in sheepskins, but puffing furiously at his chibouk, and giving vent to his indignation in a long string of curses, loud and deep, against the marauders, whom he designated as "vile dogs of Kaffirs (unbelievers) of unchaste parentage," &c.

When I could get in a word, I advised him to send some of his people to follow up the trail as soon as it became light enough to see the marks left by the horses' feet; but he, with true Mussulman apathy, declared that a pursuit would be useless, as the plunderers had got too long a start.

Of this I did not feel at all sure, knowing the extreme difficulty of getting over the ground in the dark, in a wooded country; so I determined to give chase with my own people, accompanied by the herdsman who had shown us the bear's lair the day before, and a couple of young men of the tribe, who professed not only to know the country well, but also imagined they could hit upon the haunts of the cattle-lifters.

Having buried our superfluous baggage, we set off in light marching order as soon as the day broke; and falling upon the trail almost immediately, followed it up in Indian file, as fast as the rocky nature of the ground permitted. It appeared that the culprits were six in number, as there were marks of two having remained in charge of six horses some short distance off, whilst four others prowled about our bivouac in search of plunder.

After a fatiguing ride of several hours' duration, over hill and dale, through woods and across rivers, we came to a marshy swamp which bore the appearance of having recently been disturbed by horses' hoofs; so on we pushed with renewed vigour, and I refrained from letting drive at seven gigantic cranes, who, regardless of our presence, continued to wade less than two hundred yards distant, which was a sore temptation, as they appeared of a rare kind, and I would have got them all in line with a little judicious stalking.

There could be no doubt of our being on the track of the right party, as in several places I perceived the trail of my baggage-pony, which was shod with the broad Turkish shoe on the fore-feet, whereas none of the other animals had any. Towards noon, after clambering up the steep rocky side of a low ridge of hills, I perceived, in the ravine below, a light column of smoke curling up from some broken ground, and, after a careful investigation with my field-glass, I saw several horses with their fore-feet hobbled, grazing by the banks of a small stream, which, I had no doubt, belonged to the marauders.

After a brief consultation with my followers, I directed Kuchuk and three others to accompany me in a reconnaissance, whilst the rest of the party took charge of the horses and kept a look-out on the road. As my men were well-armed, and I could fully depend upon their pluck, I did not much fear the result of a contest, but was rather afraid lest the pillagers, knowing the country, might slip through our hand with their booty, so I struck off from the track, and made a circuitous route by crossing the ravine some distance below the place where I saw the smoke, and again gaining it on the opposite height, from whence, with the aid of my glass, I could see the objects of our search reclining round a fire, apparently very jolly on the strength of their success.

After having made as careful a survey as the wooded nature of the ground would allow, we advanced towards them as noiselessly as possible, keeping well under cover, until we came to the edge of the open where the horses were grazing, from whence we got a full view of the party, which appeared to be five in number; one of whom was washing his mouth in the stream, a second superintending the cooking, and the others smoking and lolling about on the ground, evidently quite unsuspicious of danger.

Knowing the effect of a surprise, I determined, if possible, to accomplish our purpose without bloodshed, and observing their rude firearms resting against a boulder of rock, I resolved to get as near as possible by stalking, and then make a simultaneous dash.

By dint of creeping on our hands and knees, and taking advantage of the cover of bushes, rocks, and undulations in the ground, we got to within a dozen yards of the three fellows lying down, on whom we made a rush, and, after a momentary struggle, overpowered by laying about us with the butt-end of our rifles. The two others bolted into the jungle on the first alarm, where further pursuit was useless, and a sixth, who was acting as scout a short distance in the rear, fell into the hands of our other party

Having disarmed and pinioned our prisoners, one of whom had his arm broken in the scuffle, and secured the horses, (ten in number, including our own re:aptured,) we rejoined the rest of the party, and after a hasty meal set out on our return.

Our captives, who were a sullen, "ill-favoured, hang-dog looking" set of fellows, proved to belong to a mountain tribe from the other side of Pitzounda, who were returning from an unsuccessful foray in Mingrelia, when they caught sight of our cattle and attempted a *razée.*

We arrived in camp late in the afternoon, and great was the old Bey's joy at the recovery of his animals, which he had made up his mind he would never see again. The prisoners were all recognised as being old offenders; and, according to the law of the tribes, as the mildest punishment, would have been sold as slaves in the interior; but this I would not allow, as I intended, by making an example, to deter another attempt being made on my cattle: so the gang, after branding each of them indelibly with a heated horse-shoe, on the right shoulder, turned them adrift, minus their arms, horses, and kalpacs, (high caps of black sheepskin,) warning them that they might expect no mercy if found again anywhere near our camp.

The Bey had heard of another bear, and had sent out some of his people to make sure of his whereabouts; but, as the haunt was said to be nearer the "konak" than where we were, it was determined to return there on the morrow. I selected one of the captured horses for my own use, presented another to the Bey, a third to the herdsman who showed me the bear's haunt, and then gave the others, with the captured arms, as prizes to the best marksmen in the tribe.

CHAPTER XXIII.

CIRCASSIA—*continued.*

On the sale of Circassian females, and extenuating circumstances. —Their character.—An exploring trip premeditated.—The start.—A Russian fort.—Bustard-shooting.—Forest scenery. — Difficulties *en route.* — Trout-fishing. — Mosquitoes. — A lovely valley.—Wild-cattle hunt.—An awkward predicament. —A bull and cow slain.—Mode of preserving the flesh.—More game afoot.—The ascent of the first range.—Mountain scenery.—Mount El-Bruz in the distance.—Difficult travelling.—A bear started.—A long shot.—Strange feelings.—A frightful chasm, and exciting moment.—Journey along the ridge.—The descent.—Wolves.—A Circassian hamlet.—Hospitality. —A noble race.—A Durbar, and the result of our consultation.

AMONGST the various localities to which erratic fate has directed my steps, there are few that have so many agreeable souvenirs associated in my recollection as Circassia; and I wonder that more travellers and sportsmen do not turn their wanderings towards a country which, although pre-eminent throughout the world for magnificence of scenery, is yet a *terra incognita.* In these days of steam and rail, it were an easy matter for the lover of the picturesque, or the sportsman—instead of forming one of that horde of sight-seers annually discharged on the Continent—to take his lounge one afternoon in Rotten Row, and that day fortnight to find himself sipping coffee in the midst of a circle of mountaineers, in one of the romantic gorges of the Caucasus; where a man's worth is not estimated by the length of his pocket, but according to the gifts bestowed upon him by Nature, and the manner in which he makes use of them. Yes, my gentle reader, notwithstanding the tales you may have heard of the barbarity of the Circassians, in selling their daughters to the panders of Osmanli harems, and the maidens' passive apathetic resignation to such a fate, I maintain that it is the force of circumstances alone that has brought this revolting custom about. It must be remembered that the gallant tribes of the mountains have been engaged in a bloody war, against fearful odds, for the last eighty years: consequently there has been a continual drain upon the male population—the number of men falling annually in battle against the invaders far exceeding the number of male children born. Such having been the case for nearly a century, naturally enough there is a great disproportion between the sexes, and, notwithstanding that polygamy exists, it is a matter of difficulty for all the "gentler sex" to obtain protectors; and, as "*antiquated spinsters*" are of a genus unknown in the Caucasus, it is not to be wondered at that the inhabitants are willing to dispose of their extra produce, not required for home consumption, to the Turks; who make good husbands, are of the same faith, and much akin in habits and manners. The custom of admitting foreigners and prisoners of war into the tribes, was doubtlessly adopted in order to make up for the loss of men killed in battle, and not from any great partiality towards strangers. During my sojourn in the country—to which time my mind often reverts as being the happiest of my life — I found that, among these unsophisticated people, the possession of large hoards of the "yellow metal" does not constitute the value of the man; and the most beautiful maidens of the world estimate their lovers' worth by the qualities they display—not their possessions. There, a bold spirit, a cool head in the time of danger, a good shot, a skilful horseman, and a strong arm that can defend his own, is looked upon as a rich man and a suitable "partie;" if, withal, he possesses a kind heart, nothing more is required to make a home happy in Circassia. But, Heigh Allah! I must check myself upon such subjects, and put the curb upon my pen, or it will run upon other reminiscences of the past than those connected with "The Hunting Grounds."

I had passed many happy days in the konak of the Bey and amongst other friendly tribes, when one afternoon, as I was returning from a successful deer-stalking expedition, I fell in with a young mountaineer who was *en route* to his home, close to

Mount El-Bruz. After some conversation, I made up my mind to take a trip to that part of the country, under his guidance, and, if possible, to make an ascent of the "Father of Mountains." The same evening I communicated my intention to my followers, who made their preparations accordingly; and the next morning, after quite a tender leave-taking from our worthy host and his people, to whom we promised to return, a start was effected. For the first four or five miles after leaving the konak, we had the advantage of a bridle-path, which had been formed many years ago by the Russians, for the purpose of keeping up a communication with one of their outposts, a small fort, or rather redoubt, constructed on an isolated hill which commanded the entrance of a deeply-wooded gorge. The work, in which embrasures and platforms for eight pieces of cannon were still visible, had evidently been intended to prevent the aggressive incursions of the mountain tribes, but it did not appear to have been inhabited for some years, as the barrack was roofless and the flagstaff had rotted away. Our guide told me that this had been the scene of many a hard conflict between the Muscovite troops and the mountaineers, and his statement was confirmed by the numerous graves, some of which were marked by tombstones bearing Greek or Russian inscriptions, and others by rude wooden crosses.

On the slope and round the base of the hill were

clearings in the low scrub-jungle, which at one time had evidently been fenced in and cultivated, having perhaps served the garrison as pasture-lands and corn-fields. As I was taking a sketch of the little stronghold from one of these places, the "Hadjee" informed me that he had seen several very large birds go down in a patch of low jungle close at hand. From his description, I imagined that they were cranes, having seen several of a very large species wading in a swamp *en route*, and being desirous of obtaining a specimen, I loaded my gun with a couple of Eley's green long-range cartridges, and accompanied him to the spot where he had marked the birds alight. I had beaten about the place for some time without seeing anything, and was about to give up the pursuit, when, as I was turning round a low copse, a covey of bustard (*Otis tarda*) suddenly got up from a small undulating plain close to a watercourse, and I had the good fortune to bring down a couple of them, right and left, before they could get fairly upon the wing. One, a hen, fell dead, the shot having taken effect in the back part of the head and neck, but the second, a fine old cock, was only winged, and ran at an immense pace. Luckily "El Moro," my pointer, attracted by the report of my gun, came up and assisted me, otherwise I should have had no chance of catching him, notwithstanding I was in fair running condition. He proved to be a splendid specimen, the wings measuring more than four feet and a half from tip to tip. His weight I imagined to have been but little short of forty pounds, as he was in excellent condition, and by far the largest bird of the species I have hitherto seen, although I have killed many on the plains in India.

Having dined, we started again *en route*, and, on leaving the fort, made our way along tracks with which both Cassim and our guide appeared familiar, but which it would have been hazardous for a stranger to have attempted to follow without the aid of an experienced guide, as the country is so intersected by innumerable watercourses, meandering through dense labyrinths of wood, each of which so closely resembles the other, that a traveller once bewildered could hardly ever extricate himself, landmarks of any kind being few and far between. Now and then even our guide appeared puzzled, and had to climb some huge boulder of rock, or lofty tree, in order to make sure of the route, by observing the appearance of the mountains which formed the horizon of this sea of woods. On such occasions as these, had I not been an old forest-ranger accustomed to pilot my way by compass through trackless woods, I might perhaps have shared in the feelings of some of my followers, who, from time to time, showed symptoms of uneasiness as we wandered through apparently boundless depths of forest. The route was wild in the extreme, often leading across long extents of marshes, unhealthy swamps, and innumerable small rivers and streams, which our horses were generally able to ford, but sometimes had to swim. Now and then we had a good deal of trouble to cross, on account of the force of the current; and on one occasion we nearly lost one of our number, who got into a quicksand, and was only saved by our throwing him branches, with which he supported himself until we managed to draw him out with a rope.

We rode for ten or twelve miles along the base of thickly-wooded hills, until we came to a good-sized stream, running between high steep banks, fringed in places with willow and large trees, somewhat resembling the sycamore, which our guide informed us was a branch of the River Kodor, the same we had forded near the embouchure when accompanying the Turkish army from Suchum Kaleh. Here we determined to bivouac, and whilst my people were engaged in culinary operations, I strolled up the river with Ahmed and Kuchuk, on the look-out for a chance shot at deer, as I had seen a few slots during our march. Suddenly turning round a bend in the river, I observed some smoke a short distance ahead, which, after a careful reconnaissance, we approached, and found a party of Abassians catching fish in ingenious traps made of willows, which are laid in the most likely places in the stream. They had upwards of two dozen very fine fish, chiefly trout, which seemed exactly to resemble the English species, being formed and speckled without any distinguishable difference.

I got two glorious fellows, weighing about five pounds each, in exchange for a silver quarter-franc piece, which made a welcome addition to our supper. Our camp this night appeared to be the head-quarters of the mosquito tribes, for they settled upon us in myriads, keeping up a perpetual hum, and not allowing a moment's rest. It was positively amusing at times to hear the exclamations and growling of some of the people who were driven almost wild with continued torture. Strange to say, they scarcely molested me, although the faces of some of the others were much swollen by the multiplicity of their stings. With those sleep was out of the question, so they made a huge fire, round which they got some relief.

Sunrise saw us again *en route*, and after a most delightful ride of about ten miles up the river, through glorious woods of gigantic oak, beech, and walnut, or glades of rich nutritious grasses, we entered a most picturesque valley, which for beauty of scenery and rich fertility far exceeded anything that I had hitherto seen. On each side rose densely-wooded hills, here and there broken into gorgeously-coloured cliffs and dark winding ravines, whilst every turn displayed lovely vistas, stately avenues, groves of blossoming shrubs, clumps of gigantic forest-trees covered with festoons of the wild vine, and green slopes clothed with delicious verdure, forming a park-like scene far surpassing any of our finest demesnes in Old England.

As I looked around, I noticed many objects that brought "home scenes" vividly to mind, for, amongst the vegetation indigenous to southern climes, I noticed the wild plum, cherry, white-thorn, daisy, clover, larkspur, primrose, violet, and forget-me-not; besides which the full round notes of the blackbird and the warbling of the missel-thrush were heard high above the melody of the other sylvan choristers. An exclamation of surprise from Ahmed recalled me from this very agreeable reverie, directing my attention into a widely different channel, for, on passing close to a small piece of dense cover, I distinctly heard the snapping of sticks, followed by the tread of some heavy animal over dry vegetation, and almost immediately a mighty wild bull and three cows tore across the plain. To loosen my rifle and spring from my saddle was the work of a moment, and, taking a steady aim, I planted one bullet in his hind-quarter, the only part visible, as he was bolting away, and the second in his broad massive shoulder as he swerved round on receiving the first wound. This last made him bite the dust; but he soon regained his legs, and with a loud bellow and roar of rage made direct for the opposite height. I immediately gave chase, and, after a sharp burst, got up alongside my quarry, from whose side a stream of blood was spurting as he ran. Drawing my revolver from my holster, I aimed behind the ear; but my horse being fidgety and not accustomed to such kind of work, shied round at the moment, and the shot did not take effect. In the twinkling of an eye, before I could recock the pistol or get my horse out of his way, the bull charged, rolling us both over from the violence of the shock, and falling himself on his knees with the exertion. Luckily, although my horse was slightly gored in the shoulder, I was not in the least hurt with the purl; and before my antagonist could repeat his little game I sprang to my feet, and plunging my long hunting-knife into his chest, he staggered forward a few paces, and dropped on his side dead. In the meantime my followers gave chase to the rest of the herd, and a young cow, in first-rate condition for the table, fell after a desperate charge, in which she unhorsed one or two of their number, although without doing any serious damage. These cattle, which much resemble in appearance the largest of our Scotch oxen, generally go in herds of eight or ten, and the people of the country say that they are the most formidable animals in the forest, neither the bear nor the wolf ever daring to meddle with them. The bull I killed (which was the only one seen during my sojourn in that part—although we several times came across their trails) was a most savage-looking brute, having an immensely broad chest, deep shoulders, muscular fore-arms, short thick curved horns, and large dewlap. The general colour was black, with dirty white under the belly and inside the thighs and legs, and the height at the shoulder nearly sixteen hands.

Having now much more flesh than we could consume before it became tainted, I thought it advisable to halt where we were and "jerk" some of the meat, which we did, by cutting it in strips and hanging it for several hours over a large wood-fire. We grilled some steaks on the embers almost before they became cold, and to my surprise they were remarkably tender. We salted the tongues as well as we could, keeping them for the ascent—and the marrow Hoossain made into pastics that would have excited the admiration of poor old Soyer himself. During the night our fire attracted some deer; but Ali, who first perceived them, and fired a couple of shots, did not manage to bag any, although they did not go away unscathed, as when day broke blood was found upon their trail, which we did not follow up, as it led in a contrary direction to our route.

For some hours our course lay parallel and almost on the same level as the bed of the stream; but it now began to ascend gradually, and at last we found ourselves scrambling up the face of a steep scarped cliff, from a chasm in the base of which the torrent burst, as it were, from the womb of the mountain. Our guide evidently knew the country well, for the route was admirably chosen, and he led us up the steepest ascents with an easy inclination that would have done credit to the most able engineer. The surface of the rock, without being so very smooth as to render our horses' footing insecure, presented no very serious obstacle, so that we got on famously, and by noon reached a natural clearing in the woods, carpeted with rich indigenous grasses and flowers of the most delicate tints, and intersected with numerous small streams of crystal clearness, that flowed in little murmuring cascades down the side of the mountain.

We continued to ascend until dusk, when we encamped for the night under the lee of a huge mass of black granite, which exposure to the weather had made as smooth as if it had been artificially polished. Rising with the sun the following morning, and invigorated by the bracing air, we gained the tableland on the summit, after a tramp of about four hours' duration.

It was from this spot that we got the first uninterrupted view of the mighty El-Bruz, on whose snow-clad summit the sky seemed to rest. It appeared so distinctly defined that I did not imagine it was more than fifteen miles off, and was much surprised when our guide assured me that it was nearly twelve *saat*, or about three times that distance.

Our route now became much more difficult for the horses, as we had to make our way for several miles in an easterly direction along the tortuous ridge of this range, sometimes clambering up craggy cliffs so steep that every moment I was afraid of my horse losing his balance and falling backwards with me, and at other times having to descend rocky slopes and ledges with scarcely any inequalities in their surface to afford foothold. Often the men had infinite trouble with their animals before they could get them to attempt some of the descents; and frequently one of them, slipping, would come sliding against the rest, knocking others off their legs, which it required great exertion and floundering to regain. I took care to avoid such accidents by keeping well ahead; but sometimes even my horse, which was remarkable for its sure-footedness, would come on to his knees, and remain a fixture, fearing, if he stirred, to roll down the whole way. We avoided all the higher peaks, which were covered with snow, and tried to preserve our level as much as possible, although at times we traversed valleys so walled-in that the rays of the sun could never penetrate except at noonday. As we were descending a steep ravine of this kind, Abdulla pointed out to me an enormous bear, scrambling, hand over hand, up the stumps and bush on the other side; and, jumping off my horse, I made use of a slab of rock as a rest, and gave him both barrels simultaneously. Although the distance was nearly five hundred yards, my shots evidently took effect, for he rolled over several times before he could regain his legs, when he looked fiercely round and growled most savagely. I hastily reloaded, but he had in the meantime given leg-bail, so I directed two of the gang to remain where we were to mark the place, and direct me in case I should not be able to make straight for it, and then gave chase. It was no easy work to scramble up the rocky slope; but at last we got upon his trail, and soon found gouts of blood which, although not sufficient to lead me to suppose that he was mortally wounded, proved that my shots, even at that long range, had taken effect. As the trail diverged considerably from our route, we gave up the pursuit; and, after halting a short time to cook a meal, by a beautiful stream gushing out of the live rock, the water of which was so cold that it gave me a violent toothache, again pushed forward.

After a weary march and much slipping and scrambling over most difficult ground, we ascended from a ravine to an elevated ridge covered with stunted grass, along which we travelled ten or twelve miles, enjoying a magnificent prospect on each hand of apparently boundless ranges of snow-capped mountains and interminable forest. An inexpressible feeling of silent contemplation and awe seemed to pervade the entire company, as we rode along for miles without exchanging an observation; indeed, the solemn silence of uninvaded nature gave birth to strange emotions bordering on fear, which seemed inexplicable, considering the scenes that each and every one of my party had gone through.

From this we ascended a ridge of high rocks, in some places covered with low scrub, where we encamped for the night, as we found some difficulty in crossing a mountain-torrent that came tumbling over a bed of huge boulders of green and black granite with a roar like thunder.

The next morning, having crossed this obstruction, we clambered over the last crest of the mountain, a deep valley only lying between us and the El-Bruz, and commenced our descent in single file by a long spur, along the back or ridge of which we pursued our course for some miles without any feeling of insecurity, as the sides, though steep, were densely wooded, and obscured the terrors of the view. Suddenly, as we were skirting a scarped cliff, we came to a sharp angle where we had to pass a narrow ledge or shelf jutting out of the live rock, on which there was scarcely room for a goat to turn. I was leading, my horse being the most sure-footed, but here he stopped dead short with a strange snort and shudder, that first made me feel the imminence of my danger, throwing out his legs as if bent upon going no further. A foaming river was roaring some hundreds of feet below, so that we could hardly hear ourselves speak; and if I could I would have dismounted to reconnoitre, but this was perfectly impossible. I could not turn, and must advance: but *auri sacra fames, quid non mortalia pectora cogis?* What looked impossible was soon made practicable. Delay was dangerous, so I loosened the reins, gently urged my horse forward, and at the same time gave him the spur. With a grunt of despair, and eyes distended, he craned his neck forward, and, after a fearful effort, managed to gain a place where the pass became broader, when he broke out into a profuse perspiration from terror. As soon as I was able to draw a full breath, I ordered my followers to dismount and go over first, leading their horses with a cord, in which manner all managed to get over safely. It was an anxious moment, and I do not think any inducement would cause me to repeat the feat; for, although a fearless horseman, and endued with a sailor's eye, my heart often palpitates when I think of that perilous scramble.

We continued to descend until nearly dusk, when we halted for the night in the dense forest that clothes the lower spurs of these mountains, lighting huge fires to keep away the wolves, which kind of "vermin" were to be met with in packs, and bears' tracks were not at all uncommon. Frequently during the night we were alarmed by their infernal howling close at hand, but they did not dare to approach our fire. The next morning we got into the plain, and towards noon arrived at a Circassian konac, where we were made extremely welcome, more especially when our guide, who was well known in the hamlet, told them that I was an Englishman who had fought against the Russians, both in the Crimea and in Asia Minor, for at first they had taken me for one of "*the Faithful.*" A comfortable log-hut was placed at my disposal, with a shed for the horses, and Hoossain obtained a bountiful supply of fowls, eggs, corn-flour, and half a sheep, which was soon converted into a savoury mess. After we had refreshed the inner man, we held a "durbar," at which all the elders, and indeed most of the inhabitants of the hamlet attended; and never, either in civilised or savage life, have I seen a finer-looking race than the specimens then before me. The men were all of noble stature, stalwart, and muscular to a degree, with highly intelligent countenances and strikingly handsome features, the lower part of which were generally covered with long flowing beards. The women were extremely beautiful, with finely-chiselled features, lustrous eyes, and pearly teeth, which they disclosed in gracious and fascinating smiles, that lighted up their faces with the most bewitching radiance. They wore no head-dress, generally speaking, except their luxuriant tresses, which flowed in unconfined freedom over their shoulders, although during my stay among them I noticed some in jaunty-looking scarlet caps. Their hands were beautiful, and when they walked their flowing drapery revealed the exquisite symmetry of their legs and feet, which throughout the world are unrivalled. We all sat down in a semicircle in front of the door of my hut, the women a little distance behind the men, and, after Hoossain and Abdulla had served the greater part of the assembly with coffee, "chibouks" were lighted, when, with an air of great ceremony, I commenced a speech in Turkish, eked out with Hindostanee, which was translated by Abdulla, for the benefit of that part of my audience who could not understand the former language.

I explained my views, announcing my intention of exploring the El-Bruz, (which I could see caused supercilious smiles amongst some of the party,) and finished off by presenting the chief with a pair of brass-mounted pistols, a looking-glass, some scarlet cloth, and a piece of gold-lace for his harem. Although evidently much pleased with my little attention—for he was profuse in his thanks and offers of service—he shook his head and looked grave when I again brought the El-Bruz on the *tapis*, assuring me that the ascent was impossible, not only on account of the depth of snow, but also because it was inhabited by evil spirits, such as "gins," "afrits," and "gholes," who would not allow any mortal to penetrate into their sanctuaries. I made light of his fears, repeating the Mussulman creed—"*Allah e Allah, Mahomed Roosool il hum du lilla,*" and declared that I would make the attempt even if I knew the place to be the haunt of all the shytans of Jehannum.* This was a "clincher," and after some discussion between Ishmael, (our guide,) Cassim, and some of the elders of the tribe, it was settled that two of their number should accompany us, as they knew more about the mountain than any one else, having been obliged at one time to take refuge there when pur-

* Shytans of Jehannum—demons of the infernal regions.

sued by a predatory hostile party. These gave me to understand that there was a deserted konac some distance up the mountain, up to which point our horses could go, so I resolved to make the necessary preparations that evening, and start for the place early the next morning. What little superfluous baggage I had I left in charge of the chief, and then ordered Hoossain, Kuchuk, and Cassim to accompany me with the two young men of the tribe, as I did not care to have too many about me, and the rest were to take charge of the horses at the foot of the mountain.

This being arranged, and provisions, ropes, blankets, and waterproof-sheeting being packed and divided, so that each had about equal weight, I had poles cut so as to serve as "alpenstocks;" and early the next morning we started, accompanied for a short distance by the greater part of the tribe, who wished us God-speed and luck on our undertaking. After a ride of about six hours' duration through the woods we began to ascend, and in the afternoon arrived at the deserted konac, which was situated on a projecting spur. Here we put up for the night, making ourselves as comfortable as possible; Ali and his party keeping watch whilst mine slept, so as to be fresh for work on the morrow. All my followers wanted to accompany me, but it could not be, so after a plentiful breakfast we bade them adieu, and set out on our perilous expedition.

CHAPTER XXIV.

CIRCASSIA—*continued.*—THE ASCENT OF MOUNT EL-BRUZ.

Forest scenery.—The first halt.—A glacier.—A beautiful panorama.—Sunrise.—A lammergeier slain.—Glacier travelling.—Eternal snow.—Avalanches.—The lower summit attained.—Our exultation.—A description of the higher summit.—The impossibility of reaching it.—Grand scenery.—Intense glare.—The descent commenced.—A sudden death.—Kuchuk's last resting-place.—Fatiguing fag.—The bivouac in the pine-forest.—An ibex killed.—Return.—Finale.

THE forest glowed with the most vivid autumn tints; the foliage of the different trees exhibiting every shade, from the brightest orange to the deepest red; and contrasted strangely with the peculiarly rich colouring of masses of rocks here and there intermingled, forming a picture, of Nature's painting, which surpassed all the efforts of an artist to depict. Ferns nearly six feet in height, and of a species I had not previously seen, grew in the greatest profusion, whilst indigenous myrtle, box, laurel, rhododendron, and gigantic heath-bushes, grew in the greatest profusion on every side. The ground was carpeted with the most exquisitely beautiful flowers, amongst which I noticed bracken (*Pteris acquilina*) of a deep orange colour, blue, purple, and white monkshood, heath-bells, columbine, anemones, forget-me-nots, pansies, ranunculi, violets, and a delicate-looking creeper with scarlet bloom which grew amid the rocks, most of which were covered with mosses of every hue and shade. After several hours' severe toil, the appearance of the forest became very much changed; the oak, beech, sycamore, poplar, walnut, chesnut, ash, birch, and other trees of the plains, giving place to lofty pines, covered with many-coloured lichen, larch, and gigantic cedars, some of which, evidently of a great age, had at last succumbed to the violence of the storms, for many were lying prostrate. Day was now drawing to a close, so we began to make the necessary preparations for passing the night, which were not difficult to men like mine, the greater part of whose lives had been spent in the open air. Following up a foaming torrent that came tumbling down the side of the mountain, over huge boulders of granite, with a roar like thunder, we came to a cleft in the rocks, which was soon converted into a fortress impregnable to either bears or wolves, the only assailants likely to be found in these wild regions. Our blankets and waterproofs were unrolled, and we were soon all reclining round the blazing logs of an immense camp-fire, on the side of which two brass kettles, containing our evening repast, were bubbling away merrily. Mine were a motley crew, a rough and reckless lot of desperate men, of different race and creeds, bound by no tie, and heeding no law, yet perfect unanimity existed amongst them. Wild songs were sung, strange tales were told; and many a hoarse peal of merriment rang through the night air, as the jest went round. Loudly they laughed, and little they recked for the morrow. The moon was nearly at the full, and her silver light made the open parts of the forest as clear as day; but I set the watch early, and bid my followers take what repose they could, as I knew that they would have a hard fag on the morrow.

The queen of the night was still high in the heavens, when we began to make preparations for a start by packing up our baggage in the smallest space possible, and after a cup of hot coffee and *eau de vie* to keep out the night air, we were again *en route.* We soon left the forest behind, and, after crossing a belt of dwarf-pine, with an undergrowth of savin and juniper bushes almost waist-high, we came to a wilderness of rocks and beetling crags; having every now and then to clamber up steep slopes covered with huge boulders of granite and masses of fallen *débris,* which were readily set in motion. We were obliged to be very careful, and ascend like skirmishers in extended order, as, every few yards we went, huge fragments came rolling down, which would have caused severe injury had they struck any of us. After several hours' severe toil we clambered a ridge of broken rocks piled on each other in great confusion, which up to this time had entirely hidden the higher part of the mountain, and the overwhelming sublimity of the scene that then broke upon our view for the first time, amply compensated for the fatigue we had undergone. We had reached the edge of a huge glacier, which, like a mighty river suddenly frozen, appeared to flow down a gorge in the side of the mountain, and extended for some miles both above and below the ridge on which we were standing. Dense foliage and huge masses of rock intervening, had prevented our getting a glimpse of it before, notwithstanding we had attained an altitude much above the lower part, which seemed to have cleft its way far into the heart of the forest.

The panorama from this point was magnificent, for at the end of the glacier—which in some parts was dazzling white, and in others of the colours of the sapphire and the amethyst—where it appeared to blend with masses of eternal snow, rose the stupendous summit of the "Father of Mountains," towering in silent majesty like a glittering mass of cold alabaster. Seating ourselves on a smooth slab of rock, we spent some time in gazing on the surpassingly-beautiful scene spread below and around, and I made a futile attempt to sketch it; but it was labour under difficulties, for the cold became so intense that I could scarcely hold my pencil, and had to jump and caper about every moment in order to prevent my limbs from becoming benumbed. Besides this, the longer the eye dwelt upon the scene, the vaster and more magnificent became its gigantic and stately proportions; and again and again I put down my pencil, feeling the impossibility of doing justice to it. At last, after a great trial of patience, I managed to complete a tolerably correct outline, which I filled in with the aid of my glass, endeavouring at the same time to impress the scene so correctly on my mind that not a single important feature should be forgotten.

Whilst so employed, the rays of the rising sun were just beginning to tinge the summits of the loftiest ranges on the eastern horizon (where our guide pointed out to me Mount Kazbek towering high above the rest,) and by degrees each peak, precipice, and ridge assumed a delicate rose-colour, which deepened every moment until it became tinged with a gorgeous golden tint that gradually paled as the glorious luminary of day ascended in the heavens, when after a short time the virgin snow was again left in its unsullied whiteness.

No description could convey an idea of the intense grandeur of the scene before us, which displayed a richness of colouring far surpassing the painter's art to depict. Mountains divided by deep, dark, densely-wooded ravines lay beneath us, and the valley from which we commenced the ascent was bathed in a rich violet hue. Castellated peaks and masses of rock of every shape and form rose in all directions, and many foaming torrents and cascades glistened like silver on the rugged sides of the mountain. The only sounds that broke the intense silence that reigned over the whole face of nature, were the roaring of distant avalanches, the melancholy cry of the eagle, or the shrill whistle of the marmot as, alarmed at our intrusion on his domains, he scrambled into his burrow under the rocks.

The bracing freshness of the air and the magnificence of the scenery had the effect of enduing us all with an exuberant overflow of joyous animation and exhilaration of spirits, as for several minutes we amused ourselves in testing our strength by seeing who could throw farthest over the glacier, or hurl the largest fragments of rock down the steep slope. Whilst so amusing ourselves, a pair of immense lammergeier came soaring over our heads. I immediately unslung my rifle, which I carried across my back, and let drive a couple of shots, but both were without effect, the distance being too great. A lucky thought flashed across my mind, which I immediately put into execution. I took a red silk pocket-handkerchief, and, fastening a stone in the centre, I threw it into the air several times; and when I saw that it had attracted their attention, I threw it as far as I could down the slope before me. It hardly fell when both made a swoop towards it, and came well within distance. I threw up my rifle, hit the leading bird hard with the first barrel, and brought him down with the second; but I had a difficult task to get to him, as the descent was very precipitous and covered with loose stones and shingle. He proved to be a magnificent specimen, his wings measuring nearly ten feet from tip to tip. I plucked out his wing-feathers and cut off the head and claws as trophies, but I had not time to take his skin, which I felt extremely sorry for. Whilst engaged in this task, the female kept hovering round about, uttering strange sad cries, and several times I thought she would have attacked me, so I gave her a shot which made her go to the right-about.

We now clambered down upon the glacier, which by its appearance from the height would, I thought, prove easier travelling than along the craggy side of the mountain; but I soon found out my mistake, as the surface, which I imagined to be tolerably even, proved undulating, rugged, and much broken up by crevices and chasms of immense depth and perpendicular wall-like sides, which varied from a few inches to many yards in width. After a wearisome tramp of about a mile we came to a line of masses of rock, piled one upon another, over which we had great difficulty in making our way. As these obstructions appeared frequent, and we lost much ground by seeking to avoid fissures that we dared not leap, I determined to return once more to the rocky ramparts on the side, and after a difficult climb was once again on *terra firma*, and felt more at home than on the surface of the glacier, whose continual cracking, creaking, and heaving, made us feel nervous lest it might open directly under our feet and engulf us, which seemed very possible, as we twice saw the ice sink, give way, and tear asunder, forming fearful yawning chasms of unknown depths.

After several hours' continued exertion we got to an altitude high above the head of the glacier, and the aspect of the scenery became entirely changed; deep snow lay in all the gorges and ravines, and no vegetation was seen except here and there a patch of gentian or a few flowers of such intensely-brilliant blue that they seemed to reflect the colour of the sky overhead. The slope of the ridge up which we made our way was furrowed with deep fissures and gullies, presenting a stern and monotonous appearance, and here and there covered with huge, shapeless boulders of detached granite, piled one upon another in wild confusion. A strange depressing sense of desolation and dismal solitude reigned in this wilderness of rocks and beetling crags: even our voices seemed to re-echo with a strange unearthly sound. After a fatiguing climb up a narrow fissure in the mountain, filled with loose stones and fragments of rock, that rolled from under the feet at every step, we gained a grass-covered slope, which, although steep, afforded great relief after our fag up the bed of the watercourse. As we plodded along we saw a troop of ibex scampering along a craggy ridge many hundred feet below us, yet the air was so rare that we distinctly heard the clatter of their hoofs against the rocks, and the rolling of the pebbles they displaced, and shortly afterwards we saw a flight of butterflies that followed our course for some distance, frequently alighting on our persons. The ibex were the last we saw of animal life; flowers became extremely rare, and no insects were to be seen, for very shortly afterwards we reached the eternal snow, which, to our surprise, proved far easier travelling than the naked rock.

We now tied ourselves together with ropes provided for the purpose, allowing about ten feet between each man, which proved a very necessary precaution, as every now and again one or another of our number would sink up to his middle in holes concealed by the snow, notwithstanding we endeavoured to find them out by sounding the way with our staves. For several hours we continued to make our way up the height, only stopping for a moment now and then to refresh ourselves with a mouthful of brandy, until at last we all of us began to feel more or less affected with a difficulty in breathing, more particularly Kuchuk, the Nubian, who was by far the most powerful man amongst us. This feeling wore off after a time, returning at intervals; and the extreme elasticity and pureness of the air prevented us from then feeling the fatigue attendant on our continued exertions. I myself, although often breathless from floundering in the snow, did not at any time feel exhausted: a few minutes' rest would recruit my strength, and excitement kept me from flagging.

The only interruption to the solemn silence that reigned in that high altitude was the continual rumbling and roaring of avalanches, from which at times our route became extremely dangerous. Once I thought it would be all up with us, as the entire side of the mountain seemed to be giving way, and an enormous mass, containing thousands of tons of earth and rock, came tearing past us with a roar far exceeding that of the artillery at Sevastopol, increasing in velocity, and overwhelming everything in its course. It was a moment pregnant with peril, more especially as, immediately afterwards, huge boulders of rock and *débris* broke away and came spinning down the slope as if the invisible gigantic fiends, who are said to reside in these regions, were playing at bowls. However, my companions were Mussulmen and fatalists, and—if my long residence in the East had not imbued me with the same feelings—I was reckless and insensible to fear, for as soon as the storm had passed we continued our route. Another long and tedious fag, and we had attained our object, for we stood upon the "*lower bluff*" of the summit of the El-Bruz, being most likely the first of the human race who had ever set foot upon it.

It was a moment of intense gratification, far surpassing every preconceived idea, for the panorama that suddenly burst upon our eyes was so grand, so overpoweringly sublime, that inexpressible feelings of awe and strange emotions, impossible to define, seemed to pervade the whole of our number. I was the first to scramble up, and gave vent to the exuberance of my exhilaration by a loud huzzah, the Briton's cry,

> "Whene'er" his "soul is up and pulse beats high—
> Whether it hail the wine-cup or the fight,
> And bid each arm be strong or bid each heart be light."

It is heard when he expresses his devotion and greets his Queen;—it rings through the air in the van of the fight, above the pealing of death-shots or the shrieks of the dying;—it is the shout of victory when the field is won, and may be heard round the social board when friend meets friend, and the glorious past is brought to mind. It rang throughout the country as the final adieu of thousands as they marched to embark for the seat of war, and after a lapse of years it was re-echoed by the few who returned, covered with wounds and honour, but broken down in health and spirits, when they were welcomed home by their Sovereign and grateful countrymen. My gentle reader, my voice has swelled that cry on all of these occasions, but never did it burst from my bosom with such an intense feeling of satisfaction without alloy as when I first placed foot upon the mighty El-Bruz.

I mounted a heap of rocks that lay piled in confusion along a craggy ridge jutting out of the snow, as it appeared to be the highest point, and surveyed at leisure the wonderful scene before me. The higher summit still towered like a mass of sparkling alabaster, some three thousand feet above the crest upon which I was standing, but even had the day not been so far advanced I could not have made any attempt to reach it, as a scarped precipice over six hundred feet in depth, an inaccessible glacier, and a ridge of bluff peaks divided us, although it looked almost within the range of my rifle. Could I even have descended and made a circuit of the lower summit, the glacier was an obstacle that would have been insurmountable, as in it were stupendous icebergs and wave upon wave of precipitous ridges with steep scarped sides, apparently inaccessible to the foot of man, which gave me the idea of numberless rocky islands in a tempestuous ocean suddenly frozen. In the valleys and undulations between were innumerable blue and violet streaks, which, with the aid of my glass, I made out to be deep fissures and yawning chasms so wide as to appear perfectly impassable, although some seemed arched over with natural bridges of ice. Here and there, scattered over the surface, dark masses of rock and fantastically-grouped aiguilles and pinnacles appeared like the domes, spires, and minarets of far-distant Eastern cities, whilst the massive ridges of ice forcibly reminded me of lines of defence and fortifications on the largest scale, the effect of which was somewhat heightened by the continual cracking and breaking of the ice, which often resembled a well kept-up file-firing, varied by rolling volleys of musketry, whilst at intervals the roaring of avalanches sounded like salvoes of heavy artillery.

Those who have not witnessed cannot conceive the solemn grandeur of the scene then before us, and description can convey but a very faint idea of it. The firmament was of that intensely-deep blue peculiar to the waves of the Mediterranean at certain times, and contrasted strangely with the dazzling whiteness of the eternal snow, which lay spread out like the vast winding-sheet of a dead world. The sun, too, shone with a peculiarly strange unearthly light, more like that of the moon, as if his rays were not sufficiently powerful to penetrate the atmosphere. For some time I was too much bewildered and overpowered by emotion to fix my mind attentively on the grand panorama stretched before me, but after a time I distinguished, in the south-east, the lofty peak of Mount Kasbec, towering high above ranges of mountains, rising one behind another, and diversified with the richest colouring. To the westward, overlooking the ranges of mountains we had passed, lay the blue expanse of the Euxine, glistening in the light of the sun like a sheet of burnished silver; and far away, in a north-easterly direction, over fields of eternal snow, vast glaciers, and a sea of mountain-ranges, intersected by deep, dark, densely-wooded ravines, were the plains of the Kuban, veined by shining rivers. To the south-east, on the verge of the horizon, was a dense mist, which, notwithstanding the distance, I have no doubt hung over the Caspian. It was a glorious sight; and I remained gazing as long as I could endure the biting cold, notwithstanding that I felt half blinded by the strange reflection of the sun from the snow, for the broad peak of my hunting-cap had no effect in keeping out the glare; and we were each obliged to fasten a strip of my silk handkerchief across our eyes, in order to enable us to see the way. Having refastened the ropes we commenced the descent, and had made our way a considerable distance down the first ridge, by following our own tracks, when suddenly I heard a cry of alarm behind, and simultaneously felt the cord jerk. I turned and saw Hoossain supporting the Nubian, who was stretched senseless on the snow. At first I thought he was in a fit, and rubbed his forehead with snow, but on further examination I found breathing suspended, the pulse and heart still, and I knew all was over. I always carried a knife in which there was a lancet, so I opened the veins in his arms and temples, but could hardly squeeze out a drop of blood. He was dead, and I believe the cause to have been an affection of the heart. It was a melancholy end to our hitherto successful enterprise, but nothing could be done. We unfastened the cord which attached him to the others, and laid him gently down to take his last sleep, on a ledge of rock, where his body would remain as undisturbed as if buried in the deepest grave, for we were still far above any indications of animal life. After a long weary tramp we regained the ridge of rocks overlooking the glacier, by which time the sun was nearly down, and we had to wait some time before the moon got sufficiently high to light us on our way. Once we missed the track, and found ourselves clambering up the smooth face of a rock, where a false step or a slip would have precipitated us into a dark yawning chasm below, so deep that we could not hear huge rocks, which we saw rolling down the slope, when they struck the bottom. Luckily it was gloriously clear night, and the moon shone with a brilliancy rarely seen, except in the tropics. Now and then a meteor darted across the firmament, leaving a long train of light after it, and then vanished from our sight.

At last we reached the first vegetation, and towards midnight entered a belt of pine-forest, where we felt so utterly done-up with fatigue that we were obliged to halt. After some trouble we made a huge fire, and, having divided what brandy we had left amongst us, rolled ourselves up in our blankets, too tired even to eat or prepare coffee. Towards morning, having somewhat recovered, I felt ravenous, and, although so stiff that I could hardly crawl, managed to awake Hoossain, who got some water and made coffee, which, with biscuits and the remains of our provisions, once more set us on our legs.

We did not, however, think of moving until the sun was high in the heavens. As we were skirting the belt of pines, endeavouring to find out our old track, I caught sight of a magnificent solitary old buck-ibex, perched on a peak some short distance below us, and, after some careful stalking, managed to roll him over. He proved a splendid specimen, his coat being very silky nearly white, and fifteen inches in length. His horns measured thirty-four inches. I cut off his head and skin, and we made the best of our way to the deserted konac, where we arrived just before sunset. We all lay down round the fire, whilst Ali and his party prepared our food, and, after a long sleep, got up much refreshed, though still fearfully stiff—indeed that feeling did not entirely wear off for a fortnight.

Towards noon we mounted our horses and rode into the hamlet, where the old chief welcomed us as if we had risen from the dead. Here we remained a few days to recruit, and had every reason to be highly satisfied with our stay, for we were most hospitably treated by the whole tribe.

We then returned to our old friend the Illori Bey, with whom we passed a merry week; after which we made our way to Souchum Kaleh, where we embarked in a steamer for Constantinople.

PART III.—ALGERIA.

CHAPTER XXV.

A SPORTING RECONNAISSANCE IN ALGERIA.

The origin of the expedition.—The start.—Paris.—Difficulty about the importation of gunpowder.—A ruse.—Marseilles. —The voyage.—Stora.—Bône.—French hospitality.—Lake Fedzara. — Ain-Mokra. — Convivial evening. — Songs. — The trail of a lion. — Small-game shooting. — Lions afoot.— Night-watching.—Uncomfortable position.—The lion again. — His currishness. — Preparations for a trip inland. — Philippeville. — Roman remains. — The kindness of the French authorities.—Our journey.—A strange Jehu.—Constantine.—The game of Algeria.

THE origin of this expedition was as follows:— Monsieur Jules Gérard of the French army, the celebrated "*Tueur des Leons,*" having formed the nucleus of the Algerian Sporting Club, (in which are to be found the names of most of the sporting noblemen and gentry in France,) kindly sent me a prospectus, and I thought it was a pity that the

British public should not be aware of the splendid field for sport of all kinds that was within four days' journey of their shores. Although I considered that the formation of a club for sportsmen of all nations, on a permanent and substantial foundation, was an extremely desirable project, yet I foresaw that there were certain difficulties in the way which nothing but what military men would term a "reconnaissance in force," would ever be able successfully to surmount. I therefore proposed the present trip, and, joined by a few gentlemen who had the same object in view, made every preparation for a start. Unfortunately Monsieur Jules Gérard (who would have been of great assistance) was unable to accompany us, so that we had many disadvantages to labour against on arrival in the country; and the weather proving unfavourable during the greater part of our sojourn, "the bag" was small in comparison with what might have been made under more favourable circumstances.

On Sunday afternoon, the 7th of February, 1858, a number of four-wheelers were seen drawn up in a row in front of a certain house, not a hundred yards away from the statue of the great Napier, round which a gaping crowd were assembled, and from the *sotto voce* conjectures that were made, it was evident that the public had not decided whether there was to be a wedding or a funeral procession.

Their suspense, however, was not of long duration, for almost immediately after the arrival of the cabs, sundry watermen and individuals of that genus proceeded to load the exterior of each vehicle with portmanteaus, camp-beds, and other divers-shaped packages, among which gun-cases appeared to predominate. Some of the bystanders, more curious than the rest, scrutinised the directions and labels on the boxes, and expressed their astonishment on seeing on each a lion and the words, "Algerian Sporting Expedition, Philippeville, Algeria, *viâ* Paris and Marseilles."

When the traps were all arranged, a number of gentlemen entered the cabs, and the word being given, "To the London Bridge Railway Station," away they drove, and the explorers of the new hunting grounds were fairly started. After a short consultation with a very civil superintendent, tickets were taken to Paris, *viâ* Newhaven and Dieppe, and the baggage registered throughout, so as not to be subject to any troublesome inspection from either custom-house officers or gendarmes, until arrival at its destination.

At six P.M. we took our places in the carriages, the signal whistle was heard, the engine gave a responsive grunt, and we had begun our journey to Algeria.

At half-past eight we arrived at Newhaven, and put up at the London and Paris Hotel, where we found the people not the most civil in the world, and the sheets of our beds unquestionably damp.

The refreshments were very so-so, but we found the charges extremely moderate.

Monday, 8th.—After an unsatisfactory breakfast, left Newhaven by the "Dieppe" steamer, at a quarter to ten, and, after an unpleasant voyage over a nasty chopping sea, we arrived at Dieppe at four P.M.

Put up at the Hôtel de Londres, where we got some refreshment, and at seven P.M. started by train to Paris, *viâ* Rouen.

Arrived at Paris at midnight, and put up at the Hôtel des Deux Mondes, Rue d'Antin, where we got very handsomely furnished suites of rooms, and a very fair supper before we turned in.

Tuesday, 9th.—Sir William F——, the President of our Association, a jolly old Baronet from the north of England, and another member joined us, having gone on a couple of days in advance. He rather shocked our nerves by telling us that the French authorities had seized his English powder, and would not allow him to have it on payment of any duty. It was in vain he showed a letter from the French ambassador in London, authorising the carriage of arms and ammunition through France; they ignored his authority, and kept the powder. This piece of news made us all look very blue, for we had a hundredweight amongst our traps, which we looked upon as our greatest treasure, and we held a consultation as to what had best be done under the circumstances. We also had a letter to the *chef au douane* (head of the customs,) but as the first one had proved useless, we had no faith that ours would prove of more avail.

All our traps were still at the custom-house, and ten A.M. was the time appointed for the examination. The hour was fast approaching, and as yet no plan had been fixed upon to elude the vigilance of the gendarmes, when I proposed to reconnoitre the ground; and accordingly got into a trap, drove down to the custom-house, and demanded a portmanteau containing uniform, clothes, &c. This, with several gun-cases, was given up after a slight examination, and carried off in triumph to the hotel. I then donned my uniform, which is decorated with sundry bits of H.M.'s "Silver," and, accompanied by our worthy President in full Highland costume, and the other members of the Association, with chasseurs and gillies in Lincoln-green and kilts, we started off in a body to the "*Douane*."

On entering the railway station we evidently caused some excitement, for the officials seemed rather taken aback at our appearance. I asked at once for the *chef*, and, acting as spokesman for the rest, demanded that all our baggage might be delivered up as soon as possible. The officials were all *extremely* polite, and in a few moments it was before us. Then came the momentous period—bunches of keys were presented, which were most courteously declined with sundry bows and scrapes.

Two of the chasseurs opened a carpet-bag containing clothes, a hamper of saddlery, and a camp-bed or two; the goods were chalked with sundry hieroglyphics, and, after another series of salutations, were mounted on vehicles, and the game was played and won.

On arrival at the hotel, three cheers were given by all hands on account of the success.

Went to the theatre in the Boulevards des Italiens, and finished up the night at a *bal masqué*, where our worthy president, whose kilt caused intense sensation, astonished the natives in a *pas seul*, (a Lancashire jig,) and obtained unbounded applause.

Wednesday, 10*th*.—Got our ammunition safely packed in a large case, which we labelled *Comestibles*" to escape observation, and drove about the town paying sundry visits.

After dinner set off by the eight o'clock P.M. express for Marseilles, *viâ* Lyons. Arrived at Lyons at seven A.M., (on Tuesday, 11th,) got a tolerable breakfast, arrived at Marseilles at four P.M., put up at the Hôtel de Bristol, got a very decent dinner, and went to the Café Alkazer, a first-rate establishment of the sort, where we heard some very good music. Adjourned from there to the theatre, and finished off at a ball, where the Con. Con. seemed to be the order of the evening.

Friday, 12*th*.—After some little trouble regarding our passports, we took our passage by the

Messageries Imperial steamer *Oasis*, from Marseilles to Bône, *viâ* Philippeville. Embarked at half-past eleven, got under weigh at twelve, with a wind from the S.E. dead in our teeth. Coasted along the French shore as far as Toulon, and then made direct south. Had rather a rough night, there being much wind and a heavy swell.

Our fellow-passengers were chiefly French officers returning from leave; very few of whom appeared at dinner, they being but poor sailors. Some of our party, too, looked uncommonly white about the gills, whilst with others the sea air had only the effect of sharpening their appetites; and they made up for the rest.

Saturday, 13*th*.—A good deal of sea on, and strong adverse winds from the east. Rolled about a good deal, much to the dissatisfaction of many of the passengers. The living on board very good, and the captain and officers extremely civil and polite.

Sunday, 14*th*.—Made the land, distance twelve leagues, at eight A.M., which proved to be Cape Atia; came within a mile of it at noon, and kept along the mountainous coast of Kabylia, until nearly four P.M., when we rounded a bluff point, and entered the Gulf of Stora; and the lighthouse, on a small rocky island, came in view, with the little town of Stora. Philippeville (built on the site of the old Roman town Rusicada) was about two and a half miles to the eastward.

A large barracks and hospital form conspicuous objects on entering; and the town, which is built upon a slope, has a very picturesque appearance, as it lies at the foot of steep and well-wooded hills. Maltese boatmen soon surrounded the vessel; and, after much confusion, most of the passengers landed at Stora. Our party remained on board, as it was growing dusk.

Monday, 15*th*.—Went on shore in a Maltese boat; found the town remarkably clean, and well provided with very fair shops. Put up at the Hôtel de France, which we found very comfortable quarters.

Were engaged nearly all day in going from office to office, procuring our *permis de chasse* or game-certificates. Found all the French authorities extremely civil, polite, and ready to help us. Heard very good accounts of game, and were altogether much pleased with the appearance of the country. Returned on board to dine and sleep.

Tuesday, 16*th*.—Sketched the coast from the deck. Our good steamer, the *Oasis*, remained for two days to discharge, and take in cargo for Tunis.

The instructions of M. Jules Gérard were laid before the party, and followed to the letter. They were to the effect, "that if the party found the weather fine on arrival at Philippeville, they were to proceed at once to Bône, (which is some eighty miles further to the eastward,) and, taking a guide from the Chef du Bureau Arabe, were to establish themselves in the Caravansary of Ain Mokra, on the border of the Lake Fedzara."

The weather was beautiful at Philippeville, like May in England ; so, after having looked about the place, we re-embarked once more, and, at six P.M., started for Bône, where we arrived at about two A.M. on Ash Wednesday, the 17th of February.

We were very much struck with the beautiful scenery about Bône when we got up at sunrise. On an abrupt cliff, (Cape de Garde,) projecting into the sea, is the lighthouse, and near it a handsome-looking country-house, which we afterwards found to be a *café*.

On another eminence is a Mussulman marabout, or shrine, erected to the memory of some holy man. On a commanding height is the Fort of Bône, in which are about three thousand felons, who are condemned to hard labour. They were busy making a winding road from the sea to the fort, and swarmed on the height thick as bees, guarded by a large number of French soldiers.

Below the fort, to the eastward, is situated the town of Bône, encircled by the old Moorish walls of other days, which the French keep in excellent repair. The most conspicuous buildings are a large barracks, facing the sea, and a government stores, rising high above the houses of the town, which are mostly built with terraced roofs. Farther to the eastward of the town is an old Moorish bridge, of several arches, said to have been built by the Romans, which connects the town with the beautiful olive-covered hill of St Augustin, at the foot of which are several substantially-built country houses and farms, besides a mosque, a small barracks, and a depôt for cattle and baggage animals for the use of the French army.

We landed at six A.M., and, entering the town by a gate which is evidently of French construction—as there are still traces to be seen of the old Moorish one close to,—proceeded to the Customhouse, where our baggage was passed at once without the slightest examination or hindrance.

We then ascended a rather steep and narrow street, leading to the Grande Place, and took up our abode in the Hôtel de France. After breakfast, we left cards on General Périgot, commanding the subdivision of Bône, on M. le Marquis de Gantès, the Sous-Préfet, and Captain Guyon Vernier, Chef du Bureau Arabe, (the *beau-idéal* of a Light Cavalry officer,) from each of whom we received the greatest kindness and attention. They proffered their services in any way in which they could assist the party. M. Guyon Vernier provided us with an interpreter and a cook, both very necessary adjuncts to our establishment, and in the afternoon lent us horses, and took us over the town and the adjacent country. Dined at the Hôtel de France, which we found to be an establishment needing many reforms, as both the bedrooms and *salle à manger* are dirty, the attendance bad, and the living abominable. The charges are moderate. We found the *cuisine* of the Café Ourse (kept by a good-looking damsel, weighing some eighteen stone more or less, whom we designated "the Stout Party") much better; indeed, we had every reason to be satisfied both with the cleanliness of the place and the cooking.

Thursday, 18*th*.—Was engaged the whole day in purchasing wine, spirits, and supplies of all kinds for our expedition. Heard from some of the officers of the 70th Regiment de Ligne that woodcocks had been extremely scarce this season in comparison with other years.

Visited the town, and strolled about the public promenade outside the walls, where the band of the 70th played several pieces from different operas in an efficient manner. Bands of French regiments are much stronger than English ones. That of the 70th consisted of fifty performers, exclusive of the drums. Had a wretched dinner at the Hôtel de France. Visited a *café chantant* in the evening, where we heard some tolerable singing.

Friday, 19*th*.—The Chef du Bureau Arabe kindly procured for our party a large open carriage, saddle-horses, and baggage-mules, and M. de Burg, a large landholder, kindly lent us a large waggon, with a fine team of six mules, to carry our supplies; and at about noon we left Bône for the Caravansary of Ain Mokra, accompanied by M. Guyon Vernier and a party of mounted Arabs.

The road, which was tolerably good, wound along a valley about a couple of miles broad, some portion of which was cultivated, but the greater part was overgrown with a curious kind of wild bulbous plant, which much resembles our daffodil, and lilies of different kinds.

On either side rose hills some six hundred feet in height, covered with low jungle and brushwood, which M. Vernier informed us were composed chiefly of iron-ore, which yielded eighty-six per cent. of metal, fully equal to that imported from Sweden On one of the hills, to the left of the road, a mining company has been established, and a tramway formed to convey the metal to Bône.

We started three or four hares and a partridge *en route*, as we rode along. At a short distance from the town is a large loop-holed building, which was formerly the limit of the French jurisdiction, and M. Vernier informed us that he had been present at several skirmishes with the Arabs at that point some fifteen years ago.

After a pleasant ride of about two hours, a turn in the valley gave us a view of the Lake Fedzara, and we were all much delighted with the scenery and with our prospects of sport, for clouds of duck were seen hovering over the reeds, which were at some distance from the edge of the water. The lake is about sixteen miles in length, and varies from four to ten in breadth. The road winds along the northern bank between the lake and a long range of wooded hills, some small portions of which are cultivated. The edge of the lake is surrounded by rushes, averaging nearly three feet in height, and here and there are patches of brushwood and thorn-bushes. We rode along the edge of the lake for about two hours, the only houses we passed being those of two invalid French soldiers, who are employed in mending the road.

We passed three Arab encampments, all at some short distance from the road, and were considerably annoyed by their numerous dogs barking and yelping at our horses' heels.

At sunset we arrived at the Caravansary of Ain Mokra, where we sat down to a substantial dinner, provided by the *maitre d'hôtel*, a Frenchman of the name of Bosquet, who is in charge of the building. Our ride had sharpened our appetites, and we did ample justice to our good cheer. After dinner we had a brew, and singing was the order of the night. Our *vivandière* particularly distinguished herself on this occasion, and was warmly applauded. Another of our party, from the north of the Tweed, was not behindhand. The president's hunting-song was very justly encored, and brought forth roars of laughter. As the rule of the house was that every one should chant when his turn came round, or take a dose of Epsom salts hot, there was no escape. I insert the words of my songs, which I composed when laid up on my back from wounds in hospital, and time hung heavily on my hands :—

HOMEWARD BOUND.*

The sun was sinking in the west
  Below the deep blue sea;
His rays still gilt the billows' crest,
  And land lay on our lee.
Darkly it loom'd above the wave,
  As twilight gather'd round;
Each heart was sad, each soldier grave,
  Though we were homeward bound.

For one all loved lay on the deck,
  Who never would rise more;
His eys were fix'd on that dark speck
  They said was England's shore.
His brow was chill—all pain was past—
  Tears stood in every eye;
The shades of death were gathering fast—
  His time was come to die.

His heart was in his father's hall,
  He fancied friends were nigh;
At times he 'd on his mother call,
  And bid her not to sigh.

---

* The preceding lines were written from an incident during the late war, an account of which appeared in one of the English newspapers. A transport, conveying the wounded soldiers from the Crimea, had been telegraphed as having arrived at Spithead. No sooner was the anchor down than the vessel was crowded by the friends and relatives of the invalids, and among them came an old gentleman to look after the disembarkation of his only son, a youth of eighteen, who had been reported among the severely wounded. On arrival on board, the afflicted father was told that his son had breathed his last the evening before, within sight of land. The shock was too great for the old man to bear, and he died suddenly on hearing the news.

We heard him try to breathe the prayer
  Which she perchance had taught:
Veterans wept as they stood there,
  With whom that boy had fought.

The night closed round—a mournful wail
  Was heard along the deep;
To all on board it told the tale—
  Our friend had sunk to sleep.
Bright morning broke—the freshening breeze
  Our good ship onward bore;
We saw the cliffs and stately trees
  Of dear Old England's shore.

The anchor fell with grating sound,
  Our perils now were o'er,
And dear ones greet the homeward-bound
  They 'd thought to see no more.
Friends crowded round: one hale old man
  Gazed on with troubled air;
Each soldier's face he seem'd to scan,
  But no one knew him there.

At last he breathed the lost one's name—
  Each soldier turn'd away.
Again he ask'd—the captain came,
  But knew not what to say.
A tear roll'd from the sailor's eye—
  He pointed o'er his head,
Where Britain's banner, half-mast high,
  Proclaim'd that one was dead.

He took the mourner by the hand,
  And led him to the corse;
Surrounded by our weeping band,
  He told him of his loss.
The old man kiss'd the pallid cheek,
  And knelt down by the dead,
As if in prayer: he did not speak.
  He rose not—life had fled.

SONG.—THE BASHI-BAZOUK TO HIS HORSE, "DESERT-BORN." *

Come, rouse thee, my charger, prepare for the fray;
For trumpets are braying, and we must away!
The booming of cannon sounds loud on the wind;
When fame's to be won, we must ne'er be behind.
Let those who prefer it dwell in a fix'd home,
But we, my heart's treasure, together will roam!
For Islam is threaten'd—the Sultan has need
Of the Bashi-bazouk and his brave Arab steed.

CHORUS.

I'm mounted! I'm mounted! I'm away like the wind;
No steed in the desert can leave me behind.
Al-ham-du-lillah! †—I fear not a foe;
I'm free as the breezes that o'er the sands blow!

My own "Desert-born," dost remember the day,
When Cossack hordes hover'd around us at bay,
And we charged through the mass like a whirwind's blast,
And gain'd the vast steppe when the danger was past?
How the foes howl'd with rage as they watch'd our flight,
And follow'd our course till the fall of the night!
I laugh'd at their efforts—for, unmatch'd in speed,
I knew none could reach us, my brave Arab steed!

CHORUS.

I'm mounted! I'm mounted! I'm away like the wind;
No steed in the desert can leave me behind.
Al-ham-du-lillah!—I fear not a foe;
I'm free as the breezes that o'er the sands blow!

---

* "Desert-born," a favourite Arab charger, killed at the battle of Inkermann.

† "Thanks be to God!" a common Arabic expression.

We've traversed the land, and we've sail'd o'er the main—
Now the hour's near at hand to set forth again.
Fearless of danger, we roam in all weather;
No peril can daunt us while we are together.
No maiden so fair but she causes remorse:
I have known none with thee, my own gallant horse!
I never found friend in the hour of my need
True as thee, "Desert-born," my brave Arab steed!

CHORUS.

I'm mounted! I'm mounted! I'm away like the wind:
No steed in the desert can leave me behind.
Al-ham-du-lillah!—I fear not a foe;
I'm free as the breezes that o'er the sands blow!

THE WOUNDED HIGHLANDER.

RECITATIVE.

The eve the Alma's heights were won,
As o'er the field I trod,
I mark'd a wounded Highlander
Lie bleeding on the sod.
His brother strove to stanch the wound;
Alas! it was in vain:
Dark crimson streams flow'd on the ground;
And he sang this sad strain:—

"Ye maunna weep for me, Willie!
Oh dinna greet sae sair:
Ye'll follow me ere lang, laddie,
When we shall part na mair!
Like yonder setting sun, Willie,
E'en sae my course is run;
But he will rise again, laddie,
And I shall then be gone!

"Maybe when ye 'll gae back, Willie,
To our hame by the burn,
Ye 'll tell them a' the tale, laddie,
O' him wha 'll no return.
Ye 'll tell them how I fought, Willie,
Like sodger true and brave!
'Twill ease my mither's heart, laddie,
When I am in the grave.

"There 's ane wha sair will greet, Willie—
The news, oh! gently brek,
For she was a' in a' to me;
Ye 'll lo'e her for my sake!
Oh 'tis sair hard to dee, Willie,
And leave her a' alone!
It 's but for her I greet, laddie—
For her when I am gone.

"Oh dinna mind my words, Willie,
And dinna, dinna sigh;
I wadna ca' life back again—
'Tis for my Queen I die!
And 'tis a glorious day, Willie,
As e'er yon sun set on.
Ye 'll comfort a' at hame, laddie,
When I am deid an' gone!

"Now fauld me to your heart, Willie,
The nicht air 's fearfu' keen!
And kiss me ere I gae, laddie!
There 's darkness o'er my een.
I ken I 'm sinking fast, Willie,
The cauld strikes to the bone!
Ye 'll comfort a' at hame, laddie,
When I am deid an' gone!"

Close in his brother's arms,
Lock'd in his fast embrace,

He pass'd away as if in sleep,
  A smile upon his face.
We cut a lock of curling hair,
  That o'er his brow did wave;
Then by the Alma's rippling stream
  We dug the soldier's grave.

Saturday, 20th.—Sir William, M. Guyon Vernier, and I rode out to reconnoitre the country, and visited the "douar" (encampment) of an Arab tribe, about five miles from Ain Mokra, where we saw the pugs of a lion who had carried off a sheep the night previous, and tracked him to a hill covered with low wood. Here we bade adieu to M. Guyon Vernier, who had to go on duty towards Cape de Fer, and returned to Ain Mokra by the lake, where we saw thousands of duck, teal, and snipe; bagged twenty snipe, one hare, three partridges, two teal, two quail, and a water-rail.

At night we watched by a watercourse, which the lion had passed twice the evening before; and heard him roaring at the distance of a quarter of a mile, but did not get a sight of him. The night dark and showery.

Shot, along the borders of the lake, forty snipe, one duck, and two water-rail. Mr A—— watched for the lion, and heard him roar during the night, but did not see him.

Monday, 22d.—After breakfast, was preparing my gear for a day's snipe-shooting on the lake, when an Arab Sheikh came to the caravansary, and informed me that a lion and lioness had killed two cows in his douar the night previous. I immediately mounted, and, accompanied by Mahomed (my servant and interpreter) and a "spahi," (Arab irregular cavalry trooper,) who carried my spare guns, galloped to the scene of action. The douar consisted of about thirty *gourbis,* or huts, some thatched, and others made of black camel's-hair cloth, forming the habitation of men, women, children, cattle, and dogs of every description, from the well-bred "sloghee," (Arab greyhound,) to the yelping, snarling cur.

About a hundred paces from the douar several vultures were busy picking what remained of the carcasses of the two cows, and, on examination of the ground, I found the footprints of two lions, a hyena, and several jackals and dogs.

Accompanied by the "wakeef," or head man of the douar, I went to a hill, about eleven miles' distance, where they said the lions had been seen to go; but after a long search found no pugs, so I returned once more to the douar. Here I got a drink of sour milk, and again examined the ground where the cattle had been killed. After some little difficulty, I got upon the trail of the two lions, (which was in places partially obliterated by the footprints of men and cattle,) and followed it up hill and down dale for some eight miles, when, in a deep and densely-wooded ravine, I found the lair.

Had I been alone I might, perhaps, have got a shot, for the place where they had been sleeping after their feast was warm with the heat of their bodies when I arrived, and unmistakable signs showed they had been there very lately; but the noise made by the Arabs, who would talk among themselves, in spite of my remonstrance, scared them away.

I tracked them through dense wood for a short distance, when my *olfactories* informed me that a putrid carcass was not far off, and, guided by the smell, I made my way through the underwood, and came across the dead body of a young lion, something more than a year old. It bore the marks (as a coroner would say) of a violent death, for the neck, chest, and belly were gashed and ripped open as if with a knife. On examining the ground round about, I found the footprints of a large boar, who had evidently intruded into the lair and killed "the youthful scion of the Royal House," though not without a violent struggle, for the grass and herbage was trodden down, and bore the marks of a severe fight. I cut off the forelock and some claws, and made the Arabs cut off the head. It was too far gone to skin.

I then returned to the head of the ravine, where there were several old marks of the lions having frequently passed, and constructed a kind of rifle-pit, which I concealed with branches of trees, at a point which commanded two paths, on both of which I could perceive lion-pugs. Here I remained all night, and, although I heard the lions roar at a distance, I saw nothing on either of them. I twice heard a hog pass during the night, but it was very dark, and I could not get a shot. I also heard the cry of a hyena, and several packs of jackals.

Tuesday, 23d.—I returned to the douar early in the morning, and made a breakfast of eggs and gallets, (a kind of wheaten cake made of flour and milk, and baked on an iron plate.) Shot three hares and a brace of partridges for food, and strolled about the jungle until near sunset, when, having made a game-dinner, I took post in the same place as last night, and, about ten o'clock, I heard the unmistakable sounds which told me the king of beasts was afoot.

At first the sound appeared to come from the bottom of the ravine, but afterwards it seemed much nearer, and I lay very still on the *qui vive,* fully expecting I should hear his footsteps before long, though the night was so dark that I hardly hoped to get a fair shot. I lay listening for nearly an hour to no purpose, when suddenly I heard him roar on the hill behind the place where I was posted, though how he got there I do not know. The night was very dark and showery, but as I had first-rate arms, and a Cording's waterproof-sheet to keep all dry, I did not fear any miss-fires. I remained at my post on the crest of the hill until nearly three o'clock in the morning, at times hearing the lion roar, more or less distinctly, as he roamed about, when, becoming impatient, and feeling an old wound ache from change of weather and my cramped position, I wrapped my waterproof round my gun, and placed it against a tree, and, armed with my double rifle and revolver, sallied out towards the point where I fancied the lion was.

Guided by his roar, which very much resembles the noise made by a bull, followed by several grunts, though, of course, much louder, I scrambled through the brushwood until I got so near that I could distinctly hear him breathe, or rather snore, as he moved along.

Rain was now falling very heavily; my clothes were wet through and through, and the night was so dark that I could hardly see two yards before me. I lay down and placed my ear to the ground every now and then, creeping on with the greatest caution, fearing that my footsteps might betray me.

I could distinctly hear the lion making a curious moaning sound and grunting, within fifty paces from me, and at times I thought I heard a rustling among the bushes as if he was coming towards me, but I saw nothing.

This game must have lasted nearly an hour, and I was getting nearly tired of it, when, as I was creeping along on my hands and knees, I suddenly fell down a steep ravine, about six feet deep, among a lot of thorny bushes. A stream of water, nearly a foot in depth, was flowing at the bottom, and I again fell into this, rifle and all, as I was striving to regain my footing.

Whilst in this predicament I heard a crackling of the brushwood, and a loud roar close to, and I saw the dark outline of the lion scrambling up the opposite bank. I threw up my rifle and pulled the trigger, but the charge was wet, and the caps only exploded. What would I then have given for a breech-loader, when, had I even suspected the first charge to be damp, I could have substituted a fresh cartridge in two seconds.

The noise of my fall must have alarmed the lion, for I heard him no more that night. My face, hands, and legs, were full of thorns, my clothes were soaking wet through, my left wrist felt sprained, and all my bones ached with fever, so I groped about for the bank of the ravine, against which I leaned till morning, when I examined the ground.

Wednesday, 24*th*.—The lion's pugs were very distinctly imprinted in the mud, and at one time he had cleaned his claws against the trunk of a cork-tree, not twenty yards from where I must have been standing. I found my rifle-pit again, after some trouble got my gun and waterproof-sheet, and returned to the douar, where the Arabs made a bush-fire, at which I dried my clothes. I then mounted my horse and rode down to Ain Mokra, and, the weather having cleared up, strolled along the edge of the lake, and killed twelve and a half couple of snipe, of which I lost four couple in the rushes for want of a dog. Found two of the party had killed fifty-two head of small game in my absence, viz., snipe, duck, hares, and partridge.

Thursday, 25th.—Got up rather feverish, bones aching, and unfit for work. Two of the party went with Monsieur D——, a French officer, after hog. They saw two, but could not get a shot. Killed twenty-two head of small game, and a mungoose, or ratton.

One of the party (Mr C——) fired at a panther with small shot as it was skulking through the bushes.

Friday, 26th.—At three P.M. an Arab came from the douar of the "caid" (chief) of the Lachdar tribe with the news that a lion had carried off a cow in the night, and begging me to come at once. Accompanied by Mr B——, I mounted my horse and galloped off towards the place, and as we were going along the main road, at about four miles from Ain Mokra, we met a man and a woman, with the utmost fright depicted on their countenances, who told us that they had just seen a lion cross the road. On examination of the ground his pugs were distinctly visible, and we tracked them on horseback for some distance, until the sun had nearly gone down.

We then made the best of our time to get to the douar, where the caid received us very hospitably, and offered us food, which we declined, as we had already dined.

We had not been more than half an hour in the

encampment when the roar of a lion was distinctly heard, and shortly afterwards we heard another answering in the distance.

The caid sent his French servant and two Arabs with us to a small clearing near the douar, where, he said, the lion had been seen prowling about for three nights previous.

On arrival we found two Arabs posted in a tree for the chance of a shot, should the lion make his appearance. As we imagined that they might "make game" of us in the dark, we ordered them down and sent them back with the French servant and the other Arab to the douar. We then carefully reconnoitred the ground, and took up our post behind a bush in the centre of the plain, from whence we could see all around. The moon was rising fast, and the night was beautifully fine, and almost as light as day. We heard a lion and lioness roaring near, and at times a third answering in the distance.

We remained until nearly eleven P.M., waiting impatiently for his appearance, but he did not come.

A lynx was crying close to us, and a pack of jackals twice rushed howling across the clearing, but the lion was still far off as ever, as we could tell from his voice.

His roar seemed to come from a low and densely-wooded hill about half a mile's distance. We held a short consultation, and agreed to follow up by the sound of his voice, and after a good deal of scrambling through the wood we got to another small plain, where we waited until we heard him roar. There was a continual barking of dogs and lowing of cattle from the Arab douars, and at times we heard the distant discharge of firearms. I noticed the lion roared immediately after a donkey brayed or a bull made a louder noise than usual. We listened attentively for the roar, and then made our way as quietly as possible towards the spot from whence we imagined it to proceed. At last we came pretty near, as his breathing and grunting were distinctly heard, and the lioness was moaning in a rather higher key. A dense wood was before us, and they seemed about fifty paces distant. I put fresh caps on my rifle, slung my gun over my left shoulder, and crept forward as noiselessly as possible to the place where I thought the lions were lying. Their grunting seemed to proceed from behind a large bush some ten paces distant, and once both Mr B—— and myself thought we could perceive a pair of eyes. I stole forward, making as little noise as possible, but could perceive nothing. I dropped my rifle into the hollow of my arm and picked up a large stone, which I threw into the bush, where I was pretty certain he was, fully expecting him to bound out and give one of us a shot.

The stone fell with a crash in the bush; a low growl and a rustling were heard, but nothing appeared, and, after waiting about a quarter of an hour near the place, we had the mortification of hearing him roar about half a mile away. The brute had stolen off like a cur.

Again and again did we follow him up, but he always got wind of us, and bolted without giving us the chance of a shot. At last, after much difficulty, we got close to him once more; and this time we thought he seemed inclined to show fight, for we heard him growling in a most savage manner from some deep cover at the bottom of a ravine. I posted Mr B—— on a small eminence, which commanded a view on all sides, and then crept forward as noiselessly as possible to try and cut off his retreat. Whilst so doing, the lioness came to rejoin the lion, (whose growling must have been a summons for her attendance,) and I caught a glimpse of her as she was bounding through the bushes, and could have fired a snap shot, (which I wish now I had done), but that I wanted to bag the lion, which the Arabs said was a large one, with a fine black mane.

I crawled on my hands and knees for some time, until I came to the edge of a steep chasm, about ten feet deep, at the bottom of which was dense cover. There I remained for nearly ten minutes listening to the noise, which appeared to come from some thick bush, behind which, when the clouds rolled away from the face of the moon, I could perceive a dark body, in which at times I thought I saw a slight movement. I watched for some time.

but could see nothing, though the growling was still heard now and again; and at times I fancied I saw something stirring. I drew my pistol, and fired a double shot at what I thought was the body of the lion, in order to make him show face; a loud growl followed, we heard a crashing among the underwood, and the brute had stolen away without showing fight, for in about ten minutes we heard him roar about half a mile off.

The moon now became overclouded, and our chance was up for the time, so we returned to the douar, where the caid had prepared a tent for us, in which we slept very comfortably rolled up in our blankets.

The third lion was heard roaring in the distance, as he lurked round a neighbouring douar.

Saturday, 27th.—The caid sent us a substantial breakfast, which consisted of hard-boiled eggs, hot gallets, made of fine white flour, milk, butter, and a huge dish of "kouskous," the staple food of the Arabs, which is made of wheaten flour, damped and rolled into small grains like millet-seeds, which are afterwards dried, and boiled up with mutton and fowl, or with milk and sugar. Strolled about the jungle all day, visiting the trail of the lions we had been after in the night. The pugs of the lion were nearly eighteen inches in circumference, those of the lioness about fourteen. The jungle in this part of the country is chiefly composed of a beautiful heather, (now in flower,) the myrtle, of which the

Arabs eat the berries, (now ripe,) the laburnum, (in flower,) and several kinds of thorny shrubs, one of which bears a yellow flower, and is called by the French "Jaune d'Espagne."

There is no large timber: cork-trees, few of which are more than a foot in diameter, are the most common.

The Arab who lost his cow the night before our arrival came to us with a doleful story, saying that he was a poor man, and that his brother would make him pay for it, if he did not kill the lion, as it was his turn to watch the cattle on that night. His real name is Taib, but Mr B—— christened him "Corbeau," (on account of our having found him perched in a tree last night,) and the Arabs have confirmed the cognomen.

During the next fortnight we had a good deal of wet weather, and did little but shoot small game, of which we killed heavy bags. Nothing more was heard about the lions, and although we daily took long walks in the most likely places, we saw no fresh tracks.

Wednesday, 10th March.—Had a consulation as to our future proceedings, at which it was determined to start at once for Constantine, and from thence towards the southward, *viâ* Melila, Bathna, and Biscara, should the weather permit. Engaged a diligence, said to be capable of containing twenty-three passengers, for our party, and made arrangements to start at six A.M. on Friday morning.

Visited the *Circle des Officeurs*, an establishment of recent date, most delightfully situated on the crest of a hill overlooking the sea, containing a reading-room well supplied with French newspapers and periodicals, a tolerably well-stocked library, and a Buvette, where écarté, piquet, and whist, well moistened with vermuth and absinth, seemed to be the order of the day. Our party were made honorary members of the establishment, and experienced the greatest hospitality and kindness from the French officers.

Some Roman antiquities are to be seen in the environs of Philippeville, the cisterns at Stora are worthy of a visit; and every now and then one meets with a column or block of marble which bears traces of the sculptor's hand.

Some short time ago, in excavating the foundation of a house in the main street, a marble statue of the Emperor Vespasian was found, beautifully carved, and well proportioned, but, unfortunately, one arm is broken, and the face is partially disfigured; otherwise it is in a very good state of preservation, and forms a conspicuous object in the Grande Place, opposite the church.

Thursday, 11th.—M. Lapasset, Lieut.-Col. d'Etat Major, commanding the subdivision of Philippeville, called after breakfast, and offered our party every assistance to facilitate our departure on our journey southward; indeed, his kind advice, and that of Captain Cousin, Chef du Bureau Arabe, and Monsieur le Commandant Lebarte, of the 71st regiment of the line, were of the most material service.

Took a box at the theatre for a ball given by the town for the benefit of the poor, where we spent a very agreeable evening. I counted forty-nine ladies who danced, besides many others in the boxes. Observed that crinoline has not gone down in Algeria, whatever it may have done in Paris.

Friday, 12*th*.—At six A.M. "our trap," if I may so call the clumsy, rumbling, creaking vehicle which came rolling down the street like a ship in a storm, groaning as if it was aware of the rough treatment it would receive before arrival at Constantine ; and at seven our goods and chattels were hoisted on the top, our *vivandière* stowed in the *coupé*, and ourselves snugly packed outside and in. Too-too-too ! went a hunting-horn, crack went the whip, round went the wheels, and our seven horses set off at a hand-gallop, which lasted for a few hundred yards past the barrier gates, when their pace sunk by degrees into a shuffling walk , and at about four miles from the town we were brought to a standstill, the ruts being nearly two feet deep. Our driver, the queerest fish for a son of Jehu that ever mounted a box, did not appear in the least disconcerted : he flung down the ribbons, and, coolly dismounting from his seat, opened a boot and took out a quantity of pickaxes and spades, which he distributed among the passengers, all of whom were expected to try their hands at road-making. Some gathered stones from the wayside to fill up the ruts, others dug up the road so as to make it as level as possible; and at last, with the assistance of eight extra mules, making a team of fifteen in all, and the combined force of our whole party pushing and pulling, amid the shouts, oaths, prayers, protestations, groans, yells, and frantic shrieks of our conductor and driver, we managed to extricate the wheels, and were once more *en route.* The passengers were, however, obliged to walk in many places; and some of them accomplished many miles on foot, to avoid the disagreeable jolting of our unwieldy machine.

We passed through a most beautiful country, the road winding amongst well-wooded hills, to St Charles, a small fortified village about fifteen miles from Philippeville, on the confluence of the rivers Saf-Saf and Oued Zerga.

Our driver assured us that lions were very numerous in this part of the country, that on two occasions within the last month he had fallen in with them on the road during the night, and once one followed the diligence for three miles, to the great consternation of the horses and passengers. Leaving St Charles we passed through the villages of Gastonville and El Arrouch, where we changed horses; and about one P.M. we arrived at El Kantour, (the Gap,) where we dined.

Should the proposed railway be constructed between Philippeville and Constantine, the cost between El Arrouch and El Kantour will be something enormous, on account of the fearful cuttings, excavations, and tunnellings that will have to be made. The winding of the road round the ravines and hills makes the distance more than three times that by which the crow flies, and even then some of the heights are very steep, so that we had to get out and walk, as the horses could not pull us up.

The aspect of the country completely changes after passing El Kantour. The hills are bleak and rocky, and there is no wood to be seen. We passed a few roadside inns and cabarets *en route*, but the country appeared thinly populated until we arrived within a few miles from Constantine, where we saw a few ill-cultivated farms and gardens, in some of which we noticed a few date-palms for the first time.

The ascent leading to the ancient capital of the Numidian kings is very steep, and it was dark before we passed through the Port de la Brèche and pulled up at the Bureau des Diligences, where we were evidently expected, for we were immediately surrounded by touters and agents from all the different hotels, who annoyed us so much by pulling about our luggage, poking cards in our faces, quarrelling, fighting, and abusing each other, that we were obliged, in self-defence, to keep them at a distance with the drivers' whips.

We put up at the Hôtel des Colonies, a new building on "La Place," where we found tolerably clean rooms, but a very poor supper, after having partaken of which we "turned in," being extremely tired and shaken with our journey.

Saturday, 13th.—When we got up this morning we were most disagreeably surprised to find that a complete change had taken place in the weather, frost having set in during the night; and the wind was bitterly cold and raw, though yesterday in the plains we had experienced the heat of summer in England. Towards noon the sun came out, and we walked about the town, which is most curiously placed on a perpendicularly-scarped height, which is divided from another mountain by a steep chasm or ravine about fifty yards broad and two hundred feet in depth, at the bottom of which flows the river Oued el Rummel, (the River of Sand.)

An old Roman stone-bridge, of two rows of arches, formerly connected the town with the surrounding country; but it was carried away a short time ago, having stood for centuries, and the funds of the town not being in a sufficiently flourishing state to repair it, the soldiers have constructed a kind of steep winding road down the sides of the ravine, which enters the town at the ancient gateway El Kantara, (of the Bridge.) There are two other gates, one the Port de la Brèche, by which we entered, and the other a small postern, leading down into the ravine by a steep path, impassable for carriages.

The town is surrounded by an old Moorish crenated wall, which bears the unmistakable marks of the French cannon when they took the place. The streets are extremely narrow, dirty, and badly paved, and the houses ill built, with flat roofs, much resembling those of the worst parts of the suburbs of Stamboul. The French have constructed a handsome fortified barracks, called La Casbah, and several cafés and shops: otherwise Constantine is but little changed, and much resembles a third-rate town in Turkey; and, although the second capital of Algeria, would be considered but a paltry village were it in India.

The evening wet and raw. Sat round a wood-fire in the hotel with much pleasure.

Sunday, 14th.—The weather cold and disagreeable; snow and rain falling all day.

Called on General Gastu, the Commandant of the Division of Constantine, who lives in the old Moorish palace formerly belonging to the Bey of Constantine.

It is a low irregular building, having a courtyard in the centre, with an oriental verandah all round, supported by small columns of very fine marble of different colours. It is, however, altogether but a poor specimen of Moorish architecture.

In the courtyard the General has some fine specimens of ostriches and gazelles, from the deserts near Biscara, which latter much resemble our Indian antelope in form, except that they have not such fine horns.

In the evening some of our party attended a *bal masqué*, where they were much amused by the diversity of costume.

Monday, 15th.—The weather wet and disagreeable; remained in the hotel the greater part of the day. Received an invitation to a ball given by the General at the palace. Visited the house of M. Jules Gérard, the lion-slayer, one room of which is very curiously painted in the oriental style, with Arabic inscriptions and devices; and were shown the arms of honour presented to him by the ex-royal family of France, the Emperor of Austria, and divers sheiks and Arab chiefs, by whom he is much beloved and esteemed, not only for his coolness and address in lion-hunting, but also on account of his knowledge of the Mussulman character, and his familiarity with their language, habits, and customs.

His kindness, integrity, and anxious solicitude for their welfare, whilst employed in the Bureau Arabe, were very justly appreciated by the sons of Ishmael; and in the goorbis of the douars a stranger is often interrogated as to the happiness of the "conqueror of the lion," and as to his probable return.

Tuesday, 16th.—The weather still unpropitious; snow and sleet falling in the morning. It, however, cleared up a little in the afternoon, and we visited the tomb of the old Roman banker, which was discovered some short time ago to the left of the Port de la Brèche, by the side of the scarp.

The tomb consists of two stories, the lower about ten feet below the surface of the ground, and is in the form of a square, which is covered with some very fine tesselated pavement, in very good preservation, with arched vaults all round, containing bones. On a huge stone slab, which had covered a coffin, with much difficulty I copied the following inscription, which was not an easy task, there being no division between the words :—*

HICEGOQVITACEOVERSIBVSMEA +-+TADEMONSTROLVCEMCLARAFRVI
TVSETTEMPORASVMMAPRAECILIVSCIRTENSILAREARGENTARI
AMLXIBVIARTEMTYDISINMEMIRAFVILSEMPERETVERITASOMNISOM
NIBVSCOMMVNISEGOECVINNOMISERTVSVBIOVERITVSIVXVRIASEMPERFRVITVSCVM
CARISAMICISTALEMPOSTORBITVMDOMINAEVALERIAENONINVENIPVDICAEVITAMCVNPOTVI
GRATAMHABVICVNCONIVGESANCTAMNATALESHONESTEMEOSCENTVMCELEBRAVIFELICES
ADVENITPOSTREMADIESVTSPERITVSITVSINANIAMEMPRARELIQVATTITVLOSQVOSLEGESVIVVSMEE
MORTIPARAVITVOEVI++T+FORTVNAMNO+AMMEDESERVITIPSASEOVINITALESEHICVOSE+ORE'CTOVENITAR—

After a sojourn of a week at Constantine, a letter was received from M. Jules Gérard stating that he

* The Rev. Mr Blakesley, who visited the tomb some months after us, being a first-rate classical scholar, was able to make out the epitaph, notwithstanding the numerous mistakes of the stone-cutter. It should have been :—"Hic ego qui taceo versibus mea fata demonstro, lucem claram fruitus et tempora sumana. Præcilius, Cirtensi Lare, argentariam exhibui artem. Fides in me mira fuit semper et veritas omnis omnibus communis. Ego cui non misertus ubique? Risus luxuriam semper fruitus cum caris amicis, talem post obitum Dominæ Valeriæ non inveni. Pudice vitam cum potui gratam habui cum conjuge sanctâ. Natales honestæ meos centum celebravi felices. At venit postrema dies ut spiritus inania membra relinquat. Titulos quos legis, vivus meæ morti paravi ut voluit Fortuna. Nunquam me deseruit ipsa. Sequimini tales: hinc vos exspecto. Venite."

would not be able to join our expedition, as he could not get an extension of his leave of absence, so, the weather still continuing extremely unpropitious for shooting excursions, we resolved to go about and see as much of the country as we could, and I believe we were all highly satisfied with our trip, feeling convinced that Algeria is a splendid field either for the sportsman, the tourist, or the invalid.

The probable expenses of a trip will be as follows:—Travelling expenses (first-class throughout) from London, £20; hotel expenses for three months, £60; hunting expenses, comprising beaters, trackers, horse hire, boat hire, (for wildfowl on the lakes,) and sundries, £20: probable total of expenditure for three months' sport, £100. The probable additional expense with a servant will be rather more than one-third of the above, say £40. I need hardly observe that this does not include the items Château Margot or Lafitte; but each can make his own arrangements, so as to suit his inclination or his means.

The sportsman need only carry his arms, ammunition, and personal baggage. He will find everything else he requires in Algeria.

Small game of all kinds is to be found at a very short distance from the town, so that the sportsman need not go farther daily than ten miles, (or even less,) returning to sleep at the hotel. In order to shoot at greater distances, he should provide himself with a tent. if he wishes to do the thing comfortably.

Large Game.

The following animals are to be met with in this part:—The lion, the panther, the wild-boar, deer, antelope, and the jungle-sheep; also a kind of mountain-deer.

The Lion.—The best manner of pursuing this sport is by tracking his footprints to his lair, and killing him when he charges. The Arabs are *fair* trackers, and will conduct the sportsman to his usual haunts. Then everything depends on the hunter's own steadiness, shooting, and the goodness of his arms.

The Panther.—This animal may be killed by tracking, or hunted with dogs, that attract its attention and give the sportsman opportunities of taking fair aim.

The Wild-boar is found in great abundance. Ten hunters, accompanied by people who know the country, may kill fifty in a day. Alone, they may not see a tusk in a week. The boar avoids the neighbourhood of the lion and panther. Hog-hunting is followed in this country either by tracking, or with greyhounds, on horseback, or by beating. It remains for the English sportsman to ride down the gray boar, spear in hand, as is done in India. Hog are to be found close to the town; they even sometimes enter the gardens during the night.

Deer are to be found of various kinds, they are best killed by stalking.

Antelope and *Jungle-sheep* are killed either by stalking or forming a battue.

The Mountain-deer is found in the mountainous districts only, and is killed in the same way as the chamois, which it very much resembles in its habits.

Small game is very abundant throughout the country, and consists of red-partridge, hares, jungle-fowl, (poule de Carthage,) bustard, and quail, which are to be found in great quantities. On the lakes all kinds of water-fowl are to be found, from the duck to the swan; besides which, woodcock and snipe are very numerous in the season. The sportsman may fill a cart with waterfowl; it is only a question of how much ammunition he has got with him.

The abundance of game in this country is very easily accounted for. In the first place, the inhabitants—the Arabs—shoot little or nothing, and the French in Algeria do as the Arabs; so that all kinds of game, large and small, live in a state of undisturbed peace, and multiply accordingly.

Large game, such as lions and panthers, have been driven into the wildest part of the country by the advance of civilisation, and the sportsman may lose much time in finding out their haunts, if not accompanied by those initiated. M. Jules Gérard spent upwards of *six hundred nights* in the forest before he killed his twenty-sixth lion; so whoever would tread in his footsteps should not be discouraged by want of success in the first instance.

PART IV.

PRACTICAL HINTS ON FIREARMS AND THEIR USE.

CHAPTER XXVI.

The advantages of breech-loading guns and rifles.—The different systems.—Advice on purchasing firearms.—The theory of rifle practice.—Aiming, position, judging distance, and practical hints on shooting.—On the colour of sportsmen's dress.—Table of experiments with targets.

AT a time when cannon and rifles form the subject of so much discussion and conversation in every circle, it were well if sportsmen would give some consideration to the *breech-loading* system, as adapted to sporting-arms. Cannon and small-arms are both in a transition state, and in the course of a few years we may expect to see great changes in the armament of our land and naval forces, for Sir William Armstrong and Mr Whitworth, of Manchester, have satisfactorily proved that rifled cannon on the *breech-loading* system exceed all others in *length of range, power of penetration,* and *accuracy of fire;* and all our first-class gunmakers—amongst whom I may enumerate Purdey, Lancaster, Lang, Westley Richards, Boss, Moore, Terry, Needham, Whitton and Daw, and Leetch—are manufacturing small-arms (both guns and rifles) that load at the breech, of one description or another. Lancaster, Westley Richards, Terry, and Leetch have peculiar systems of their own invention, but most of the others have adopted that of La Faucheux, which, although it has been invented for upwards of five-and-twenty years, was very little known in this country until that excellent shot and practical mechanic Mr Lang, of "Old Red House" notoriety, took it up; and it is to him that we are indebted for the efficient carrying out and improvement of a principle, which is almost as great an era in gun-making as the invention of the copper cap.

The following are some of the great advantages that the new system has over the old for fowling-pieces.

I shall begin with the extreme *facility* and *quickness in the loading,* whereby any person armed with a breech-loader can load and fire at least six shots in the same time that another with a common gun takes to load and fire two, with much *greater com-*

parative safety, as with a breech-loader the muzzle of the gun can never by any chance be directed towards the person of the loader; no mistake can be made, such as putting two charges of powder or shot into one barrel; there is no chance of losing a hand by pouring powder from a flask down the muzzle of a gun recently discharged, in which, perhaps, a bit of lighted tow, or, what is oftener the case, a small piece of cork (got among the powder in opening the canister) may remain—an accident which may happen to the most careful sportsman. Again, one is always enabled to see clearly through the barrels, and can be certain that no dirt or obstruction has got in, which is a great advantage, as many people have been injured by guns bursting from the muzzle being accidentally plugged up with clay, which may have got in whilst jumping a ditch, climbing over a fence, or stumbling in an uneven turnip-field. The sportsman can never meet with an accident by loading one barrel whilst the other is on full-cock, which the ramming down of a wad or the catching of a twig might cause to go off; and when game is abundant, in the hurry of reloading or the excitement of the moment, accidents from this cause frequently occur: also there is no danger of an unlucky cap flying and endangering the eyesight—not a very uncommon occurrence.

As to the *pleasantness* of shooting, both to self and company, there can be no doubt; for what an advantage it is for sportsmen, when beating country, to be able to load without halting or breaking the line, and making all the rest of the company wait until the operation is finished. Who has not been put off his shooting by having to wait whilst some nervous, fidgety old gentleman hunts in a dozen different pockets to find his powder-flask, wadding, shot-bag, and caps, which are all dispensed with by using a breech-loader? What an advantage it is, when shooting in fens or swamps, to be able to load without putting the butt of your gun in the mud or water, whereby you soil your clothes when you put it up to the shoulder and make yourself uncomfortable for the rest of the day. Also, what sportsman, after a heavy day's shooting, has not found his hands blackened and sticky from exploded gunpowder, and sometimes raw and blistered from constantly ramming down the charge? And in cold weather who has not found loading with a common gun, and putting on the caps, distress him beyond measure, more especially if he has been obliged to pull off his warm gloves before he is able to effect it at last?

Another great advantage is to be able to change the charge in a moment, according to the game to be met with, instead of the old tedious method of drawing the shot with the screw of the ramrod; and also to be able to load without noise, as, when game is plentiful, the noise of ramming down an obstinate wad frequently puts up birds on all sides.

A sportsman armed with a breech-loader can reload almost as soon as a keeper can hand him a second gun and receive the one discharged, which does away with the necessity of having a man at one's heels with a loaded gun—an objectionable practice, as a trip or stumble might so easily occasion an accident.

Breech-loaders *foul very little*, as the thick elastic mercurial waddings which enter the breech are fully a size larger than the bore of the muzzle; consequently, being forcibly driven through the barrel with the force of the powder, each discharge carries away any refuse or accumulation that may have been left by the one previous, and at the end of a long day's shooting the barrel is just as free from foulness as at the beginning; also, the explosion of the charge does not take place in the breech, but in the paper cartridge, which comes out uninjured, containing the *débris* of the burnt powder, which in the ordinary gun is driven into the chamber and nipple every time it is reloaded, until the latter becomes clogged up, and miss-fires are the consequence.

The *ease of cleaning* is also very apparent, for nothing is required but the passing of a little tow through the barrel once or twice, and afterwards wiping with an oiled rod; whereas, with an ordinary gun, the dirt is forced in the breech and through the nipple, and frequent washing out of the barrels is required, which is never the case with a breech-loader.

There is less recoil in a breech-loader than in a muzzle-loader of the same size and weight, which I account for by its construction rendering it necessary to have more weight of metal at the breech; and also because at the bottom of the cartridge of the breech-loader there is a tight roll of paper, about one-eighth of an inch in thickness, which (like the buffer of a railway carriage) gives with the action of the powder and lessens the recoil.

After five years' experience with breech-loaders, during which I have made a series of practical experiments, I have come to the conclusion that they shoot rather *harder* than ordinary muzzle-loading guns; and my way of accounting for this fact is, that all *windage* is prevented, (by the wadding used being a size larger than the bore;) besides which, I think they will *burn more powder*, and of a larger grain than that in general use for percussion-guns, which is stronger, because there is more air that facilitates combustion between the grains. I also consider that they shoot *quicker*, because there is no long communication (the nipple) between the point of ignition and the charge, the explosion of the cap taking place in the centre of the powder, which is inflamed *almost* simultaneously; for it is an error to suppose that gunpowder explodes instantaneously, as, however rapid its progress, it takes a certain time in travelling from the first grain to the last.

The sportsman can easily make up his own cartridges at the rate of about half a gross in an hour, or, if he prefers it, he can purchase them all ready from any gunmaker.

When all the advantages of the breech-loader are contrasted with the known disadvantages of the muzzle-loader, it is difficult to account for the prejudice that has existed against them for so many years; for, notwithstanding that the present system was introduced by La Faucheux a quarter of a century ago, it is only lately that it has come into general use amongst sportsmen. Numerous objections have been urged against the system, but none appear to have had any substantial foundation; and I shall not enter into them, although I am aware that there are many sportsmen of the old school who, from prejudice, will not even deign to give it a trial: with them arguments and facts are both equally lost.

In the pursuit of large game, breech-loading arms are infinitely preferable; for until the last few years the hunter was always obliged, when waging war with the denizens of the forest, to keep up a battery of several guns and rifles, which, to say nothing of the expense of the first outlay, and the continual wear and tear, &c., was attended by several serious disadvantages, some half-dozen of which I shall enumerate. In the first place, Two or three gun-bearers are required to each sportsman, whose duty it is to pass up the spare guns as fast as those in hand are discharged: now it is a great disadvantage for a hunter, when on trail or stalking, to have a number of persons at his heels, on account of the extra noise they must necessarily make in forcing their way through cover, which often gives alarm to the game and prevents him from getting a shot. Secondly, It is a great drawback, when in the pursuit of some dangerous animal, when a *faux pas* might be attended with fatal consequences, to have any other than yourself to look after. Thirdly, It is not pleasant to have loaded firearms carried in the rear by inexperienced hands, with whom an accident from carelessness is as likely to occur as not. Fourthly, It is not a comfortable feeling to have to depend upon the coolness and courage of your followers; and many a sportsman has found himself in an awkward position by his gun-bearers having been seized with a panic, and bolted, leaving him, with both barrels discharged, in the presence of a wounded and infuriated animal, when nothing but some lucky chance can prevent a catastrophe. Fifthly, It frequently happens, in hunting in different parts of the country, that the sportsman (if he does not keep in his pay a shekar-gang of his own, which is expensive work) has to intrust his spare guns to men of whom he knows nothing, who may be tempted to decamp with them—not a very unfrequent occurrence.* Sixthly, It is a great annoyance to a tired sportsman, after a hard day's fag, to have to clean four or five

* Lieutenant Rice, of the Bombay army, lost all his guns in this manner.

double guns and rifles, which task he dare not intrust his followers to perform, as there are times when a miss-fire might be attended with the most serious consequences. Happily for the sportsman of the present day, all these disagreeable contingencies may now be avoided by making use of rifles on the breech-loading system. Now, independent of gun-bearers, he may roam through the forest alone, careless as to what animal he may meet, for he knows that, should his first shots not take deadly effect, he can reload in the twinkling of an eye, and keep up a running fire, against which nothing can stand, instead of having to bolt under cover to reload, (in case a spare gun is not at hand,) returning breathless, and often with unsteady hand, from having to use sheer force in jamming an obstinate ball down a foul barrel. When mounted, a rifle on the breech-loading system has immense advantages, as it can be easily reloaded, without in any way interfering with the management of the horse; whereas with the old muzzle-loader the sportsman was entirely powerless whilst drawing his ramrod and ramming home the bullet. He who has once used a breech-loading gun or rifle will no more think of going back to a muzzle-loader, than the crack marksman at Hythe would return to old "Brown Bess."

Lang's breech-loading rifles have either three or four broad grooves, (I prefer the latter;) and the projectile used is of a cylindro-conical shape, very similar to that used by General Jacobs, of the

Scinde Horse. With one of his double rifles, forty bore, and 7½ lbs. in weight, a bull's-eye three inches in diameter has been struck thirteen times in eighteen shots, at a hundred yards, firing right and left barrels alternately, and the other shots were all within four inches from the centre. At three hundred yards, bullet after bullet was put in the area of a foot square, which is almost as close shooting as can be got out of a double rifle. For great precision at long distances, single ones must be used; as in every double rifle, where one sight has to serve, the barrels must *converge*, consequently the lines of trajectory must *cross* at some point, and although up to five hundred yards the lateral deflection may not be very material, they can never exhibit the precision of single barrels at long distances.

Mr Westley Richards, of Birmingham, has invented a breech-loader that has been highly approved of by the authorities, and it is a most excellent weapon either for military or sporting purposes, although the system of Messrs Terry and Calisher has been preferred; for, by order of the Secretary of State for War, a contract has been entered into with that firm for the immediate supply of their carbines for the use of several cavalry regiments. The *Times*, speaking of its great advantages over the old system, says:—" The Small-arms Committee have submitted the carbine to the severest tests, making a most favourable report on its peculiar advantages, and hence its adoption in the army. Only some few months ago Terry's rifle was subjected to a test by Captain Richard Hewlett, of the *Excellent* gunnery-ship, and one thousand eight hundred rounds were fired without the carbine requiring to be cleaned or missing fire. The same carbine was tested on South Sea Common, by order of the Lieutenant-Governor, Major-General the Hon. Sir James Yorke Scarlett, and twenty-five rounds were fired at three hundred yards' range from the butt; and the General himself made a centre hit. An officer on the ground, one of the instructors of musketry, then took the instrument, and struck the target afloat twice out of three times, at a distance of one thousand and fifty yards; yet the barrel is but thirty inches in length." It is my opinion that this rifle is one of the most serviceable weapons that an Indian officer could possess, as it is a most formidable instrument, whether in the field, against an enemy, or in the dense deep jungle, the haunts of the tiger and the elephant.

Arms are still in a transition state, and it is yet a matter of doubt as to which principle is the best. From the numerous experiments I have made and witnessed, I consider that, *for accuracy of fire,* nothing equals the system of Mr Joseph Whitworth of Manchester, his rifle with the *hexagonal bore* and elongated projectile having "distanced" every other at long ranges in a course of experimental trials lately made at the School of Musketry at Hythe; besides which *the trajectory is lower than any other system.* He uses a short barrel, having a hexagonal bore and a very quick turn; for whereas the Enfield rifle has only one turn in 6 feet 6 inches, and therefore only half a turn in the barrel of the Enfield, which is 3 feet 3 inches, he has a 45-inch bore, with one turn in *twenty* inches, which rotation is sufficient with a bullet of the requisite specific gravity. Mr Whitworth has reached such a pitch of accuracy, that in a shed excluded from the influence of wind, and firing from a beautifully-contrived rest, at five hundred yards he can put any number of consecutive balls within a space less than that occupied by a five-shilling piece; and it is said that he will not be contented until he can throw a bullet from the barrel of one rifle into the barrel of another placed at five hundred yards' distance. His ordinary rifles are guaranteed, in the hands of a good marksman, to be true at the same distance within eight inches. When his rifle was tested at Hythe with a Regulation Enfield, the efficiency of the one as compared with the other was as twenty to one: Colonel Wilford saying the Whitworth was better at eight hundred yards than the Enfield at five hundred. Beyond one thousand one hundred yards the Enfield must cease firing even at large masses, while Whitworth's can do business at two thousand. Indeed, rifling seems to be in its infancy, and range must only cease with the power of the human eye to take an aim. If Mr Whitworth applies his peculiar principle of rifling and extreme accuracy of boring to a breech-loader, he will produce the most finished weapon of the day. Next to the Whitworth I appreciate the advantages that Mr Lancaster's eliptical rifling has over other systems, as it gives excellent practice, and, *the bore being smooth*, is not liable to harbour rust or wear away. This rifle has given admirable results, and has the great advantage of not fouling nearly so easily as the Regulation and other pieces, and also admits of being cleared far more easily.

I shall conclude my remarks by observing that the market in the present day is deluged with arms that are made *to sell*, and not to shoot; and the public should be on their guard, so as not to allow themselves to be taken in by spurious imitations; for there are unscrupulous *vendors* who do not hesitate to engrave the names of first-class gunmakers upon guns of inferior workmanship, and sell them to the uninitiated as "bargains." Young sportsmen, in selecting a gun, should always go to a maker of note, who, for the sake of his own credit and reputation, would not allow an arm that is unsound, or of inferior workmanship, to leave his establishment bearing his name, which, in first-class work, is always engraved in full, with address. He may have to pay a long figure in comparison with the cost of the inferior article, and, perhaps, something for "the name;" but he is sure of a good weapon, which will prove far better worth the money in the long run, and need not be apprehensive of accidents from defective workmanship or unsound material. Inferior guns, "made to sell," are now-a-days got up so well, that at first sight they resemble A 1 guns of best material and first-class workmanship; but the practical sportsman, on taking them in hand, soon discovers the counterfeit. There is no "*music*" in the locks; the strength of the mainsprings, as well as the *pull* of the triggers, is unequal; the barrels are imperfectly bored, or rough and unpolished in the interior, and perhaps the gauge shows that they are not of exactly the same calibre. Again, the lock-plate and mountings are not fitted and let in with that peculiar nicety that distinguishes first-class London work; and the stock, in spite of a thick coat of French polish and varnish, betrays "*greenness*," being made of unseasoned wood. I have seen some of these inferior guns throw shot pretty fairly to begin with, but after a short time they invariably fall off, both in their strength and regularity of shooting, become shaky, and even dangerous; for the locks (being made of soft metal instead of the best tempered steel) begin to wear, and are no longer to be depended upon. It is a mistaken policy, and false economy, to purchase any other than a first-class gun, which, with ordinary care, will last longer than half a dozen cheap ones of inferior workmanship, and give infinitely more satisfaction, to say nothing of the great additional security against accidents.

Perhaps the following hints on rifle-shooting may prove useful to those who have not had the benefit of an efficient instructor.

Riflemen are not made in a day, but it is an established fact that any one gifted with perfect vision can, with *instruction* and *practice*, become an efficient marksman; therefore, none should be discouraged or despair, as perseverance must lead to ultimate success.

First commencing with the *theory* of rifle practice, which must be fully understood before the rifleman can hope to be an expert shot at all ranges, I shall afterwards enter upon the *practical* part of his initiation.

The first point for consideration is the barrel of the rifle, which, (in the Enfield pattern,) it may be observed, has three spiral grooves cut in the interior, or *bore*, at an equal distance from each other, of even depth, and making half a turn in the length of the barrel, which is three feet three inches. These grooves, otherwise termed the *rifling*, give the bullet (an elongated cylindro-conical projectile) a spiral motion, sometimes called the *spin* or *twist*, as it flies through the air, point foremost, rotatory on its own axis. This very much increases the accuracy of the flight of the bullet, as it serves to keep it in its true course, and prevents any inclination it may have to deviate from it, owing to irregularity in shape or weight.

The diameter of the bore of an Enfield rifle is

·577, but that of the bullet is rather less, in order to facilitate the loading. This difference in size—*i.e.*, the difference between the circumference of the bullet and the bore—leaves a space between the bullet and the bore, termed the *windage*, which was the principal cause of the inefficiency of the old "Brown Bess," for two reasons: the first, because a great part of the explosive force, or gas generated by the ignition of the powder, was lost, as it escaped by the space between the bullet and the side of the bore; and, secondly, because this irregular escape caused the ball to rebound from side to side in the barrel, instead of passing evenly through the bore, and the consequence of this was, that it took an erratic impetus throughout its flight.

The Enfield bullet is, however, so constructed as to do away with these objections. Although the circumference is much less than that of the bore, so as to enter the barrel easily in loading, *all windage is effectually prevented*, as in the base of the projectile is a hollow, into which is fitted a small wooden *cup*, or *plug*, which, by the force of the explosion of the charge, acts like a wedge,* and expands and enlarges the lower part of the bullet, making it fit the barrel tightly, and *take the rifling*, so that in its passage through the barrel it is constrained to turn

* This theory, although adopted by the School of Musketry at Hythe, is contradicted by several competent authorities; and I believe there is reason to doubt its accuracy. *Vide* Major John Boucher's excellent work for the use of Volunteer Riflemen.

with the grooves, and thus receives the spinning movement on its longer axis, which not only ensures accuracy of flight, but also always keeps its point forward. By the bullet being thus expanded, and so much enlarged as to fit the barrel and grooves tightly, none of the explosive power of the gas engendered by the ignition of the charge is allowed to escape, but the whole propelling force acts upon the projectile. There is also a much better chance of the whole of the powder being burnt.

The barrel is a tube of iron, of which the sides of the interior, or *bore,* are parallel, but those of the exterior converge, it being necessary that the metal of the breech-end should be very much thicker than at the muzzle, towards which it gradually tapers, as it has to stand the force of the explosion of the charge. In consequence of this contraction, every barrel has in itself a certain degree of elevation—but of this more anon.

The *axis* of the barrel is an imaginary line drawn through the centre of the bore, and parallel to the interior sides.

The *line of fire* is the continuation of the axis in a straight line, and marks the direction the bullet would take on leaving the barrel, *propelled by the explosion* of the charge, were it not that it is also acted upon by the *power of gravity,* which attracts it towards the earth, and the *resistance the air offers to its passage,* which is always in direct opposition to its flight.

The *trajectory* is the actual course of the bullet, which always describes a curve—a fact easily accounted for, as, from the moment it leaves the muzzle, the force of the gunpowder drives it forward, and gravity draws it downward, so that by yielding to both forces—*i.e.*, by moving onwards and downwards at the same time—it must travel in a curve diverging more and more below the line of fire, until at last, the propelling power being expended, it falls to the earth. Hence it follows, that if the axis of a barrel is directed upon the bull's-eye of a target, at one hundred yards' distance, the bullet will strike about one foot five inches below; the power of gravity naving made it deviate from the line of fire, and drawn it towards the earth, one foot and five inches, in a flight of one hundred yards. Therefore, if the barrel were as thick at the muzzle as it is at the breech, it would be necessary to aim one foot five inches above the mark in order to hit it; but this is not the case, for, as I have before observed, every barrel has in itself a certain degree of elevation, on account of the increased thickness of metal at the breech-end. The Enfield rifle-barrel has elevation in itself for about seventy-five yards.

The *point-blank* range of a rifle is the distance that it will throw a ball before grazing the ground, the barrel being held with its axis parallel to the ground at the height of four feet six inches above it. The point-blank range of the Enfield rifle is about two hundred paces.

The *line of sight*, or aim, is an imaginary straight line taken from the pupil of the eye through the centre of the back-sight, along the top of the fore-sight, to the object intended to be hit. The back-sight is so arranged as to give the proper elevation for different distances. The farther the object is to be aimed at, the greater the elevation required; and this is given by raising the sliding bar of the back-sight, which is marked with lines up to nine hundred yards.

Accuracy of shooting is greatly dependent upon the sights being carefully adjusted, and fitted exactly parallel to the axis of the barrel. If the back-sight is too much inclined to the right, or the front-sight too much to the left, the rifle will shoot to the right of the mark aimed at; in the same manner, if the back-sight is placed too much to the left, or the fore-sight too much to the right, the gun will carry to the left; and the greater the distance, the greater, in proportion, will be the deviation. Every rifle, therefore, ought to be carefully sighted and shot before it is placed in a novice's hands, as non-success in practice on account of an ill-sighted weapon would not be his fault, and might serve to discourage him.

The mechanical routine necessary to be gone through before the tyro can become an efficient marksman consists of *Aiming Drill*, *Position Drill*, *Judging Distance Drill*, and *Practice in Firing*.

AIMING DRILL is necessary to familiarise the uninitiated with the use of the sights, teaching him how to "*align*" his rifle, or "*aim*" correctly at a mark. The practice of this drill exercises the eye, strengthening and developing the sight in the same manner that continued exertion increases the power of the limbs. The following standard rules should be carefully observed :—

I.—*The rifle should always be held with the sights perfectly upright*, as it is only in this position that the *line of sight*, the *line of fire*, and *trajectory*, are in the same vertical plane. If the butt of the rifle is not held *vertically*, but is "canted" either to the right or the left, so that *the perpendicular of the back-sight with the axis* of the barrel is not preserved, the ball will strike to the right if the sight inclines to the left, and *vice versâ* ; and in firing at long ranges, a very slight deviation in this respect will cause a wide deflection.

II.—The "*aim*" or "*line of sight*" should be taken along the centre of the notch of the back-sight and the top of the fore-sight, which should cover the centre of the object aimed at.

III.—The eye should be fixed *steadfastly* on the mark aimed at, and not on the barrel or fore-sight, which latter will be easily brought into the alignment if the eye is fixed as directed.

IV.—In aiming, the left eye should be closed. Aiming drill is generally taught with a "traversing-rest," or, if that is not at hand, a tripod with a sandbag on the top, standing about four feet eight inches from the ground (or the average height of a man's shoulder) will answer every purpose; and the novice is required to align his rifle with the proper elevation upon objects at distances varying from fifty to nine hundred yards. Each time he has aligned his rifle he steps aside, in order that the instructor may take his place and see if the aim be correct. This practice should be continued until the novice has no difficulty in aligning his rifle on the bull's-eye at all distances. Up to three hundred yards, the bull's-eye is eight inches in diameter, and above that distance two feet.

POSITION DRILL is absolutely necessary to ensure good practice at long ranges. It *habituates* the novice to correct positions, and enables him to fire steadily in all situations. It gives him a perfect command over his weapon, and enables the eye and hand to act together, so that the left hand raises the rifle at once to bear upon the object, for the eye to take aim; and at the same moment the fore-finger of the right hand acts upon the trigger.

To establish the natural connexion between the eye and the hand, constant practice is required; and the novice should be accustomed to handle his rifle *both with and without the bayonet,* being put through all the motions of firing *standing and kneeling,* with the same precision as if actually practising with ball-cartridge.

At the School of Musketry at Hythe, recruits are taught to fire standing at all distances up to three hundred yards, and kneeling at every longer range. The best position for taking a steady aim without artificial appliances is by kneeling on the right knee and sitting on the right heel, the rifle being firmly grasped and steadied by the left hand, the left elbow resting on the left knee so as to form a support.

Should the novice meet with any difficulty in aiming correctly, the inspector should cause him to snap caps at a lighted candle placed about a yard distant, when, if the aim is properly directed, the candle will be extinguished. The novice should be attentively watched during this practice until all tendency to wink or flinch is overcome, and his countenance shows that he has become indifferent to the report.

This practice is *most excellent* for forming "*marksmen,*" for besides saving ammunition, it may be continually resorted to, even in a room, the bull's-eye being a small black wafer on the wall at one end and the stand taken at the other. By snapping caps only the young beginner is enabled to see whether the muzzle of the barrel wavers when he presses the trigger, which he cannot properly ascertain when firing ball, on account of the smoke of the discharge. The constant handling of the rifle in a proper manner, by aiming at various objects at different distances, enables "the finger to work in unison with the eye," and gives great steadiness of position before, during, and after pressing the trigger, which is all that is required in making good ball-practice at a target of which the distance is known.

Blank-Cartridge Firing.—Before the novice be allowed to fire a ball, he should practise a certain routine of blank-cartridge firing, in order to further the same object for which he was exercised in snapping caps, as well as to the "*recoil*" or "kick," which is a backward motion caused by the force of the explosion of the powder acting against the breech of the barrel at the same time as against the bullet. The *force of the recoil* depends upon the *charge* of powder, the weight of the bullet, the weight of the rifle, the windage, the rifling of the barrel, the boring of the barrel, (whether purely cylindrical or otherwise,) the friction, and the foulness, which much increases the resistance offered by the air to the bullet passing up the barrel. The instructor should impress upon the novice the necessity of pressing the heel of the butt well and firmly into the hollow of the shoulder, as the more confidently a man "stands up" to his rifle, the less likelihood there is of random shooting.

The position of the body, arms, and hands, and the manner of pressing the trigger, as also the position of the head when taking aim, are to be duly watched both in this and the former exercise, in order to discover and correct those errors which are fatal to good shooting, and which cannot be so successfully corrected when firing ball.

Judging Distance Drill.—One of the greatest

essentials in a well-trained marksman is the capability to estimate distances correctly, as good shooting cannot be made unless the distance is previously ascertained and the proper elevation given to the back-sight. At long ranges it requires great practice to judge distance accurately; but there is always a ready method of ascertaining it practically, by firing, and watching whether the bullet strikes the ground over or under the object aimed at. If over, he will lower the sliding bar of the back-sight; if under, he will raise it. Practice over all kinds of ground is the best means of teaching a novice how to judge distance correctly by the eye, and any one possessing good vision may train himself most effectually in this art for all practical purposes. This, however, can only be accomplished by continual practice and careful observation. When engaged in ball-practice at a target placed at known distances, the tyro should carefully notice the *apparent* height of the markers at each range, remembering that in fine clear weather objects standing in a strong light will appear much nearer than they really are, and *vice versâ* in cloudy and damp weather.

At fifty yards, the features of a man may be clearly identified, and his complexion, arms, accoutrements, and dress distinctly perceived, the buttons and the badge on his forage-cap being distinguishable. At one hundred yards, the features become indistinct, the buttons appear in a line, and the badge can be only faintly discerned. At two hundred yards, the face appears like a whitish ball under the line of the cap, and the buttons and badge become invisible. These distances should constitute the first practice, the second would embrace distances from two to four hundred yards; and the third, from four hundred to one thousand yards or more. At five hundred yards no features are visible, and the head looks like a ball upon the shoulders, the neck being hardly visible.

The instructor will desire the novice to mark the size of the men at each distance, and point out any difference he may discern in their appearance. He will also desire him to take notice of the position of the sun, the character of the background, and the state of the atmosphere at the time, in order that he may be accustomed to their altered appearance under different circumstances.

After some days' exercise in Judging Distance Drill, the proficiency of the novice may be tested by his being practised to judge the distance of objects placed at unknown ranges.

TARGET PRACTICE.—The novice having been thoroughly instructed in "*aiming*," "*position*," and "*judging distance*" drill, can commence "*target practice*," when his efficiency will be tested.

The following hints may prove useful to the novice:—

At the moment of *pressing* the trigger the act of respiration should be suspended, to ensure greater steadiness of aim.

When once the aim is clearly taken, all delay in pressing the trigger is prejudical to good shooting, as, if the rifle is held at the "present" too long, a "*wavering*" of the muzzle takes place, and an uncertain shot is the consequence.

In taking aim at a target, fix the eye steadfastly on the bull's-eye, grasping the rifle *firmly with the left hand* "well forward," (according to its balance,) the butt being *pressed home* into the hollow of the shoulder; the right hand, with the exception of the forefinger, *lightly* clasping the small of the stock behind the trigger-guard, so as to steady and preserve the butt in a vertical position; then, holding the breath, place the forefinger well round the trigger, feeling it lightly, and raise the muzzle gradually and steadily until the fore-sight is seen through the centre of the notch of the back-sight covering the centre of the bull's-eye, when the motion should be arrested, and the trigger simultaneously pressed without the slightest jerk, the eye being rigidly fixed on the object aimed at, and the whole of the body *immobile.*

The great "knack" in rifle-practice is to accustom *the hand and eye to work together*, so that the trigger be pressed simultaneously with the object being "covered," as it is almost an impossibility to retain an aim.

Care should be taken that the aim is not lost in pressing the trigger, which, if the lock is well made, should not "pull too strongly."

After the trigger is pressed—keeping the rifle to

the shoulder—a perfect immobility of body should be retained, and the eye kept steadfastly upon the object aimed at, and the deflection noted.

In aligning a rifle at a mark, the position of the head with reference to the butt will vary according to the range and the elevation required. At short distances the shoulder is a little raised and the head bent forward, (not sideways,) the cheek resting against the small part of the butt, so that the object aimed at is seen through the notch in the back-sight. At longer ranges, the head must be raised and the shoulder lowered; and at the farthest distances, if the stock of the rifle is too much bent, the heel of the butt may rest against the breast or side instead of the shoulder. As heavy firing in this position is inconvenient, it is perhaps better in this case to allow for the necessary elevation by *firing high*, or aiming above the object intended to be hit, as the recoil is often felt severely when the heel of the butt only rests against the shoulder.

Careless loading is conducive to irregular firing. The exact charge of powder that the rifle will burn should be correctly ascertained and strictly adhered to, for a little more or a little less will cause a great vertical deviation in the flight of the bullet. Care should be taken to keep the barrel upright when pouring in the charge, so that the grains of powder may not adhere to the sides of the barrel, which would foul and impede the passage of the bullet.

The bullet should not fit too *loosely*, nor yet be so large as to require hammering, in order to force it down, as in the former case it is liable "to strip," (or pass out of the barrel without taking the rifling, and gaining the spiral motion,) and in the latter it will have ragged edges, which will cause it to diverge from its true direction in its flight through the air.

In *pressing* down the bullet, although great care should be taken to drive it properly *home*, much force should not be employed, as by *ramming* and *jamming* with the ramrod the shape of the bullet is altered and spoiled, which much affects its true flight, and the powder is "mealed" and "caked," by which the strength of the charge is much diminished, as a certain amount of air is necessary to ensure thorough combustion.

The base of the bullet should rest evenly upon the powder, and its axis be in line with that of the barrel.

For fine shooting, care should be taken that there is no hidden defect in the bullet, for if any part be hollow or imperfect, the centre of gravity will not be in the line of the axis, and consequently there will be a deviation in its flight.

I shall now notice the causes of irregular firing, over which the rifleman can have no control, but which may, to a certain extent, be rendered less injurious to "the score," if the following observations are carefully attended to :—

First, *the wind* affects the flight of the bullet to a considerable extent in firing at long distances, diverting it from its true course, and accelerating or retarding its progress according as it blows *with* or *against* it. When the wind blows from a quarter exactly *opposite* to the direction of the bullet, it experiences a greater resistance in its flight, and accordingly more *elevation* should be given. Should the wind blow exactly from the shooter to the target, the resistance will be *less* than ordinary, and consequently *less* elevation than ordinary is required. Allowances should be made according to the strength of the current of air. If the wind blows from the *right*, aim to the *right*, as the deflection will be to the *left*, and *vice versâ* if from the *left*.

If the course of the wind *forms an angle* to the direction of the bullet, aim must be taken, and allowances made accordingly. Thus, if the wind blows from the *right* and *contrary*, the deviation will be to the *left* and *low:* therefore, in order to strike the bull's-eye, aim should be taken to the *right* and *high;* and to the *left* and *high* if the current of air is *contrary*, and from the *left*.

If the wind blows from the *right* and *rear*, on aiming direct at the bull's-eye, the deflection of the bullet will be to the *left* and *high:* therefore, in such a case, aim should be taken to the *right* and *low;* or to the *left* and *low*, if the current of air comes from the *left* and *rear*.

Correct judgment in making the proper allowances for the effect of various winds upon the flight of the projectile, can only be gained by practice in all kinds of weather, but the above hints may assist the novice.

The *state of the atmosphere* considerably affects the *range* of the bullet. In damp weather, when the atmosphere is dense, its resistance to the flight of the bullet is *increased,* and consequently *greater elevation* should be given. In fine clear weather, on the contrary, the resistance is *less,* and the bullet *rises,* therefore *less* elevation is required. Humidity in the atmosphere also affects the range of the bullet in a different manner, as it has a certain influence on ignition of gunpowder, which in damp weather is not so rapid as in fine; therefore, on such days, larger charges should be used than in hot summer days.

The *position of the sun* is sometimes liable to influence the correct aim, as if it shines from the *right* it lightens up the *right* side of the front-sight, and the *left* side of the notch of the back-sight, throwing the *left* of the front-sight and the *right* of the back-sight into the shade; therefore, if the firer is not careful in aiming properly, the "line of sight" is liable to pass from the *left* of the centre of the notch of the back-sight and the *right* of the front-sight, the effect of which would be that the bullet would strike to the *left,* and *vice versâ* if the sun shines from the *left.* Sun-shades are sometimes used to obviate this difficulty.

It must be obvious to all, that the flight of the bullet occupies a certain time, and in firing at *moving* objects a certain allowance should be made accordingly, and great judgment is required in this point when firing at long ranges. For instance, in deer-stalking, if a deer is running *transversely* either to the right or left, a sportsman aiming directly at the shoulder would most likely either strike the hind-quarter or miss by shooting behind, as, in the time between the *discharge* of his rifle and the *impact* or striking of the bullet, the quarry would have moved forward a certain distance. The following hints on this point may aid the novice:—

In firing at anything moving, it is advisable to "cover" the object and allow the muzzle to follow it for some distance before pulling the trigger, in order to ascertain the velocity of the motion and the allowances required to be made.

If the object is directly *approaching* the person firing, the muzzle of the barrel should be gradually *lowered*, the finger feeling the trigger all the time, and aim should be taken *low*.

If the object is *retiring*, the muzzle of the rifle should be raised, (more or less according to the distance and the velocity of motion of the object,) and aim taken *high*.

If the object is moving across, either to the *right* or *left*, aim should be taken *well forward*, after having followed the motion with the object well covered for some time.

Should the object be *ascending* a hill, fire *high*; if *descending*, fire low; if diagonally, *in front*.

The best colour for the dress of a sportsman is *gray* or *brown*, being less distinguishable than any other.

The following tables were constructed with great care from a series of experiments I made with targets of different coloured cloth, under various circumstances and at different distances, in order to serve the newly-raised volunteer corps in the selection of the most suitable colour for their uniform. The figure 1 denotes the most visible, 7 the least so, 0 invisible:—

Colours.	At Three Hundred Yards.								At Six Hundred Yards.								
	Open Country.	Wooded Country.	Rocky Ground.	Sea Shore.	Over Water.	Against Sky.	Against Earthworks.	Agst. Stone Fortificns.	Open Country.	Wooded Country.	Rocky Ground.	Sea Shore.	Over Water.	Against Sky.	Against Earthworks.	Agst. Stone Fortificns.	One Mile.
Scarlet........	4	3	4	3	2	4	5	4	4	2	5	3	2	3	5	4	5
Green (Rifle)	3	6	5	4	4	2	4	3	3	7	4	5	4	4	4	3	3
Blue (Royal)	2	4	4	3	5	3	3	2	2	6	3	4	5	4	3	2	2
White..........	1	1	1	2	1	4	1	2	1	1	1	1	1	5	1	2	1
Gray..........	7	6	7	7	7	6	6	7	6	7	0	7	0	7	0	7	6
Brown (dead leaf)........	7	7	7	6	6	5	7	6	7	0	0	6	0	6	0	6	7

Colours.	At Three Hundred Yards Distant.											
	On a Clear Day.				On a Cloudy Day.						Bright Moonlight.	Starlight.
	Daybreak.	Sunrise.	Mid-day.	Sunset.	Daybreak.	Sunrise.	Mid-day.	Sunset.	Rain.	Rain and Fog.		
Scarlet	4	3	3	4	4	3	4	6	3	3	4	5
Green (Rifle)	3	4	4	3	7	7	3	0	4	4	3	4
Blue (Royal)	2	5	3	2	6	6	3	0	4	4	3	4
White	1	1	1	1	1	1	1	1	2	2	1	1
Gray	7	6	7	5	0	0	5	0	6	6	0	0
Brown (dead leaf)	6	7	6	6	0	0	6	0	6	7	7	7

By these tables it will be seen that gray and brown are colours that are the least distinguishable at a distance, and consequently the most suitable for light troops.

THE END